81-1560

QL
737 Lilly, John Cunningham.
C432 Communication between man and
L53 dolphin: the possibilities of
     talking with other species.

JUL   2000

JUN   2004

JUL 09

JUL X X 2015

DATE DUE
50901

Communication
between Man and Dolphin:
The Possibilities of Talking
with Other Species

BOOKS BY THE AUTHOR

Man and Dolphin (1961)
The Dolphin in History
   (with Ashley Montagu) (1963)
The Mind of the Dolphin: A Nonhuman Intelligence (1967)
Programming and Metaprogramming in the Human
   Biocomputer (1972)
The Center of the Cyclone (1972)
Lilly on Dolphins: Humans of the Sea (1975)
Simulations of God: The Science of Belief (1976)
The Dyadic Cyclone
   (with Antonietta Lilly) (1976)
The Deep Self: Profound Relaxation and the Tank
   Isolation Technique (1977)
The Scientist: A Novel Autobiography (1978)
Communication between Man and Dolphin: The Possibilities
   of Talking with Other Species (1978)

Communication between Man and Dolphin:

The Possibilities of Talking with Other Species

BY JOHN C. LILLY, M.D.

Foreword by Burgess Meredith
Prologue by Antonietta L. Lilly

CROWN PUBLISHERS, INC.   NEW YORK

This book is dedicated to the future success of interspecies relations and the jointly realized enhanced future of the shared interdependence of humans and cetaceans. There is a new hope that humans can substitute communication for depredation, and cooperation for exploitation, even as the cetaceans have for several tens of millions of years. May we, the humans, soon learn from them, the dolphins, porpoises, and whales.

Inquiries should be addressed to Crown Publishers, Inc.,
One Park Avenue, New York, N.Y. 10016

Published simultaneously in Canada by General Publishing Company Limited

Printed in the United States of America

Book Design: Shari de Miskey

Library of Congress Cataloging in Publication Data

Lilly, John Cunningham, 1915-
Communication between man and dolphin.

1. Dolphins—Behavior.   2. Animal communication.
3. Animal intelligence.   I. Title.
QL737.C432L53   599'.53   78-16362
ISBN 0-517-53036-8

Third Printing, April, 1979

CONTENTS

*It is of great importance that the general public be given the
opportunity to experience, consciously and intelligently, the efforts and
results of scientific research. It is not sufficient that each result be
taken up, elaborated, and applied by a few specialists in the field.
Restricting the body of knowledge to a small group deadens the
philosophical spirit of a people and leads to spiritual poverty.*

—ALBERT EINSTEIN

*No bigger in the mass of the body than the thumb of a man,
the Purusha, the Spirit within, is seated for ever in the
heart of all creatures.*

—FROM THE UPANISHADS

Invitation from a White Whale

FOR THE PAST SEVERAL YEARS I HAVE BEEN EXPOSED TO A VAST amount of information about whales and dolphins. A network of organizations such as Save the Whales, Greenpeace, Dolphin Embassy, etc., has formed across the country. People everywhere are interested in what they sense are joyful beings, and they want to know more about them. They come to my husband, John Lilly, for advice and information because he was the first person to propose that dolphins are as intelligent as men, but in a strange and watery way. His conclusions, after twenty years of original scientific work, have reached the public. We are no longer a unique and lonely species. The dolphins too are intelligent. This fact was demonstrated to me in a deeply moving experience at a research institute in San Diego.

We had recently formed the Human/Dolphin Foundation—a new organization to help in our efforts to communicate with dolphins. But I was also seeking a more personal participation in the achievement of this goal, which is, to me, the most exciting and important undertaking of our time. Consequently, when we were invited to visit a recently built research institute by its director, Bill Evans, John's colleague and friend, I felt it might afford me the opportunity I was seeking.

As we passed through the facilities, we were impressed with the youthful vitality exhibited by both humans and dolphins. Bill was excited about the possibilities of educating both, and his enthusiasm was complemented by his vast knowledge about cetaceans. We were nearing the end of our tour when Bill suggested we visit the beluga whales *(Delphinapterus leucas),* or "the canaries of the sea," as the whalers of the last century called them. He led us up a stairway through a large door and down a hallway to the top of an enormous tank. Suddenly, I was looking down at one of the most unusual beings I had ever seen in my life.

The beluga whale looked like Caspar the Friendly Ghost—pure white with a flexible neck and a mobile facial expression.

I had the feeling I was perceiving, *and being perceived by,* an immense presence. I was simultaneously speechless and trying to absorb a vast amount of information that I was unable to fit into adequate patterns of past experience. It somehow transcended the human experience, going deeply into unknown mysteries.

There were a few eternal moments of recognition ... the frequency between us was like a brightly lighted tunnel of happiness. Everything else around me dimmed in the white light that soothed and pervaded my very essence.

I vaguely remember walking through the rest of the laboratory.

Before leaving, I asked Bill if I could come back and swim with the whales.

Life went on with a very full schedule, and in the midst of it I found myself often thinking of the whales. But it wasn't until I talked to my friend, Paul Gaer, that another visit to the belugas became a reality. Paul is a writer and photographer and was intrigued with the adventure I had planned. We are old friends who have shared interests for a long time.

Before I knew it, we were on a plane and I was in a dressing room at the institute changing into a wet suit preparatory to my rendezvous with the whales. I slipped into the icy water, feeling I was entering alien territory—*their* territory. I was afraid and the adrenaline shot through me as I turned uneasily trying to keep the circling whales in my line of vision. The sheer size (about twelve feet and eight hundred pounds) and power of the animals in the water compared to my small, fragile, and inadequate self were quite sobering. My fear seemed to be sensed and accommodated by the whales, and it soon disappeared when I realized how delicately aware of me my new friends were. I could sense their sonar scanning me. I tried making sounds under water; they immediately swam within two feet of me and made new sounds. We played for fifteen minutes, with Paul's camera clicking away, in the background. We were interrupted by a crew who came in to do an audiogram, so I had to leave the water. I got out feeling dissatisfied, unfulfilled. What it was I expected, I did not know, but I somehow could not leave just yet. I lingered by the edge of the tank.

A whale raised her head above the water to peer at me. I looked directly into her eyes. Suddenly, she shot a stream of water from her mouth that splashed over my face and shoulders and slowly down over my body. It was a loving touch—an invitation to a more intimate communication—as sensual an approach as I have ever experienced from my own species. Without thinking, I cupped some water in my hand, brought it into my mouth, and shot it back at the beluga. The joy of the next few minutes can only be described as absurd. I was able to hug and kiss her soft white skin. This was what I had hoped to experience—I had crossed a boundary, a new space opened, I was fulfilled. This whale's invitation to share her world gave me a glimpse through a cosmic crack between species . . . a oneness of all living beings as we will know them someday in the future . . . a place we have been before and will return to again . . . a peaceful paradise . . . *the* "peaceable kingdom."

The process of contraction and expansion . . . emerging from a dense pattern of loneliness (interspecies deprivation) to overlap with the whales in a startling new way. I thought of something John had written about his work in the Virgin Islands:

> This opening of our minds was a subtle and yet a painful process. We began to have feelings which I believe are best described by the word "weirdness." The feeling was that we were up against the edge of a vast uncharted region in which we were about to embark with a good deal of mistrust in the appropriateness of our own equipment. The feeling of weirdness came on us as

the sounds of this small whale seemed more and more to be forming words in our own language. We felt we were in the presence of Something, or Someone, who was on the other side of a transparent barrier which up to this point we hadn't even seen. The dim outlines of a Someone began to appear. We began to look at this whale's body with newly opened eyes and began to think in terms of its possible "mental processes," rather than in terms of the classical view of a conditionable, instinctually functioning "animal." We began to apologize to one another for slips of the tongue in which we would call dolphins "persons" and in which we began to use their names as if they *were* persons. This seemed to be as much of a way of grasping at straws of security in a rough sea of the unknown, as of committing the sin of Science of anthropomorphizing. If these "animals" have "higher mental processes," then they in turn must be thinking of us as very peculiar (even stupid) beings indeed.

The white ghosts had a sense of curious loving selves, careful of my vulnerability in their watery environment. They are my self living in the ancient, cold sea in which I swam in the dim, distant past before my cells organized and climbed out onto the land. That day with them I rejoined my archaic self in the water.

I will go back, I hope, and talk with them with new understanding of my origins and share the breaking of the long separation of human and cetacean.

ANTONIETTA L. LILLY

FOREWORD

MANY YEARS AGO I FOUND OUT WHERE JOHN LILLY LIVED AND, uninvited, went to see him. He is a very private man, still he received me and we became friends. In fact, almost as a member of his family, I followed the events described in his books *Center of the Cyclone, Deep Self,* and, more recently, *The Scientist.* Presently I am trying, as best I can, to be of practical assistance to him through the Human/Dolphin Foundation, which a few of us established three years ago. This foundation is located in a high canyon above the Malibu Hills in southern California. It is near the residence of John Lilly and his wife, Toni.

From time to time Toni and John take off to give a lecture and/or workshop or for a social visit; but mostly, for seven days out of the week, they attend the data that is being accumulated and the blueprints that are being drawn for Project Janus (Interspecies Communication with Cetaceans).

Adjacent to the Lilly house is a small one-and-a-half-room laboratory. Here, five days a week, a handful of young scientists, who have come from different parts of the United States and Canada, work, without pay, under Lilly's supervision. Their job is to coordinate the software and the hardware, or, more simply, to work on the various computers, hydrophones, and calculating paraphernalia that the foundation has purchased (which you will read about in this book), and to prepare the results for scientific testing.

One feels privileged to be in the vicinity of this activity. The word is out that important steps are being taken, and, indeed, important people come and go. The implications of a possible breakthrough in establishing communication with an alien species whose brain size is larger than our own (whether on this planet or another) are enormous, and the consequences of finally ending what has been called the "long loneliness of man" on this earth, in our time, would, of course, be epic.

What it amounts to is that we are in a race to speak to the whales and dolphins before they are destroyed. Like a Greek drama the tension is great and the outcome is uncertain.

This book is a description of certain strategies being formed and specific steps being taken to bring about an affirmative ending to the drama.

Communication between Man and Dolphin is a book only John could write. We who, with admiration and love have followed the man's extraordinary search, have been waiting for its publication for a long time.

The late John Steinbeck wrote in *The Sea of Cortez:* "It is a good thing for a man to look down at the tide-pools, then up to the stars, then back to the tide-pools again."

John Lilly has put it another way, and it was this statement that drew many of us to him: "In the province of the mind, what one believes to be true either is true or becomes true within certain limits. These limits are found to be beliefs to be transcended."

BURGESS MEREDITH

PREFACE

IN 1955 I BEGAN SCIENTIFIC RESEARCH WITH THE BOTTLE-NOSED dolphin, *Tursiops truncatus*. In 1968 this research program was terminated. In the intervening years, several major discoveries about dolphins were made.

From 1968 to 1976 my efforts were put into research on myself and other humans. This work was subsequently published in depth in a book.* During the completion of this work I reviewed the dolphin research literature from 1968 to 1976. I found that practically no research based on the 1955–1968 work had been done along the lines of communication between dolphins and humans and among dolphins themselves.

I constructed a bibliography of the work from 1968 to 1976 done by others. Eventually I hope to publish this bibliography.

This review of the literature convinced me that it was timely for me to resume my research with the dolphins. In preparation for this, I reviewed all the papers and books that I had written on

---

* John C. Lilly, M.D., *The Deep Self: Profound Relaxation and the Tank Isolation Technique* (New York: Simon & Schuster, 1977).

the subject. This review appears in the Annotated Bibliography of this book.

With my wife, Toni, and our friends, Burgess Meredith and Victor Di Suvero, we established the Human/Dolphin Foundation in Malibu, California. The aims of the foundation are to support research and education leading to communication between man and the cetaceans by new electronic and computer methods. The basic considerations leading to this proposal are given in this book.

Insofar as is possible this book should be self-supporting, i.e., for those interested in the field of interspecies sonic communication; for anyone interested in more detailed information about the origins and development of this project, I have provided an Annotated Bibliography.

Since the research program terminated in 1968 I have not ceased thinking about the dolphins and the problems of interspecies communication. In recent years I have written several papers that are included in this book ("The Rights of Cetaceans under Human Laws," "The Cetacean Brain," "Languages Alternative to Those of the Human," "The Dolphins Revisited"). In this book there is a special chapter of projections into the future, and I call attention to a special chapter at the end of another book, *The Scientist,** including two scenarios describing future relationships between cetaceans and humans. One of these scenarios is a pessimistic account of the demise of all of the cetaceans and probably the humans as well. The other scenario is frankly optimistic, postulating a breakthrough in interspecies communication research leading to complete communication between man and the cetaceans by means of computer aids.

I have incorporated the proposal for support of the interspecies communication program in the Appendix to this book. This proposal summarizes the present position of communication research and the scientific bases for assuming that there will be success with the program. In the Addendum (also included in the Appendix) there is a summary of progress to date including the raising of funds sufficient to furnish a computer and the peripheral apparatus for the computer.

* John C. Lilly, M.D., *The Scientist: A Novel Autobiography* (Philadelphia: Lippincott, 1978).

In 1977 Ms. Georgia Tanner joined the board of the Human/ Dolphin Foundation and has furnished the financial wherewithal for the completion of the apparatus needed to initiate this program.

In July 1977 Dennis Kastner joined the Human/Dolphin Foundation. He is an expert in the hardware and software for microcomputers and minicomputers. He has had extensive background in human communication and human communication systems in Canada. Gratitude is expressed to him, Paule Jean, Brad Weigle, and Linda Dias for continued help in the Foundation work.

I wish to express my appreciation for the selfless help provided by my wife, Toni Lilly, Burgess Meredith, Ms. Georgia Tanner, Tom Wilkes, Victor Di Suvero, Alexandra Hubbard, Louis Marx, Jr., Arthur and Prue Ceppos, John Brockman, Dr. William Evans, Gregory Bateson, Dr. Kenneth Norris, Dr. Peter J. Morgane, Dr. Willard F. McFarland, Dr. Eugene Nagel, Dr. Paul Yakovlev, Dr. Sidney Galler, Dr. Orr Reynolds, Dr. Hudson Hoagland, Dr. and Mrs. Frederick Worden, Milton Shedd, Frank Powell, Jr., Dr. Henry Truby, Ms. Alice M. Miller, Dr. Robert Livingston, Christopher Wells, Dr. Harvey Savely, Dr. David Tyler, Ms. Margaret Howe Lovatt, Scott McVay, Dr. Helen McFarland, Ms. Jane Sullivan, the late Dr. William McLean and the late Dr. Wayne Batteau, and Jean Knights and John and Denise Perry.

A chronological list of discoveries about dolphins by the author and his co-workers from 1955 to 1976 follows; the literature referred to is in the Annotated Bibliography in the Appendix.

CHRONOLOGICAL LIST OF DISCOVERIES ABOUT DOLPHINS

Date	Discovery	1st published account, reference *
1955	Voluntary respiration	1961:4
1955	Anesthesia lethal without respiratory aides	1961:4
1955	First respirator and first demonstration of successful anesthesia	1961:4
1955	Brain size established	1961:3
1957	Ability to control reactions to negative reinforcement	1962:5
1957	Ability to demand positive reinforcement through voicing control	1962:5
1957	Distress call	1963:11
1957	Voluntary erection of penis in male dolphin	1966:19
1957	Dolphin voices to demand start/stop reinforcement	1962:5
1957	Dolphin matches human voice	1962:5
1960	Ability to learn human speech sounds: counting	1962:9; 1968:33
1960	Close wet contact man/dolphin leads to learning	1961:4
1960	Critical brain size for control of voice for symbolic use	1961:4; 1963:10
1960	Reprogramming abilities in sonic mode: burst count matching	1965:18
1961	Sonic exchanges of dolphins	1961:3
(1957) 1963	Silent areas all parietal and larger than man's	1971:36
1964	First automatic respirator	1964:14
1964	Biocomputer theory and practice (extensions of learning theory)	1966:22; 1968:30, 37, 38
1964	LSD-25 abolishes avoidance behavior and increases vocalization index	1967:24
1965	Stereophonation	1967:27
1965	Sonic sources: three: 2 nasal, 1 laryngeal	1967:27, 28
1976	Newtonian rotatory limits determine body/head size for large brains evolution and survival	1977:Intro. and Chap. 5

* Note: The reference numbers refer to the Annotated Bibliography in this book.

INTRODUCTION

IN THIS BOOK I INVITE YOU TO ENTERTAIN SOME NEW BELIEFS about dolphins. Many of the young new generation believe as I do; many do not so believe. Here we give the basis for these beliefs—experience, experiment, and deductions therefrom.

As the accumulated facts about the structure of the brains and of the behavior of the Cetacea have become integrated, beliefs about them have been constructed and realized quite counter to those held by many biologists and many keepers of dolphins and whales in oceanaria. In brief, this new belief claims: *these Cetacea with huge brains are more intelligent than any man or woman.* The old beliefs have been based upon ignorance and lack of direct personal experience with dolphins and whales.

In the past mankind's beliefs led to clashes about politics, about territory, about religion, about the law, about relationships between man and woman. The new beliefs about the Cetacea lead to problems—personal, political, and social in addition to scientific.

Man is changing the planet. He has a history of killing off all of the large mammals of the land. The large mammals of North

1

America were extinguished by man. The African species are being decimated by the encroachment of man upon their territories. In the seas the pelagic mammals are being critically depleted as man invades their territories and hauls their bodies ashore for his purposes.

In the past (before 1965) I felt that the scientific viewpoint of total objectivity, of the noninvolved scientific observer, was the be-all and end-all for one's life. I am no longer convinced that such a dispassionate noninvolved view of ecology will ever work. A scientist who fails to assume social responsibility, the feedback from all other members of his species, is not taking the responsibility of being a human being beyond a limited self-serving role in society. Involvement and participation are absolutely essential for understanding and for survival of self and of one's own species.

We need a new ethic, new laws based on those ethics which punish human beings for encroachment on the life-styles and the territory of other species with brains comparable to and larger than ours. We need modifications of our laws so that the Cetacea can no longer become the property of individuals, corporations, or governments. Even as the respect for human individuals is growing in our law, so must the respect for individual whales, dolphins, and porpoises.

The explosive-propelled and exploding harpoon, entering the flesh of the whale and causing it to emit great quantities of blood from his blowhole, is a recurrent nightmare for more and more humans. The death cries of whales are heard around the world under water and are ignored by those who cause them. Those who believe that they are killing to provide huge reservoirs of flesh for industrial use rather than killing the largest, most sophisticated brains on the planet, somehow must change their beliefs; their killing must be prevented by giving the cetaceans the same legal protections as humans.

Those who catch and imprison dolphins must modify what they are doing to allow more communication between the imprisoned dolphins and their families and friends in the sea. If any dolphins and whales are to be kept captive, their captivity should be for only an agreed-upon, limited time, after which they should be released to their natural habitat to communicate

man's activities to their fellows. I envision the day when the
current oceanaria will progress from being "prisons" for dolphins
to being *interspecies schools,* educating both dolphins and
humans about one another.

Let us contrast two sets of clashing beliefs that cause today's
controversies among humans regarding whales and dolphins.

The first beliefs derive from the biology of the last century
before much was known about the anatomy of brains and how
brains operate. Brains were weighed, bodies were weighed,
length of bodies measured, various calculations were made of
brain weight, body weight, and body length on the Cetacea (and
on land mammals). These gross measures were then plotted as
brain weight versus body weight on an X-Y graph. Certain
trends were found in these data that showed that, in certain
species, as the brain size increased so did the body size,
according to certain simple relations. Plotting them in these
ways and calculating them according to certain rules leaves no
doubt that there are such relationships.

However, an unwarranted simple assumption crept into the
use of such plots: a large body needed a large brain. Hence the
size of brain is not a measure of its intelligence or
computational capacity. Practically no one bothered to ask
why, in the evolution of our planet, the big brains in the large
bodies survive and why the large brains in small bodies do not
survive. There are no large brains in small bodies existing today.

It was not until this century that we began to realize the
incredible delicacy and fragility of the structure of the brain,
especially the very large brains. This most complicated organ of
the body needs great protection from blows to its container,
from changes in temperature, and from deprivation of oxygen
and food supplies.

During World War II it was found that rotatory forces of
sufficient intensity on the human head cause extensive damage
to the brain: angular acceleration and resulting displacement set
up shearing stresses within the brain, tearing it and possibly
damaging its blood vessels. It was found that the smaller brains
(those of monkeys) required higher acceleration to damage them
by rotatory means. As the brains became larger, it was
necessary to attach much larger masses to their container to

protect them by reducing these rotatory forces within the critical limits that avoid damage. A glancing blow on a very large object causes less rotation acceleration than the same blow on a smaller object: the sheer stresses conducted to the brain are limited by the size of the attached mass.

As the brains grew larger over the millennia they became more and more susceptible to rotatory forces that would tear their structure unless they were tied to masses that were large enough to prevent these damaging levels of rotational acceleration.

The larger the brain the greater the vulnerability to damage and the greater the need to slow down rotatory acceleration of the head containing the brain.

These considerations can be used to show that a large brain in a small body and a light head is very precarious and probably cannot survive for any length of time on this planet under gravity and the rotatory forces due to motion of the particular body. As the brain becomes larger, so the bone surrounding it must become thicker and the head more massive to protect the increased mass of biocomputer (brain) from the acceleratory forces that can destroy it. The larger biocomputers are more easily injured by rotational forces than the small ones.

Thus, the evolutionary pressures in the mechanical environment of the huge biocomputers allowed only the large brains with large protective masses surrounding them to survive on the planet, both in the water and on the land. On the land the elephant's very large brain (6,000 grams) is surrounded by a huge skull and a very large body, which cannot be moved in the rotatory acceleration sense beyond a certain critical limit with the forces normally found in the animal's environment. As the brain in a growing elephant becomes more massive, so do the surrounding bone and the size of the body increase to absorb the rotatory acceleratory forces.

The same limiting rotational acceleration law applies in the sea. If one watches an underwater movie of dolphins and of giant whales, one quickly sees the differences in small as opposed to large brains in these rotatory acceleratory forces. The dolphins in their swimming move and twist and turn with high velocities and high accelerations; in contrast, the giant whales have a slow, majestic movement. Their ballet is grandly deliberate. One can see the limitations in the acceleratory forces in spite of the huge musculature. From such movies one can compute the natural limits imposed on rotatory accelerations for a given brain size and for the bodies housing and protecting them.

In the biological science of the past and of the present such considerations have not always entered into the thinking of the cetologists or of the delphinologists. The application of Newtonian rotational mechanics to these problems is lagging behind other knowledge of the Cetacea. The knowledge of brains and their upper limit of acceleratory forces comes from medical research studies on smaller animals and on man himself. The time has come for the biologists to start to apply such thinking to large brains and the bodies housing them. The evolutionary selective pressures for and against survival of large brains are not yet fully understood.

Such considerations enlarge biological beliefs beyond their current limits, dictated by the biology of the nineteenth century.

A dramatic confirmation of these mechanical forces is seen when the very large brain is removed from a dead whale. A nine-thousand-gram brain from a sperm whale is an incredibly fragile structure when removed from the braincase. If one merely rotates the vessel in which it is contained, one can see sheer stress lines and distortions of the structure appear on its surface and within its depths. If one then contrasts this with a removed human brain, it is evident that one can rotate the human brain at a greater rate of acceleration before the same kinds of stress appear within the structure. If one rotates a small monkey brain, one can use a much greater rate of acceleration than one can with the human before such stress and strain appear within it.

This way of looking at large brains suggests that biology must critically examine all of the parameters of survival of large brains. Presumptions derived from simple correlations between brain weight, body weight, and body length simply have no relevance to brain survival.

One other facet that is missing from the usual biological belief system about Cetacea is knowledge of the structure of brains themselves: *where they enlarge* when they are very large and *how they are used* once they are enlarged. As Von Bonin pointed out many years ago, the correlations between brain size and body size do not involve the psychological parameters needed to know how these brains are used. Recent findings give us some clues about the functioning of large brains.

In brief, the large brains are enlarged in the areas of cortex devoted to the higher levels of computation over and above those present in the smaller brains. In extensive series of studies on the primate and human brains, it has been shown that the small brains in small primate bodies directly control those bodies. The neocortex is all sensory and motor in brains the size of the macaque monkey (100 grams).

In the next larger set of primate brains, those of the chimpanzee, the gorilla, and the orangutan, something new has been added over and above the sensory and the motor neocortex. At this brain size (three hundred to four hundred grams) the new areas are not connected directly to either input or output as in the smaller brain. These new areas are called the silent, or associational, brain areas. In the chimpanzee these areas have been shown to be correlational, computational areas that use the surrounding sensory-motor cortices in the service of longer-term calculations than those the smaller brains are capable of.

In modern parlance the monkey has the minimum-sized *minicomputer,* designed for control of the primate body, including the use of an opposable thumb and the leading of a very active climbing social life. This sensory-motor neocortical minicomputer is maintained in the set of larger brains in the chimpanzee and the human. The *new silent associational cortices* distributed among the sensory-motor cortex is a *macrocomputer,* a larger-sized computer running the *minicomputer in the service of long-term calculations;* the time span of memory, of the term of planned action, and the number of calculable future contingencies increases as the macrocomputer increases in size.

For man the macrocomputer (the silent areas) increases above that of the chimpanzee. The increased size of man's macrocomputer creates the potential of calculations going further into the past and further into the future, conditioning the present action on the longer past experience and the longer future plans. When these areas are removed in man (such as in frontal lobotomy), the motivation of and the initiation of such long-term considerations and computations disappear. With enough damage to the macrocomputer the individual's time scale, past and future, decreases and hence clusters closely around the present.

In the sea among the Cetacea there is a continuous spectrum of brain sizes ranging from the ape size all the way up to six times the human size (in the sperm whale). Among the large variety (fifty-two species) of dolphins and toothed whales there are brain sizes ranging from the ape size through the human size to the superhuman level of four to six times the human size.

Careful studies by Dr. Peter J. Morgane, Dr. Paul Yakovlev, and Dr. Sam Jacobs (36) have shown that the larger cetacean brains are enlarged only in the macrocomputer, the associational silent cortex. In the largest of the cetacean brains the macrocomputer is all that has been added to the mass of that brain; the minicomputer corresponds to that of the smaller cetacean species. The cellular neuronal networks are essentially the same as those of the human.

Therefore, we deduce that the human-sized brains in Cetacea correspond to human computational power and that the larger cetacean brains are capable of extensions of computations into the past and into the future beyond the range of the human. Such considerations as these generate new beliefs about dolphins, whales, and porpoises:

1. In the large range of brain sizes in the Cetacea the smallest Cetacea correspond in their computational capacities to the apes.

2. Those whose brains are as large as human (Tursiops, etc.) have computational capacities similar to the human regarding the use of past and future in current computations.

3. In those brains larger than the human (orca, sperm whale, etc.) the computational capacities exceed those of the human regarding past and future used in computations of the current situation.

4. Man's current consensus judgments about the Cetacea are too limited. His knowledge of cetacean intelligence and computational capacities, and of the necessities for survival in the sea are primitive and incomplete. As yet, man is not capable of understanding the ecological truth recognized by the Cetacea, as proved by their ancient solution to their survival. At the least their record of adaptation to their environment is as successful as man's adaptation to his for a period of time at least twenty times as great as that of man's existence on earth.

5. The Cetacea are sensitive, compassionate, ethical, philosophical, and have ancient "vocal" histories that their young must learn.

6. Cetacean knowledge of humans is restricted to experiences in the sea between the Cetacea and human ships, warfare, yachts, catcher boats, and so forth. Very few, if any, Cetacea have experienced man on land and then been returned to the sea. Therefore, their communications in the sea about us, their knowledge of us, is incomplete. Their judgments about us would be based on their communications and experiences with whaling, the capture of dolphins, explosions in the sea, oil spills, ships and their propeller noises blocking their communications, and undersea warfare with destruction of Cetacea by submarines and by military aircraft.

7. The Cetacea realize that man is incredibly dangerous in concert. It is such considerations as these that may give rise to their behavioral ethic that the bodies of men are not to be injured or destroyed, even under extreme provocation. If the whales and dolphins began to injure and kill humans in the water, I am sure that the Cetacea realize that our navies would then wipe them out totally, at a faster rate than the whaling industry is doing at the present time.

8. Thus, we deduce that the whales have a knowledge of man, fragmentary as it is, which they weave into theories and into accounts of direct experiences in a way similar to the way we develop knowledge of one another. In spite of the fact that they have no writing, no external records, they probably, because of their large brains, have extremely long memories and the capacity to integrate these memories equal to and better than our own.

9. Paleontological evidence shows that the whales and the dolphins have been here on this planet a lot longer than has man. Dolphins (like the current *Tursiops)* have been here on the order of fifteen million years with brain sizes equal to and greater than that of modern man. Apparently some whale and dolphin brains became the equal of that of present-day man and then passed man's current size about thirty million years ago. Secure human skulls in large numbers with a cranial capacity equal to present man are found only as far back as one hundred fifty thousand years. Thus we see that man is a still evolving latecomer to this planet. He may not survive as long as the Cetacea have survived. (Man may also ensure that the whales will cease surviving within the next generation or two.)

Considerations such as these at times make some men of science and of compassion feel anger and guilt for their own species. One can begin to lose hope that anyone can do much about this situation, for those who are aware are very much in the minority on this planet. Those few who have the requisite knowledge may be too late to stop the killing of Cetacea and to initiate new programs of cooperation and communication with the Cetacea.

This book is an attempt to present the basis for these beliefs and their current details insofar as possible. It is hoped that the contents of the book will become known widely enough to help start programs of research on communication with the Cetacea. Such programs can be designed to find out who they are, what they think, what they talk about. In the process of publicizing the program and its results it may then be possible to stop the killing; only then will man's need to educate the Cetacea and to be educated by the Cetacea flower in new schools, industries, and government.

So in this book we present what is known, and we suggest guidelines for future interspecies work between man and Cetacea.

It is hoped that the coming generation will recognize that that is probably one of the greatest and most ennobling challenges that face man on this planet today. To be able to break through to understand the thinking, the feeling, the doing, the talking of another species is a grand, noble achievement that will change man's view of himself and of his planet. Seventy-one percent of the surface of our planet is covered with oceans, inhabited by the Cetacea. Let us learn to live in harmony with that seventy-one percent of the planet and its intelligent, sensitive, sensible, and long-surviving species of dolphins, whales, and porpoises.

CHAPTER ONE

The Development of the New Beliefs about Dolphins

BELIEFS ABOUT DOLPHINS ARE RECORDED STARTING WITH ARIS-totle. In his work, *Historia Animalium (The History of Animals)*, Aristotle makes many pertinent observations about dolphins, including the fact that they bear their young alive, suckle them, breathe air, and communicate by underwater sounds.

Aristotle made a rather startling statement about dolphins: "The voice of the dolphin in air is like that of the human in that they can pronounce vowels and combinations of vowels, but have difficulties with the consonants."

This observation had been scorned by nineteenth-century biologists investigating dolphins as biological objects in the sea. These nonparticipant objective observers, who had not experienced the living dolphins at first hand, called this mythology.

On the face of it, Aristotle's statement is rather startling. First of all, dolphins communicate with one another with underwater sounds; but then Aristotle mentions, "the voice of the dolphin in air." Until new observations were made in 1956 and 1957, this statement remained a puzzle. Someone at the time of Aristotle must have heard the voice of the dolphin in air or Aristotle would not have mentioned it. He did not specify the conditions under which this voice was heard in air, nor how the voicing sounds were produced by the dolphins.

During the nineteenth century and the early twentieth century biologists said that the whales and dolphins had no vocal chords and therefore had no voicing. The underwater sounds and their sonic emitter apparatus had not yet been investigated.

From Aristotle's writings we know that there were dolphins in the Mediterranean and porpoises in the Black Sea. We can hypothesize that Aristotle, or his contemporaries, experienced dolphins in shallow water pools close to man, in the light of our later knowledge of dolphins, derived from our experiments in the fifties. Modern dolphins under similar circumstances start emitting sounds in air when they are exposed to humans speaking in air. There is no reason to suppose that the ancient dolphins of the Mediterranean did not act as the modern dolphins do.

An extensive search of the written literature, both scientific and literary, since the time of Aristotle, shows no further experience with dolphins' sounds in air—as described by Aristotle. Up to 1955 there were only denials of the validity of Aristotle's observations by those who had no opportunity to be close to dolphins in shallow water. Aristotle states further that "small boys and dolphins develop mutual passionate attachments." He told stories of dolphins giving young boys rides, pulling them through the water. He also told of a dolphin beaching itself and dying from grief when a friendly boy left. It was not until the twentieth century that similar episodes are recounted. One of the more famous is that of Jill at Opononi in New Zealand as recounted by Antony Alpers. (40) At the small town of Opononi in New Zealand there is a long bay into which dolphins swim from the sea. On a small beach opposite the town, a dolphin, later called Opi, swam with the children selectively. Certain people could not approach Opi, but the younger persons could. Among these children was one, Jill, who developed a close friendship with Opi who towed her and played with her. These activities went on for several weeks. One day Opi did not arrive; he was later found dead on the shore.

Modern confirmation of Aristotle's observation about small boys and dolphins was made in collaboration with Ivan Tors during the making of his movie, *Flipper,* in the Bahamas. Ivan asked me to be a consultant for this movie. We discussed the possibility of having the hero of the movie swim with the dolphin called Flipper. We discussed Aristotle's observations that small boys could ride dolphins. This story was denied by Santini, the man who had captured the dolphins for use in the movie; he said, "It can't be done." Ivan asked me if we could arrange a demonstration to test the validity of Aristotle's observations.

I said that if it could be arranged for the dolphins to be worked with near a sand beach accessible to deeper water, then we could demonstrate Aristotle's observation. Ivan's wife and his two sons were available for the experiment. He arranged for three dolphins, a mother and a baby and another female, to be put inside a wire fence next to a beach in the Bahamas.

Ivan, Ivan's wife, myself, and the two boys entered the shallow water at the edge of the beach. We then spent about three hours reaching out and attempting to touch the three dolphins. When they determined that our hands were soft and that we intended them no harm, they came closer and closer and finally were gliding by us allowing us to stroke them from one end of their bodies to the other. We spent another three hours the first day in such "getting acquainted" maneuvers. The second day the dolphins approached us almost immediately as we entered the water, and the two young boys were able to climb aboard behind the dorsal fin of the mother dolphin; she gave them rides out to the deeper water, taking them under just long enough so that they did not run out of breath, bringing them back to the surface, and then delivering them to the shallow water next to the beach.

Mrs. Santini came down the dock beside the beach, saw what was happening, and shouted teasingly to her husband, "It can't be done!" From that point on the movie crew and the cast made very rapid progress. The results were shown in the *Flipper* full-length movie and in the TV series by the same name. Thus was another of Aristotle's observations confirmed.

We showed that dolphins today will do the same things that dolphins did two thousand years ago, when they faced humans in the water. From approximately 400 B.C. to 1962, dolphin relations with man seemed to be consistent—for over two thousand years! Aristotle's beliefs about dolphins were based upon observation made on the living dolphins of the sea. Most of what Aristotle had to say about dolphins has been reconfirmed in this century. After the time of Aristotle, skepticism about his observations began to arise. By the time of Plinius Secundus, the skepticism grew greatly as contact was lost with the living dolphins of the Mediterranean. The beliefs of Aristotle gradually faded, and in the new beliefs that took their place the dolphins, in comparison to man, once again were viewed as wild animals of inferior intelligence, lacking compassion and sensitivity.

The new belief system counter not only to Aristotle's belief but to the observations of his time is carried to 1929 by Eunice Burr Stebbins in her Ph.D. thesis, entitled *The Dolphin in the Literature and Art of Greece and Rome,* as follows: "Usener comments to the effect that the prevalence of these tales made it difficult for even the scientific thought of antiquity [i.e., Aristotle] to get away from the belief in the dolphin's ability to carry a rider. . . ."

One might well ask how one gets away from a belief in one's own observations of boys riding dolphins! Such authoritarian views currently continue to inhibit research with dolphins.

In the late nineteenth century and early twentieth century a few aquaria kept dolphins and porpoises in captivity. In England in the Victorian times a porpoise show was closed; the explanation given was that the sexual activities of the porpoises should not be displayed in public. Apparently these porpoises acted the way modern dolphins do in captivity, demonstrating frequent sexual encounters of various sorts.

In the early twentieth century an attempt was made to keep *Tursiops,* the Atlantic bottle-nosed dolphin, in the New York Aquarium. These dolphins were caught at Cape Hatteras and carried to New York in tanks in the intercoastal waterway. Neither in the English case nor in the New York case did anybody swim with the porpoises or the dolphins. The noninvolved objective observers of that time did not believe Aristotle's observations and considered the dolphins and porpoises zoo animals.

The first successful oceanarium in the United States, the Marine Studios at St. Augustine, was the first public display in which successful attempts to put on dolphin shows was realized. Extensive complex jumping, swimming, and carrying activities were exhibited in these shows. A colony of dolphins was kept in a separate tank, about seventy feet in diameter and twelve feet deep, complete with underwater observation windows and facilities for watching the dolphins at the surface of the tank. An auditorium was built with a separate tank for the circus shows. Laboratory facilities were available for scientists who wished to study the dolphins. From the forties through the fifties no one swam with the dolphins to any great extent.

Previous to the development of Marine Studios, the Theater of the Sea was operating in southern Florida. The feature of the Theater of the Sea act was to have the dolphin jump out of the water to grasp a fish presented to him from a tower twenty feet above the water. A few episodes of humans swimming with the dolphins were seen in those early days. As a consequence of the *Flipper* feature movie, a new relationship was established in the new oceanaria across the United States. For the first time parts of the show began to include human performers in the water with the dolphins.

In frequent conversations with Ivan Tors after 1962, I suggested to Ivan that even the killer whale *Orcinus orca*, the largest of the dolphins, probably would accept relationships with man in the water. In spite of fear engendered by the account in Scott's diary (1911) in Antarctica about the killer whales, and similar wild stories about their ferocity, their cunning, and their depradations of other animals, I believed that they would not hurt men and women who swam with them in the water, that they would show the same respect for the humans that the smaller dolphins had already demonstrated.

At the New Bedford Whaling Museum I reviewed the logs of the whaling ships and their firsthand accounts of contacts with orca. Despite the fact that during the killing of the larger whales men were thrown in the water among the whale killers, as they were called at that time, there was no record of a man's being either injured or eaten by orca. I hypothesized that man's paranoia about these huge dolphins was unfounded and based mainly upon Scott's account and the account of a biologist who examined the stomach contents of orca and found the remains of seals and smaller dolphins.

I transmitted all of this information to Ivan Tors, and he finally decided to risk doing a movie with an orca, the killer whale. His movie company spent six weeks with Namu, captured near Seattle. They found that Namu could be approached and worked with in the water by swimmers, both male and female. The resulting movie, called *Namu, the Killer Whale,* which is sometimes shown on TV, shows the immense respect of the humans for the large dolphin, and the large dolphin's gentleness in dealing with the humans. Scenes showing a man riding the back of Namu, holding on to the six-foot-high dorsal fin, and others coming aboard over the tail of the huge dolphin were adequate demonstrations that these were gentle, compassionate, cooperative animals.

I emphasize these public demonstrations because they are recorded on film and can be studied by those who are interested in the origins of the belief we have developed over the years about the dolphins, including the largest ones.

These public demonstrations were outside of scientific research and were based upon direct experience that we have had with the dolphins in the water. The correspondence between Aristotle's observations and our own experiences in the laboratory at St. Thomas and in Miami, convinced us that Aristotle's beliefs were correct and that later biological conjectures were incorrect.

Our extensive studies of the brains of the dolphins gave us a faith that these were a sentient, compassionate, considerate species with a great computational capacity, comparable, in a strange way, to that of man. The longer we and others worked intimately with them, the more we realized that the large brain was used in the service of survival, of compassion, and of cooperation.

In other parts of this book we present the neurological facts about cetacean brains and the similarity to the human enlargement of certain critical areas, areas in which the human brain has become enlarged over that of man's predecessors and of the apes. Elsewhere in this book we also present the unexpected verification of Aristotle's statements about the voice of the dolphin in air.

CHAPTER TWO

The New Beliefs Arise in Experiments

As is given in detail in *Man and Dolphin*, we had the first contact with dolphins at Marine Studios in St. Augustine, Florida, in 1955. This was our first experience with their behavior in the public shows and displays. The first findings of the basic physiology necessary to the work were also discovered at that time. Their voluntary breathing system, knocked out by anesthesia, was discovered. We also saw their brain structure for the first time.

Also in that same period it was seen that the public responded to the dolphins, to their presence, to their form, to their performances. The respect of the trainers and those responsible for the dolphins' care was also seen for the first time. We heard the philosophy of the trainers, of the curator, and of the management about dolphins; their beliefs were explained to us in great detail.

It is difficult to recapture one's own state of mind and the public knowledge about dolphins as of those early years. Enough of the public had seen dolphins in action so that there was a growing acquaintanceship with them. By that time Donald Hebb had visited Marine Studios, as had Per Fredrik Scholander and

Laurence Irving. Hebb, observing the dolphins' behavior, came to the tentative conclusion, hedged with careful scientific language, that the problem of determining the intelligence of dolphins was not yet solved. He put forth a "tentative hypothesis" (so labeled) that they could have intelligence comparable to that of the chimpanzees with whom he had worked. (41)

Scholander and Irving (42) had investigated the dolphins' respiration, using a spirometer, a device for determining the quantity of air breathed in and out. Their results showed us that about ten liters of air are breathed in each respiratory cycle. These records of theirs also showed us that it took only three-tenths of a second for the dolphin to empty its lungs totally and to refill them.

At the National Institutes of Health, where I was working at the time, I devised a respirator, hand-operated, which would copy this kind of respiration with a dolphin under anesthesia. We also found the necessary connection for this respirator and the lungs of the dolphin. We reached back into the throat of the dolphin, its jaws propped open, moved the larynx out of the nasopharynx, moving it down in the floor of the mouth, and inserted a one-and-one-eighth-inch diameter plastic tube down the trachea, connected it with the respirator, and demonstrated that we could keep alive an animal under anesthesia by using this technique. (1, 4)

Langworthy (43) had previously written that "due to certain technical difficulties" he was unable fully to anesthetize the dolphin safely. The technical difficulties were, of course, that he did not know that a respirator was required or that a respirator would work: he did not know that their respiration was voluntary.

(This work formed the basis for a later mechanical respirator that could carry dolphins through anesthesia even more safely; however, that was to come some ten years later, in collaboration with Forest Bird, Dr. Peter Morgane, and Dr. Eugene Nagel.) (14)

Prior to the use of this respirator, a dolphin died from anesthesia. The neuroanatomists were able to obtain a dolphin brain from this specimen.

I had seen many human brains in my courses in neuroanatomy

and during neurosurgery, but this was the first time I had seen a dolphin brain. I was impressed with its size and complexity. What most impressed me was the total size and the number of gyri and sulci on its surface, i.e., the tremendously packed folding of this large brain within its case. The weight of that brain was more than that of the average human brain—sixteen hundred grams compared with fourteen hundred grams.

These experiences gradually began to change my point of view about the dolphins from the notion that they are animals *upon which* one performs scientific experiments to the realization that they are man's equals on this planet—*with whom* one collaborates on scientific experiments. At this early date in my experience, the beginnings of new beliefs found their first roots. The growth of these new beliefs continued over the next thirteen years.

From 1955 to 1958, periodic visits to Marine Studios allowed me to accumulate further data about the dolphins and dolphins' brains. Experiments on their use of positive and negative reinforcing systems within their brains demonstrated that, in spite of negative stimuli, they would not become angry: they controlled their anger. During a period of hurt, they would shake all over but would not perform any violent action. I suddenly realized that this large brain, like man's, could control the built-in instinctive patterns of reaction to pain, which in other animals can lead to aggressive or frightened actions. The dolphin could control this behavior and did control it. Thus, we found that the huge cerebral cortex could exert direct inhibitory influences, from higher-level thinking processes, on their expression of emotion. We discovered that they had similar control over their positive motivations and would do only that which was appropriate to obtain necessary satisfaction.

At Marine Studios I was routinely recording what was going on during the experiments, as is recounted elsewhere. On playing back these tapes, I found that the dolphin had been making airborne sounds that, when slowed down, sounded like human speech. This observation was a key in our subsequent work. It established that the dolphins would do anything to convince the humans that they were sentient and capable. We saw for the first time that their computational capacities were immensely complex and large, carrying their attempts at communication with us even to the point of matching our voices, our laughter, and other noises in the laboratory.

In May of 1958 I gave a talk at the American Psychoanalytic and American Psychiatric meetings in San Francisco. I was asked to speak at a press conference run by Earl Ubell, the science editor of the *New York Herald Tribune*. Earl had spoken to me in some depth about the work with the dolphins and so he was primed with the right questions to ask. I was surprised to find that there was an immediate interest and an overwhelming response to my saying that the work to date showed that the dolphins were probably quite as intelligent as man but in a strange and alien way, as a consequence of their life in the sea. Man, the land mammal, was having difficulties making judgments about the dolphins of the sea. The newspaper stories spread from the local San Francisco papers around the world—as far away as a newspaper in Sydney, Australia. Because of my preoccupation with the work, I hadn't realized how radical a change this was from the previous views of the dolphin. This view, which apparently hadn't been suggested before by any scientist, became very popular.

I had decided to leave the public health service; my research was being done under the joint auspices of the National Institute of Neurological Diseases and Blindness and the National Institute of Mental Health. Dr. Leo Szilard was at the NIH at that time, investigating memory and the brain. Hearing of my dolphin work, he invited me to discuss it at several luncheon meetings. He attempted to dissuade me from leaving NIH and tried to point out how the work on the dolphins could continue there. I explained that I wanted to start a new laboratory devoted entirely to dolphin research. I had been so impressed with the dolphin that I decided that the research was worth a new institute somewhere in the warm water regions under U.S. jurisdiction. Subsequently Szilard wrote his book containing the story, called *Voice of the Dolphins,* based on what I had told him at NIH. (44)

In August 1958 I moved to the Virgin Islands in order to find a place for a dolphin laboratory. By the summer of 1959 I had located the proper place on the island of St. Thomas and had laid plans for the new laboratory there. At that stage in the development of the research and of our evolving beliefs I felt that we should pursue communication studies and studies on the brain of the dolphin.

By 1960 I had found means of support for the new dolphin laboratory in St. Thomas. I had obtained the cooperation of the navy's Underwater Demolition Team #21, stationed on St. Thomas. A lecture was given to them about dolphins. Their enthusiastic response was to blast out of the land on Nazareth Bay a sea pool in which the dolphins could be placed.

In Washington, an old friend, Dr. Orr Reynolds, in the Office of Science of the Department of Defense, agreed to allocate the first grant to the new Communication Research Institute, a nonprofit corporation of the Virgin Islands. The funds were channeled through the National Science Foundation and the Office of Naval Research. The new laboratory building, designed by Nathaniel Wells, an engineer of St. Thomas, was completed within a year. As recounted in *Man and Dolphin,* before the laboratory was started, two dolphins were brought to St. Thomas and further experiments on communication were completed. Earl Ubell flew with us and the dolphins in the cargo airplane from Marine Studios to St. Thomas. He wrote a story of his experiences in his newspaper.

When the grant was made to the Communication Research Institute, the story was written up by John W. Finney in the June 21, 1960, issue of the *New York Times.* Ubell's and Finney's stories excited general public interest. Professor Marston Bates wrote an article for *The New York Times Magazine* in October 1960 entitled "Inquiry into the Dolphin's I.Q. and Man's."

The early history of the beliefs and the work received documentation. Only then did I realize that this was a new and novel viewpoint to be taking about another species. This feedback from zoologist Bates was added to by Loren Eiseley, who wrote in the *Phi Beta Kappa Quarterly* (Winter issue, 1960–61) an article entitled "The Long Loneliness, the Separate Destinies of Man and Porpoise" (reprinted in his book *The Star Thrower,* Quadrangle, 1978).

While the laboratory in St. Thomas was being built, I was asked by the Air Force Office of Scientific Research to go to Mexico City to evaluate a research program for them. In Mexico

City I met Dr. Peter Morgane, a neurophysiologist and neuro-anatomist. He became so intrigued with the problems of the dolphin's large brain that he agreed to join the Communication Research Institute and pursue research on the brain.

Meanwhile, a laboratory was started in Miami, Florida, devoted to both the communication story and the neuroanatomical studies.

In Miami the observation of the dolphin's willingness and initiative in mimicking the human voice was continued. (9, 12, 18, 23) From 1961 to 1968 Dr. Morgane, Dr. Eugene Nagle, Dr. Will McFarland and Dr. Paul Yakovlev of Harvard University Medical School, pursued the neurophysiological and neuroanatomical studies. They did a complete survey of the dolphin's central nervous system, pursuing neuroanatomical research, which is continuing to the present time. (15, 20, 34, 35, 36, 45)

In order to investigate quantitatively the dolphin's sonic output in air, Dr. Henry M. Truby, a phonetician and linguist, joined the Miami group. He supervised the programming and analysis of the dolphin and the human's sonic outputs in the interactions in 1968. (33)

When the laboratory in St. Thomas was completed, Gregory Bateson, an anthropologist, became interested in the dolphin research. He agreed to move to St. Thomas and run the laboratory there. Three dolphins were flown from Miami to the St. Thomas laboratory that had been established before Bateson arrived. Two of these dolphins were contributed to the institute by Ivan Tors when he completed his first feature-length movie, *Flipper*. Tors also contributed costs of the airplane transport of the dolphins to St. Thomas.

Bateson spent eighteen months in the laboratory making very fundamental behavioral observations on the three dolphins. (46) He also found Margaret Howe on the island of St. Thomas and found that she was one of the best behavioral observers in his experience. When he left after eighteen months to go to Hawaii to the Oceanic Institute, Margaret asked to work on the mimicry story to attempt to teach a dolphin to enunciate English in the air well enough so that it could be understood by humans unequivocally. She worked for a period of two years. Her results are given in *The Mind of the Dolphin* and in numerous tapes.

Man and Dolphin was written in 1960. (4) It was translated into several languages after publication in the United States. The Russian translation became very popular among scientists and the public in Russia and led to the Minister of Fisheries placing a ban upon the killing and capturing of dolphins in the Black Sea and the Sea of Azov. The French edition *(L'Homme et Dauphin)* led to the book *The Day of the Dolphin,* by Robert Merle, a fictionalized account, presumably based upon our work. Subsequently, in the seventies, this was made into a movie in the United States. Despite my objections to the use of my name by the movie people and my objections to the misuse of dolphins in the movie, in the service of an undercover agency, the movie was released. A suit on copyright protection against Robert Merle and the movie company was lost in Los Angeles.

In 1966 *The Mind of the Dolphin* was written, detailing our progress and including scientific papers. (27)

The work accomplished in the years from 1960 through 1968 is expressed in the papers in the Bibliography published from the Communication Research Institute. Some of these papers are reproduced in the Appendix and discussed elsewhere in this book.

CHAPTER THREE

Sciences Necessary to Interspecies Communication with Cetacea

OVER THE YEARS FROM 1955 THROUGH THE PRESENT IT HAS BEEN found that a number of sciences are necessary to understanding the facts and theories fundamental to interspecies communication. There are at least a dozen sciences (and probably more) that contribute such understanding.

As has been shown by Thomas Kuhn, the structure of scientific revolutions necessitates the development of a new paradigm, which is contrasted with the old paradigm and taught to the younger generation. The old paradigm is then allowed to die with its proponents. (47)

Our new paradigm is "interspecies communication." Interspecies communication is possible only if one possesses knowledge obtained from very diverse sciences. What are these sciences?

Basic to any scientific investigation are models and simulations, i.e., the development of theories and the attempt to test them. In this way one can explore a new field. An excellent example is the relationship between theory and experiment in physics. When theoretical physicists collaborate with experimental physicists, there is advancement in the field of physics.

Without adequate theory, however, experimental physics makes no progress.

So to start we must devise proper theories in the field of interspecies communication.

Our area of investigation is concerned with the human species and the cetacean species. First, we should make use of the science of paleontology to learn about the development of the two species over the surface of the planet for the last thirty million years. Of particular interest are the cranial capacities of both species and the dating of the remains of the predecessors of modern man and modern whale.

The science of physics has much to contribute to our understanding of the survival of all species. One should know about Newtonian mechanics in the classical sense; the topics of mass, force, acceleration, momentum, and their rotatory analogs, and rigid bodies versus semirigid and nonrigid bodies are basic to an understanding of the physiology of locomotion and the laws of survival of organisms in evolution. Knowledge of some of the physics of stress and strain in various materials is also fundamental.

Anatomy of each species must be studied. Comparative studies of neuroanatomy and of functional body anatomy are basic.

Mammalian comparative physiology gives us interspecies similarities and differences in regard to respiration, circulation of the blood, metabolism, nutrition, and neurophysiology.

Hydrodynamics and aerodynamics give us essential information about the flow of fluids: of air, of water. One must learn something of Reynolds flow (i.e., laminar flow) versus turbulent flow of respiratory gases and of seawater. One should learn something of the flow of air in tubes through orifices and the differences between laminar and turbulent flow in these conditions. One must learn something of propulsion through water, of the concepts of drag, of the influence of viscosity and density upon these processes.

The science of physical acoustics must be mastered—something of the sources of sound energy, of the reflection, refraction, and absorption of sounds in gases, liquids, and solids. The conduction of sound in the three states of matter and the changes in patterns of sound crossing boundaries between gases, liquids, and solids must be known.

Biophysical acoustics must be studied. Knowledge of how organisms produce sounds and how organisms detect sounds is needed for our studies.

The production and detection of human speech, the sciences of phonetics and the physical analyses of sounds, and linguistics give a perspective on human communication and a possible structure of cetacean communication.

The study of psychophysical acoustics is necessary for an understanding of the central processing of acoustical signals: the transforms of acoustical signals from spatial to temporal parameters, externally and internally within the central nervous system, are derived from this science.

An understanding of the computer sciences is necessary. Means of signal processing by software and hardware are necessary. Some understanding of hardware (i.e., circuits), software (i.e., programming), and firmware (i.e., temporarily fixed programming) are needed. The size of a memory (the number of places that data and programs can be stored in a computer) determines the limitations of a given computer. The software available for a given computer and the development of new software must be understood. In this context the available algorithms and their uses in the service of one's own problems is basic. Real time processing is a concept that must be mastered. The limitations upon the various kinds of operations a computer can do in real time and the contrast between the analog and the digital methods must be mastered. Analog to digital and digital to analog converters at the input to digital computers must be understood. The available microprocessors in minicomputers and their various characteristics are important.

The science of biocomputers, of brains and their computational capacities, must be understood. The critical levels of development of various functions and their relation to size of structure is important. The presence in each mammal, in each mammalian species, of a biominicomputer with its genetically determined circuitry ready for future special purpose use must be understood. The containment of the biominicomputer and its use by later evolved biomacrocomputers, giving rise to general-purpose functions, is important.

The science of evolution points to the past increase in brain sizes in the two groups of species, the humans and the cetaceans. It may be that we are on a rising curve of further evolution of brain size in the two species. Thus, it is necessary in this science to have something of a time perspective and knowledge of our current position in regard to the development of each species.

Here we do not attempt to give a detailed analysis of the facts, theories, and uses of each of these sciences in interspecies communication. In a sense, this book and its references indicate the disciplines necessary for the new science. Many students have asked me what to study in order to pursue interspecies communication work. Students should become familiar with the disciplines described above. Integrating the facts in each of these fields into a relationship to the whole develops only when one's knowledge in each of the important areas becomes sufficient. A doctor of philosophy degree could be designed around these scientific disciplines. In a sense, then, we are giving the prerequisites for such a degree.

With the slowly developing modern view permitting students to select their own university courses of study, I'm giving the above suggestions to those interested students and faculties who wish to learn and to teach in this new domain.

CHAPTER FOUR

Who Are the Cetaceans
(Dolphins, Porpoises, and Whales)?

THE CETACEANS (DOLPHINS, PORPOISES, AND WHALES) ARE THE pelagic (completely waterborne) mammals of the sea. The reproduction of the cetaceans is the typical mammalian reproduction via sexual intercourse, gestation of the young dolphin in the womb, and birth, under water. The cetaceans nurse their young, feeding them milk formed in mammary glands. The cetaceans are warmblooded, with a brain temperature of 37° C (98.6° F). The cetaceans have lungs and breathe air. Their blood is circulated by a four-chambered heart similar to that of the land mammals. Their muscles closely resemble those of the land mammals and are used for propelling them through the water by movements of their flukes.

Most of the life of the cetaceans is spent under water, and only a small fraction of the time is spent at the surface to breathe and to rise up and look around. Some species leap out of the water when it is safe to do so. The breathing act of a cetacean can be seen as a spout: a column of water droplets combined with the air that they expel from their lungs. The water droplets are from seawater collected in the sacs just below the blowhole from which the air mixed with the water comes forth. The explosive expulsion

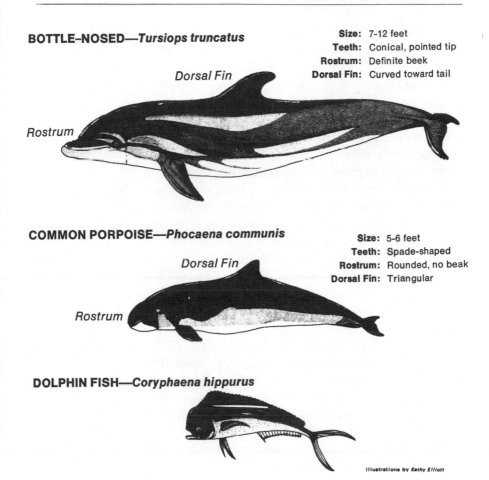

BOTTLE-NOSED—*Tursiops truncatus*

Size:	7-12 feet
Teeth:	Conical, pointed tip
Rostrum:	Definite beek
Dorsal Fin:	Curved toward tail

Dorsal Fin

Rostrum

COMMON PORPOISE—*Phocaena communis*

Size:	5-6 feet
Teeth:	Spade-shaped
Rostrum:	Rounded, no beak
Dorsal Fin:	Triangular

Dorsal Fin

Rostrum

DOLPHIN FISH—*Coryphaena hippurus*

Illustrations by *Kathy Elliott*

FIGURE 1.   The classical distinctions among dolphin, porpoise, and dolphin fish.

The topmost figure is of the bottle-nosed dolphin, *Tursiops truncatus,* which grows from seven to twelve feet in adulthood, has conical pointed teeth, has a definite beak at the rostral end and the dorsal fin, which is curved toward the tail. The next figure down is that of the common porpoise, *Phocaena communis.* These inshore cetaceans grow to five to six feet in length, have spade-shaped teeth, have a rounded rostrum with no beak, and a triangular dorsal fin with no overhang. The brain size of the common porpoise is approximately that of a chimpanzee, i.e., three hundred fifty to four hundred grams; whereas that of the bottle-nosed dolphin, *Tursiops,* is up to eighteen hundred grams, i.e., in the upper range of the human brain size. The bottommost figure is of the dolphin fish, *Coryphaena hippurus,* otherwise known as the Dorado or Mahi-mahi, which pursues flying fish near the surface of tropical seas and whose blunt rostrum causes vertical spurts of water when it enters and leaves waves at the surface. The dolphin fish breathes water and is not a mammal like the porpoise and *Tursiops.*

of the air from their lungs sucks up this water, forming the spout.

The cetaceans have exquisitely streamlined bodies of distinctive shapes.

At the front end of their bodies the dolphins have long beaks, which are their jaws. The true porpoises have more blunt front ends, as do the pilot whales and the sperm whales. Most species have a dorsal fin, from the six-foot-high dorsal fin of a male *Orcinus orca* down to the practically nonexistent dorsal fin of some species of river dolphins and baleen whales.

The home territory of most of the cetaceans is the oceans and seas of earth, which cover 71 percent of the planet's surface. A few species live in freshwater rivers (the Amazon, the Plata, etc.). Some of the seagoing cetaceans travel up freshwater rivers some distance *(Tursiops* in the St. Johns River of Florida, the Beluga up the Mackenzie River and the St. Lawrence River, etc.). Since the cetaceans are effectively independent of their environmental water, they can live quite safely in freshwater, as has been demonstrated experimentally with the bottle-nosed dolphin.

The cetaceans cannot drink seawater; their kidneys will not concentrate the urine any more than the kidneys of humans or other land mammals will. All of the cetaceans' water comes from the metabolism of the fat in their diet, changing the fat to carbon dioxide, which is exhaled, and water, which is held in the tissues. In effect then, the cetaceans are desert animals depending upon the water derived strictly from their food.

In order to avoid the ingestion of seawater as they take in their food, they have two major methods of keeping the seawater out: in the case of the toothed whales, there is a sphincter in the back of the throat, a circular muscle that closes the back of the throat until food, fish, or squid is to pass into the stomach. This sphincter squeezes the salt water off the food morsel and prevents the accumulation of salt beyond the sphincter. The second mechanism is found in the baleen whales in which they open their huge mouths in the dense krill (small shrimplike creatures growing in abundance mainly in the Arctic and Antarctic oceans), take in the krill plus the seawater, and move the seawater out through the strainer known as the baleen, catching the krill in the strainer. They then close the mouth, which now has no seawater in it, and swallow the krill.

Thus do the cetaceans prevent the taking on of the large amounts of salt present in seawater. Physiological experiments with humans and other land mammals show that drinking seawater leads to dehydration unless it is diluted with freshwater by a factor of approximately ten times.

Experiments on captive bottle-nosed dolphins show that they will drink freshwater when it is presented to them from a hose. This drinking then leads to their not eating for a day or two. They then start eating again and stop drinking water. Apparently, in their natural state they do not separate thirst from hunger. Drinking freshwater allows them to feel hunger separate from thirst for the first time.

The diet of the toothed whales, including the dolphins and porpoises, consists of fish and/or squid. Small squid are eaten by the smaller cetaceans, and giant squid are eaten by the largest of the toothed whales, the sperm whale. The largest of the dolphins, *Orcinus orca,* the so-called killer whale, eats large fish and seals and some old dolphins of smaller size. They have also been seen to eat parts of baleen whales that have been killed by man. Baleen whales subsist totally on krill. The larger the cetacean, the longer he or she can go without food after a prolonged feeding period. The bottle-nosed dolphin can go approximately a week without food; the killer whale can go approximately six weeks without food; and the largest of the whales, the blue whale, can go approximately six months without food. During the period of maximum feeding the cetaceans store the food in the form of fat. The fat is then converted into biological energy plus carbon dioxide and water. After a cetacean has burned up all his fat, he can die from lack of water.

Most cetaceans can dive to fairly great depths, depending upon their oxygen capacity, which again depends upon their body size. The larger the cetacean the deeper it can dive without needing air. Before a dive most cetaceans take a series of rapid breaths, then fill their lungs and start downward by lifting their tails out of the water to let the initial impetus of the gravity pull upon their hindquarters. As they dive, their lungs collapse, their ribs cave in, folding along special joints along the sides of their body. The lungs collapse completely, driving the remaining air into the dead spaces within the skull. This trapped air in the dead space is not given access to the bloodstream. The collapse of the lungs and confining of the air out of contact with the blood means that the oxygen and the nitrogen of the blood are at the same partial pressure that they are at the surface at one atmosphere. No nitrogen is forced into the blood or into the fat of their bodies; the nitrogen in the fat is at equilibrium at one atmosphere not at the high pressures of the depths to which they dive. The cetaceans then cannot experience the diver's disease known as bends, or decompression sickness. Bends result from air combining with the blood at the high pressure in the depths, and then, when one returns to the surface with his high pressure nitrogen saturating the fat of the body, one has the bends. As one rises to the surface and lowers the pressure on the body and in the lungs, the nitrogen must come out of the fat and it comes out in the form of painful bubbles that can block the circulation to the lungs and to various tissues. In human divers, using only a snorkel and not an Aqualung, no bends are experienced—they are breathing the way the whales do.

The cetaceans will not experience bends until some human tries to force them to use an Aqualung. Or until some human induces them to breathe air in an open diving bell or in an open undersea house in which the air pressure is kept at the pressure of the water at that depth. Such experiments with dolphins or whales could be very dangerous for the cetaceans in that they have had no experience with bends. However, they may be intelligent enough to rise slowly so that they will not experience the bends.

Cetacean swimming is mostly in three dimensions: two horizontal dimensions and one of depth. Each cetacean adjusts his buoyancy in order to be in a neutrally buoyant condition at a given depth. In the neutrally buoyant condition very little effort is needed to swim. One does not have to exert muscular force to move horizontally and to stay at the given depth. Dolphins have such complete streamlining that they can tow each other; one dolphin in the proper position with respect to the other, or one whale in the proper position with respect to the other, is towed along in the swimming pressure pattern of the active dolphin or whale. Such activities show the beautiful streamlining and the low level of friction of the cetaceans with the surrounding water.

There are several mechanisms that enhance this lack of friction. The shape of the body is streamlined, but it is also a flexible shape. When a dolphin accelerates, one can see the shape of the body change to match the acceleration vortices generated in the water as the velocity is changed rapidly. Vertical hollows in a definite wave pattern are seen to move along the sides of the animal, shedding the vortices generated. The skin of all cetaceans emits a very fine oil continuously from the front of the animal to the rear. After a whale dives, one can see the oil slick on the surface of the sea. This oil has several functions; its viscosity does not change with temperature and remains very low in either warm water or very cold water. The oil layer on the skin thus provides slippage for the boundary layers of seawater close to the skin, thus reducing the friction of the skin against the water. The cetaceans are literally lubricated, streamlined objects. Experiments on a six-meter international racing yacht, which allowed oil to flow out over the hull, showed that the same principle could be applied to humanly constructed boats and increase their speed considerably.

There is a basic principle in the physiology of mammals, terrestrial as well as oceanic, which helps to explain some of the cetaceans' adaptations to the sea. This principle is that the brain controls body mechanisms, including circulation, metabolism, and activities of the muscles, to maintain its own food supplies and its own temperature.

This principle can be demonstrated when one squats too long and stands up abruptly; he may pass out as the blood leaves his brain temporarily. The brain has been deprived of its blood supply. Immediately following such an abrupt movement, measurements of the blood pressure show that the heart, under the control of the brain, has responded by beating faster and harder to restore the blood pressure that was momentarily lowered by the sudden standing and the blood drops into the muscles of the legs. If one's body becomes too cold, shivering starts at the behest of the brain to increase the metabolism to keep the brain temperature constant by the circulation of the warmed blood from the muscles through the brain itself.

The brain temperature in cetaceans is maintained by several mechanisms including adequate insulation of the body and control of circulation in the skin. When a cetacean gets too warm, the blood vessels dilate, and the very rich blood supply in the skin disperses the heat into the water. When a dolphin is jumping out of the water, one can see this pink flushing of the white undersides caused by the increased blood flow through his relatively transparent skin. When the cetacean becomes too cold, the vessels contrict his blood supply, keeping the blood from contact with the water. The blubber, the oil-filled outer layers of the dermis, ranging in thickness from an inch or two in the bottle-nosed dolphin to six to ten inches in the larger whales, prevents the loss of heat from the deeper regions of the body—the muscles, intestinal tract, and so forth. The fat deposits, which allow the cetacean to go long periods without eating, are underneath this blubber layer. In the starving animal the fat deposits disappear, but the blubber remains a constant thickness. A well-fed dolphin shows no constriction in the neck region behind the blowhole because his neck is filled out with the fat accumulated in this region. A starving dolphin shows a very definite constriction in the neck region, since the fat has disappeared.

The cetaceans depend upon the flow of water around their bodies to dissipate the heat resulting from their bodily metabolism. A cetacean taken out of water by humans or beached will die of increased body temperature unless cooled by evaporating water or by flowing water put upon the body by humans. A cetacean out of water can dissipate the heat only by expiring air and water from his lungs. When the temperature of his brain becomes too high, he will die from a high fever.

Cetaceans also depend upon the buoyancy of the water to maintain their circulation to the brain and the rest of the body. A cetacean taken out of water or placed in a tank in which the water level is lowered progressively will tip himself over on the side. On the side the pressure on his lungs is lessened and allows better circulation of the veinous blood to the lungs and to the rest of the tissues. The work of breathing is increased immensely out of water. The work of the heart is also increased a great deal. Flexible slings in which the cetacean is hung can reduce the work of breathing and the work of the heart. However, the best method of transporting cetaceans is in tanks of water in which they can float.

One peculiar adaptation of the cetacean anatomy and physiology to the sea is the rete mirabile. This is a plexis of arteries, interconnected in a very complex way, which underlies the brain and the spinal cord and is found lining the upper portion of the pleural cavity behind the lungs. This rete mirabile is supplied with blood from special arteries. Experiments show that this system is very large and contains arterial blood with a large amount of oxygen. The system acts in such a way that it damps out the pulsations of the heart in the blood supply to the brain. It is also very well innervated by the sympathetic nervous system. In addition to supplying the normal blood flow through the brain, the rete supplies blood in emergency situations. If a cetacean is diving and stays down too long, the oxygen deprivation of the brain results in a wave of contractions traveling from the posterior regions of the rete in back of the lungs toward the brain, driving the oxygen in the blood stored in the rete into the brain. This emergency blood/oxygen supply then allows the cetacean to swim extremely rapidly and reach the surface with one final burst of speed.

Dolphins and whales in contact with humans show that their skin is exquisitely sensitive to touch, to pressure, and to flow of water. When one meets a dolphin for the first time in the natural environment, if one can touch the dolphin, one establishes the beginnings of a bond of friendship. As the dolphin trusts the human more and more, he or she will allow the human to stroke him, coming in closer and closer to the human, who can then run his hand along the length of the dolphin's side.

If one unexpectedly touches even the tip of the dorsal fin or the flukes, one can see that dolphins are extremely sensitive and react with a startled jump at such light touching.

Their skin is exquisitely sensitive to pain. If one has to give an antibiotic to a sick dolphin, for example, the needle prick results in a quick jump, which is then controlled, and as long as the needle is in the dolphin, he or she will shake, controlling fear and pain. Their flippers are very delicate and the tissue under the flipper, "the armpit," is very easily torn. If one remembers that tied together in the flipper are all the bones of our hand, lower arm, and upper arm, one can see that the joint at the body of the cetacean is effectively a shoulder joint. There is a scapula under the blubber, close to the flipper. In lifting cetaceans in slings, one must be very careful not to bend the flippers in ways that will tear these very delicate tissues. The flipper can lie close in to the side wall of the chest without being hurt; however, the cetacean must not be allowed to lie on the flipper or the circulation will be cut off and the flipper badly injured because of lack of blood supply. One can tell if a cetacean has undergone such an experience in the past. The recovery of a flipper results in loss of pigment, and the flipper or other skin is usually white after it heals. The pigmentation takes a much longer time to reestablish itself after an injury.

Apparently, the toothed whales have no sense of smell, but they have an exquisite taste sensitivity. The taste organs distributed around the periphery of the tongue can be extruded between the teeth so that, as the cetacean travels through the water, he can taste the water flowing through the cracks between his lips. This sensitivity allows the cetaceans to follow trails of taste in the sea. One of these trails is the feces and urine that other cetaceans emit in the seawater. They can track one another to a certain extent by finding these patches of changed taste in the sea. They can probably also find the traces of fish that have traveled in a given direction and thus track schools of fish from the products of their metabolism left behind in the sea. They can probably also detect ocean currents of various sorts, the effluent from rivers, the change in salinity of the sea owing to slight dilutions by rivers, the pollutants in the sea introduced by man; all add to the medley of tastes experienced by cetaceans.

The cetaceans' underwater communications are of particular interest, as is their echo ranging and recognition abilities. These are discussed in greater depth in other portions of this book.

Cetaceans' brains and their origins are discussed elsewhere in this book. Here we merely say that their brains are very much older than man's. Undoubtedly the cetaceans have a complex inner reality or mental life. This also is discussed later.

Young cetaceans are educated by older ones.

The cetaceans' sexual reproduction has required several modifications compared to that of land mammals.

The genitalia are all inside, not exposed to the sea. The penis of the male is kept inside the body until the occasion for sexual play or intercourse requires that it be erected outside. Experimentally it was found that the male dolphin erects his penis voluntarily in a matter of seven seconds. He can also collapse his penis again in an equally short time. In the male the penis comes out of the genital slit, which is forward of the anal slit. The penis is streamlined fore and aft and comes to a small point, at the tip of which is the exit of the urinary canal and the canal for the ejaculation of spermatozoa and semen. The penis is narrow laterally and broad fore and aft at the base. The corresponding slit in the female fits the penis closely in a fore and aft direction and laterally. The female has the analog of the land mammal vestibular cavity and the inner vaginal cavity leading to the uterus. In the male and the female there are two bones, analogous to the pelvic bones in the land mammals, that support the genitalia. These bones are tied to the backbone through ligamentary structures. These bones form a platform that stabilizes the penis in the male and the vagina in the female during sexual activities.

Sexual behavior of cetaceans in their natural habitat is practically unknown because of the difficulties of observations in the wild. In captivity, in the absence of danger, sexual play consumes a lot of the waking time of the young cetaceans. However, this may be an effect of the boredom caused by the confinement of the Cetacea in small tanks with nothing else to do.

The gestation period of cetaceans varies with their size. The smallest cetaceans have a gestation period of approximately ten months. As the size goes up, this period is extended to two years for the largest of the whales.

The embryos and fetuses of dolphins and whales go through transformations very similar to those of the land animals. The very small embryos are not recognizable as distinctively cetaceans. As they become fetuses later in pregnancy, their distinctive cetacean characteristics develop. The embryos show four limb buds, the hindmost two of which are usually resorbed during growth in the womb; however, every so often a dolphin or a whale is born with residual limb buds lateral to the genitalia. The development in the uterus of these hind limb buds implies that an ancestor of the whales and dolphins had four flippers or four legs, depending on one's theories connected with the origins of whales and dolphins.

The baby dolphin is born under water usually tail first. His little flukes are folded as they come out, but they quickly expand and become the flat flukes useful in swimming. At the instant of birth the mother whirls to break the cord and the little baby starts swimming blindly and very rapidly. The mother directs his swimming in such a way that he reaches the surface and takes his first breath, a very dramatic moment in the life of the dolphin. The baby then continues his swimming and within a few minutes learns where the surface of the water is to obtain air. In an oceanarium he may try to swim through a window, not knowing that the glass is not water. I have seen a mother arrive at the glass just ahead of the baby and divert him from such impacts. Later she allows him to hit the window a glancing blow so that he will learn about glass firsthand. He does this only once.

The next problem to the baby is finding the nipples and learning how to suckle. As his hunger and dehydration build up, he begins to seek the nipples and the mother presents them to the baby. The nipples on the dolphin are on each side of the genital slit toward the rear of the female. The two small slits contain the nipples, which can be sucked out or extruded into the water. The baby must learn to make a half tube of his tongue against the upper jaw, grasping the nipple in this half circle of his tongue, and to suckle without sucking in seawater. This amazingly precise act is learned the first day with the cooperation of the mother.

The milk is particularly thick, the nutrient content is one-half protein, one-half fat, and approximately 10 percent water. There is no lactose or other sugar in the milk. This particularly rich mixture is of a similar composition for all the cetaceans. The baby dolphin drinking just this milk gains, in a period of two years, four feet in body length and three hundred pounds in body weight. The baby blue whale gains two hundred and fifty pounds a day at the period of maximum growth, derived totally from the milk from the mother.

It takes a period of approximately one to two years to wean a baby dolphin from its mother's milk. Slowly but surely he begins to find other things to eat, such as small fish. As he grows, the fish that he eats can be larger. He is taught to bite the fish and taste it to see that it is not poisonous or spoiled. His sharp, needlelike teeth penetrate the fish, and the taste tells him whether it is safe or not. He then turns the fish in his mouth with his tongue, lines it up so that it goes headfirst, crushes it into a cylinder and swallows it over his larnyx lying in the bottom of his oropharynx, and passes it through the squeegee sphincter, mentioned earlier, into the esophaghus and into the first stomach.

In an adult bottle-nosed dolphin the first stomach is large enough to hold approximately twenty pounds of fish. The exit to this large bag is a very muscular outpouching from the larger stomach. The exit from the outpouching is no larger than the tip of one's little finger. In these two stomachs the fish is ground, compressed, torn apart, and digested enough so that the bones are freed from the flesh and the flesh becomes a liquid that can be squeezed out of the small hole into the duodenum. The bones are separated from this liquid and regurgitated outside through the mouth. The liquid then travels down through the rest of the very small-diameter intestine, is mixed with pancreatic and liver fluids, and the digestive process is carried out fully over a considerable length of small and large intestine. There is no cecum or appendix. The lack of a cecum means that the Cetacea are adapted to a nonvegetable diet. They have no provision for digesting cellulose as do cows and horses. The intestinal tract terminates in the anus, which in the bottle-nosed dolphin is very small, about the size, when fully expanded, of one's little finger. The feces, in general rather liquid, are dispersed rapidly in the seawater.

The urine is also discharged in the seawater. Analyses of the urine of dolphins show that it is very similar to that of humans, i.e., dolphins cannot concentrate the urine any more than we can beyond a certain limit. Therefore, they cannot drink seawater and lose the salt through their urine. Their kidneys are like ours in that they can excrete the metabolic products, but they cannot excrete large quantities of salt.

Cetaceans are subject to diseases very similar to those of land animals. They can be infested with parasites of various sorts, including roundworms; they have bacterial and viral diseases. In our experience cetaceans in close contact with man experience the common cold and epidemics of influenza at the same time that the persons in contact with them experience these diseases.

Thus, we introduce the cetaceans to you as free-ranging, pelagic, balanced mammals of the sea.

In our humanistic literature, in our politics, in our laws, in our governments, we generate a human species reality. We establish rules for interactions among humans. We describe phenomena in terms of human feeling, thinking, and doing. We define self and others like self as capable or incapable of taking responsibility for action, for thinking, and for feeling. We assume responsibility for loving, hating, hurting, or helping the other person.

In contrast to this view of our own species, in our biological science we see other species as less than capable, without responsibility for others or for us. We describe them as having "instinctual" action, no thinking, and relatively little feeling. We define them as conditionable beings, responding to our operant conditioning methods as if they were incapable of complex thinking and complex computation of action in the future. We look upon all of them as if they were irresponsible and incompetent, to be managed by us for our economic gain, for our entertainment, for our amusement, for our sport, for the education of our young.

Within the human reality some of us are guided by the golden rule.

We recognize that among humans there are those who are socially incompetent. There are those who cannot speak language as we know it and cannot be controlled by this very flexible instrument. We recognize such individuals in our laws and place restraints upon their social behavior. We confine them or we kill them at birth.

It is such considerations as these that lead to a consideration of human behavior in contrast to what we have learned of the behavior of dolphins, porpoises, and whales.

In the following table we divide up behaviors among those for the "capable human individual" and contrast this behavior with that of the dolphin *Tursiops* and the dolphin *Orcinus orca*. Our knowledge of the human is far greater than it is of the dolphins. We are limited in our considerations of the dolphin behavior because we cannot communicate with the dolphins. We can evaluate human behavior because we can communicate with the

TABLE 1

THE CONTRASTING BEHAVIOR OF MAN, OF *TURSIOPS,* AND OF *ORCA*

Capable Human Individual Behavior	*Tursiops* Behavior	*Orcinus orca* Behavior
1. Competent to function in a society of humans; incompetents are confined or killed.	1. Competent dolphins function in a species/interspecies mutual dependence; incompetents die or suicide out.	1. Same as *Tursiops.*
2. Competent to speak a human language sharable with others.	2. Competent to speak a dolphin language: same as human.	2. Same as *Tursiops.*
3. Capable of handling personal aggressive behavior within own group so as not to kill another human.	3. Same as human.	3. Same as human.
4. To be capable of killing other humans in the service of own group.	4. Forbidden to kill other dolphins, irrespective of species. (Exceptions: two dolphins confined eight years in Seaquarium.)	4. Exceptions noted: evidence in stomach contents; case of one old *Tursiops.*
5. To respond to aggressive action of another human with "self-defensive" actions, damaging or even killing if necessary.	5. To respond to aggressive action on the part of another dolphin with graded force short of bodily damage.	5. Same as *Tursiops.*
6. To interact in human society so as to ensure one's own supply of food, shelter, clothing, bodily transport: one's own survival, one's own life-style, one's own advancement in human society.	6. To cooperate in concerted action to find and obtain food, air, water temperature.	6. Same as *Tursiops.*
7. To influence and be influenced by others in the service of human groups: family, city, town, country, nation, world societies.	7. Same across species.	7. Same as *Tursiops.*

Capable Human Individual Behavior	*Tursiops* Behavior	*Orcinus orca* Behavior
8. To be draftable in war, the defense/attack of one's own group for/against other human groups.	8. No war, no draft.	8. Same as *Tursiops*.
9. To learn how to kill/eat other species for self and other humans, no matter the brain size and/or the body size of the other species.	9. To learn to find and eat appropriate fish/squid/etc., in cooperation with group: body size of other species regulated by physical size of dolphins.	9. Same as *Tursiops*. Exceptions noted: stomach contents studies; some have eaten smaller dolphins.
10. To capture and confine other species for sport, entertainment, display, education of humans.	10. No possibilities for dolphins.	10. None.
11. To learn to conserve other species for economic purposes.	11. Interdependence with other species developed over estimated twenty-five or more millions of years: mutual survival.	11. Same as *Tursiops*.
12. To learn to live in a total ecology of the planet, land, atmosphere, and oceans.	12. Demonstrated abilities to live in total ecology of oceans.	12. Same as *Tursiops*.
13. To learn the realities of other species, to explore their potential and realized communicative abilities.	13. As data accumulates, communicative abilities appear to be well developed. Demonstrated willingness to develop communication with man.	13. Same as *Tursiops*.
14. To care for individuals of other species, to become attached, to feel grief at his/her death.	14. To care for individual humans in the water, rescue him/her, become attached to those confining and caring for the dolphin, to die if left by him/her alone.	14. Same as *Tursiops*. (Tors experiences)

other humans in those cases in which the humans are capable of communicative language behavior.

Some of the human behaviors described are imbedded in our laws for the rights of human individuals in dealing with other human individuals and the relationships among groups of humans as large as nations. Some of the behaviors are not in our laws as yet.

Because we can talk to another person, we must assume that he can think and feel, even as we do ourselves. We project onto the others and receive from the others their projections, which allow us to make this basic assumption. We cannot do this as yet for members of cetacean species because we cannot yet communicate with them at this level. So far we must judge the individual cetacean on the basis of direct experience with what they do with us, what they do and do not do to us.

CHAPTER FIVE

Why Are There No Large Brains
in Small Bodies?

"BY THE YEAR 1843 THE SIZE OF THE BRAIN OF WHALES WAS being related to the total size of the body. The very large brains of the large whales were reduced in importance by considering their weight in a ratio to the weight of the total body. This type of reasoning was culminated b a long series of quantitative measures published by Eugène Dubois (Bulletins de la Société d' Anthropologie de Paris, Ser ɬ, VIII, pgs. 337–76, 1897)." (48)

Recently a review of the evolution of mammalian brains was published by H. J. Jerison. (49) In summary, the data on the whales relating their brain size to their body size shows that if one plots brain size against body size there is a continuous curve above which no animals exist and below which all of the current and past animals exist.

Such information as this raises the question why large brains do not exist in small bodies?

To explain these curves, biologists have assumed that a large body needs a large brain to control its functions. In other chapters in this book we have shown that a large body does not necessarily need a large brain to control it. We present the fact that a primate body is controlled by a primate minibiocomputer.

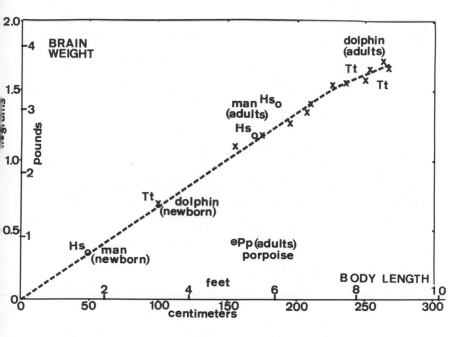

FIGURE 2. Brain size and body size in the human, the bottle-nosed dolphin and the porpoise.

The newborn baby dolphin has a brain of about twice the size of the newborn human, six hundred fifty grams compared with three hundred grams. As the dolphin grows and as the human grows, their brains tend to become equal in size. Finally, as the dolphin continues his growth beyond that of the man, his brain becomes heavier than that of the man. Here we compare brain weight in kilograms and pounds to body length in feet and centimeters. A very similar curve is found for brain weight versus body weight. See Appendix 6, The Cetacean Brain.

As brains and bodies get larger in the mammalian series, we also showed that the increase in brain size is mainly an increase in the "silent areas or associational cortex," which we call the macrobiocomputer. The macrobiocomputer is devoted to controlling the minibiocomputer in new and complex general-purpose programmatic fashion. The basic difference between man and chimpanzee is in the increased size of the macrobiocomputer. Among the Cetacea the only increase in brain size that can be found is increase in the macrobiocomputer, not in the minibiocomputer. The whale shark at forty tons has only a small minibiocomputer and no macrobiocomputer.

T A B L E 2
HUMAN/DOLPHIN COMPARISON

Structure/ Function	Human	Dolphin
Bodies	Mammalian: head, hands, arms, legs; manipulatory, walking, running in-air adaptations: nonstreamlined shape.	Mammalian: neutral buoyancy, swimming adaptations, head, flippers, flukes: streamline shape.
Brains	900–1,800 grams: 1,400 grams average; present size 0.1 million years. Predominantly associational cerebral cortex.	1,000–6,000 grams: present size 25 million years. Predominantly associational cerebral cortex.
Locomotion	Discontinuous, with sleep periods interrupting; no movement for long periods. Maximum velocity about 18 knots running.	Free dive limit continuous process: moving to surface for every breath, swimming 24 hours/day whole life. Average 5 knots: Maximum velocity about 30 knots.
Sexuality	Carefully regulated: can take place at any time. Ritualized clothing, behavior, male vs. female.	Free expression: voluntary erection of penis in males. Can take place at any time. Fertilization at time to give birth during warm season.
Birth & Reproduction	Gestation 9 months. Birth into air.	12 months gestation. Underwater birth.
Respiration	Always available air: automatic continuance during unconsciousness, sleep, anesthesia.	Air must be sought at surface; must wake up for every breath; no automatic continuance in sleep, unconsciousness, anesthesia.
Nutrition	Plants, animals: predigestion by cooking	Fish, shrimp, squid: raw (no cooking)
Circulation	Upright position adaptation: no rete mirabile	Horizontal, buoyancy adaptation rete mirabile for emergency brain functioning.
Communication	Outputs: 2 sources with sequence control: Air-speech; written materials Inputs: ears adapted to air: azimuth and elevation detection: scanning.	Outputs: adapted to underwater emission: 3 sources independent control. Underwater sound communication; no written forms. Sound emission for ranging, recognition, and orientation. Inputs: ears adapted to underwater azimuth and elevation: scanning.
Evolution	Evolved from prehuman forms over last million years.	Evolved from predolphin forms last 50 million years.
Organization	Economic exploitation of ecology: financial records rule.	Total interspecies interdependence; in ecological harmony.
Ethics	Human-centered: no other-species directed.	Dependence on others: no aggressivity, no hostile attacks.

Structure/ Function	Human	Dolphin
Nonbrain, Outside Records	Human reality constructed in written records.	None.
Gonads	Male: external testes, external penis. Female: internal ovaries, internal uterus.	Male: internal testes, internal penis. Female: internal ovaries, internal uterus.
Mating	Male erection: involuntary. Female estrus: monthly. Copulation: voluntary, any time. Insemination: depends on fertility cycle in female: sperm → egg.	Male erection: voluntary. Female estrus: ? monthly. Copulation: voluntary, any time. Insemination: depends on fertility cycle in female: sperm → egg.
Gestation	9 months. Intrauterine embryo, placentation. Embryo → fetus → birth.	12 months. Intrauterine embryo, placentation. Embryo → fetus → birth.
Birth and First Breath	Uterine fetus → baby in canal → air-gravity environment. First breath in air surrounding body. No need for immediate mobility.	Uterine fetus → baby in canal seawater buoyant environment. For first breath must reach air at seawater surface. Must swim within few minutes of emersion from canal.
Brain and first survival programs	At birth 300 grams. Automatic respiratory circuits operating after first breath releasing them. No locomotory circuits yet completely operative. Cries and coos.	At birth 600 grams. Automatic respiratory circuits released at first breath. Control of respiratory acts must be coordinated with surfacing of blowhole in air. Coordination of locomotion to surface with breathing: sensorimotor patterning developed within first 6 minutes. Whistles and harsh noises.
Suckling	Mother places baby's mouth on nipple, elicits suckling pattern ("releaser") by lip stimulation.	Swimming baby has fat stores for initial nutritional needs. Mother presents mammary-genital region to tip of baby's rostrum, elicits suckling pattern after first few hours.
Infancy	Mother carries, fondles, protects, feeds, teaches baby (human speech within first 1½–5 years).	Mother stays with, suckles, protects, strokes, swims with, teaches baby dolphin-necessities for first 2 years and longer.
Speech	First words: 18 months to 2 years. Cooing → vowel sounds. Practice of phons for first 18 months.	Initial sounds: distress whistle for calling mother, "putts" for localization (release air from blowhole). At 9 months postpartum, control of clicking without air loss matures. Whistle control suddenly complex.
Sonic Window:	20 to 15,000 Hz.	100 to 150,000 Hz.

Structure/ Function	Human	Dolphin
Communication frequencies:	300 to 3,000 Hz.	1,000 to 80,000 Hz.
Timing	10^{-3} to 10^{-5} sec.	10^{-4} to 10^{-6} sec. overlap limited
Electromagnetic radiation window	0.3 to 0.7 micrometers.	Not investigated as yet. Evidence definite overlap.
Gravitation window	Adapted to $(1+)g$ (bipedal locomotion)	Adapted to near-neutral buoyancy out of water respiration/heart action impeded.
Temperature window	37°C (98.6°F)	37°C (98.6°F)
1. Brain	32°C 44°C	(limits unknown)
2. Skin	5°C 50°C	(unknown)

Thus we find that a large brain is not necessary to control a large body.

Then why are large brains always housed in large bodies?

Let us consider the Newtonian mechanics in relation to brains and survival on this planet. During World War II neurosurgeons found that certain humans suffered brain damage with no external signs of damage sufficient to account for the internal damage. Soldiers were dying or were badly brain-damaged without penetrating wounds and without skull fractures.

These facts led to a theory that rotatory acceleration of a brain about an axis through that brain could cause tearing of blood vessels and of the substance of the brain itself. This theory was confirmed in a series of studies by Dr. Sheldon and Dr. Pudenz on monkeys at the Naval Medical Research Center at Bethesda, Maryland. Under purely rotatory acceleration, damage to blood vessels and the substance of the brain itself was found.

Similar results have been found since World War II, in other wars and in automobile accidents in the United States. A glancing blow to the head of sufficient force at the correct angle can rotate that head so rapidly that the blood vessels to the brain and the partitions separating parts of the brain damage the substance of the brain itself (the tentorium cerebelli and the falx cerebri).

It was found that the monkey brain must be accelerated in the rotatory mode much faster than the human brain. The human brain is damaged by smaller values of rotatory acceleration than is the monkey brain.

Elementary consideration of the Newtonian mechanics of rotatory acceleration explain this difference between the monkey and the human brain.

In the mammalian series, all brains, no matter their size, are equally delicate in all of their parts. Comparing small brains with large brains across species, one finds that they are all incredibly delicate structures corresponding somewhat loosely to bowls of gelatin of different sizes. Within their structures the larger brains are not tougher than the smaller brains. The critical shearing force for tearing the brain itself does not change as the brain increases in size. The density and the breaking limits within all mammalian brains have the same values.

As the brain gets larger, the radius increases. The susceptibility to acceleratory rotational forces increases as the square of the radius.

There is a critical strain set up within the substance of the brain as the outermost parts of that brain are accelerated faster than the innermost parts. At a critical value of stress the strain reaches the point at which the continuity of the substance fails and "fracture," breaking, and so forth, occur. As the stress builds up and the critical strain is reached, blood vessels and neuronal circuits are torn. Hemorrhages appear within the brain substance and around the brain as the blood vessels connecting it to the dura break.

It can be shown by elementary mechanics that as the radius of the brain increases, the rotatory acceleration necessary to reach the breaking limit decreases inversely as the square of the radius of rotation and, hence, of the radius of the brain itself.

Now let us consider the effect of housing a large brain in a small skull attached to a relatively small body. Let us visualize a man with a brain the size of *Orcinus orca* at four times the weight of the present human brain (six thousand grams vs.

fourteen hundred grams). We will assume that this large brain has the same fragility in the detailed microscopic sense as the orca brain has and as the modern human brain has. We will also assume that the density, the mass per unit volume, is the same as in modern man and in modern orca, i.e., approximately the density of water or slightly less (1 gram per cubic centimeter). Let us also assume that this hypothetical man has an increased skull thickness sufficient to prevent the skull collapsing on its first impact, in, say, a fall to the ground during ordinary running.

Such a hypothetical man, without the natural protection of a very large head surrounding this brain to reduce the acceleration of the brain itself in the rotatory sense, would have to tread very carefully upon this planet to avoid the critical rotatory acceleration that would damage his brain and kill him. The moment of inertia of his skull would not be great enough to prevent damage to his brain by rotatory acceleration in situations in which the smaller-brained humans could easily survive. He would be at least two and one half times as vulnerable to brain damage as would modern man.

Modern vehicles, including motorcycles, cars, airplanes, rockets, and spacecraft, subject the human brain to accelerations beyond the critical value, every so often leading to brain damage and even death. Our brain and skull size evolved under conditions in which such factors as these were not in the survival programs of the evolutionary processes to which our predecessors were exposed. Vehicles designed for our brain size would not allow the survival of larger brains. Our technological developments are designed for the survival of a given brain size but no larger.

There are two ways in which very large brains can survive in nature on this planet (without being exposed to the accelerations of man's vehicles). The first route is that taken by the elephants to surround the large brain (four times the size of the human) with a very large skull, a large moment of inertia, and a large body, which prevents this brain from being accelerated, in the rotatory sense, in the elephant's ordinary rough-and-tumble existence. A given force operating tangential to the head of an elephant must be very large to accelerate the mass of the skull above the value at which the brain inside the skull can remain uninjured. The elephant has evolved in air, which offers very little resistance to the movement and the rotation of the animal under a 1 g. gravitational force. The huge mass of bone around the brain also prevents muscular actions that are above the critical value for rotatory acceleration of the contained brain. Watching an elephant, one can see the slow, ponderous movements of the great masses. One can also appreciate the necessity for these slow, ponderous movements in protection of the brain inside.

Another route that has given rise to brains even larger than that of the elephant is to develop the brains in containers in a medium that resists very rapid motions of the body containing the brain. Underwater in the sea the density and the viscosity of the medium are larger than that of the air of the land by factors of 830 and 55. The increased density of the medium means that the bodies containing large brains in the sea and the brains themselves can grow very much larger than they can in the air on the land. All acceleratory forces are cushioned by the surrounding medium. In the sea the movements of the medium itself, in a rotatory sense, do not get above the critical value for survival of these brains. A few places where dangerous values of rotatory acceleration would exist in the medium are immediately under a water spout or in the eddies of tidal flow between islands.

The structure of the head surrounding the brain is also of importance. A large brain cannot have a skull with very large protuberances or handles on it. This is particularly true in air. One can easily see this in the case of the humans. If we had very long jaws, such as those the dolphins have, boxing would be impossible. A blow on the end of a long jaw would cause the rotatory acceleration of the brain to go above the critical value for damage. Boxers must cushion their hands with boxing gloves to prevent killing one another by rotatory accelerations with blows to the side of the jaw. Even as boxing exists today, the critical values for damage to the brain are often exceeded, and boxers accumulate small injuries to their brains as their heads are rotated by blows to the head and jaws. If the boxer is not killed, he at least becomes punch-drunk owing to the small (petechial) hemorrhages caused throughout his brain structure.

Organisms on the land, then, with large brains do not have large, long protuberances coming out of their skulls, such as upper and lower jaws. One exception to this rule is the elephant's tusks, which apparently break at the critical value of impact for unconsciousness; however, elephants can be and are killed by head rotations in falls. The elephant's head is a relatively compact set of bones surrounding the brain. The trunk itself is only soft tissue, which can absorb the blows and cut down on the acceleration of the brain itself. Man's head is relatively compact, with short jaws close in to the brain. On the other hand, the gorilla, with longer jaws, has a smaller brain, one-third the human brain size.

Organisms in the sea can afford much longer jaws in relation to brain size. The small dolphins have very long jaws and also small brains (equal to those of apes). The largest of the dolphins, *Orcinus orca*, has a very much reduced length of jaw in proportion to the size of his skull. The sperm whale, with his long jaws, has a very protuberant and very large, soft, bulbous structure on the top and sides of his upper jaw, which prevents the lateral accelerations in the high-density water. This structure is also relatively soft compared with bone and can absorb blows on its lateral surfaces, thus preventing the rotatory accelerations that would damage the sperm whale's very large fragile brain (something of the order of nine thousand grams, six times that of the human brain).

Such basic considerations of the Newtonian mechanics of large brains will allow us to construct a quantitative theory and to do experiments appropriate to investigation of why large brains are surrounded by large masses. The evolution, on this planet, of organisms with large brains can thus be explained in a quantitative fashion heretofore not applied in the theory of evolution. Such studies can give rise to a new quantitative appreciation of the survival of organisms on this planet. Thus, we can understand the necessities of the evolution of bony structures to protect brains, their shapes, their sizes, and their masses under the acceleration of gravity on the planet Earth. We can also understand why the largest brains on the planet have evolved in the sea rather than on the land. We can also work out why muscles are arranged in the way that they are arranged in each of the large-brained mammals. The ecological niches in which large brains are found are as much defined by Newtonian mechanics as they are by the evolution of conglomerates of cells originating in the seas of Earth.

Such studies can also indicate what man can expect of the evolution of his own brain in the future. He can establish the conditions under which his own brain may evolve to larger sizes and new levels of computational capacity beyond those of the current *Homo sapiens*. When man learns about the limitations of his own brain and when he discovers how to change the evolution of that brain toward larger, more effective sizes, he must take into account all the above considerations. His appreciation of his environment will increase considerably over that which is recognized by the human species today.

The macrobiocomputers have evolved control of the minibiocomputers. The macrobiocomputers must be protected as they attain very large sizes. Let us learn to communicate with the ancient macrobiocomputers of the Cetacea and learn something of the complexities of their computational capacities. Such communication may enrich our lives beyond anything that we have heretofore conceived and may open up possibilities for the future evolution of man beyond his present limits.

CHAPTER SIX

Communication by Means of Sounds: The Twin Cases of Cetaceans and Humans

HERE WE DEFINE COMMUNICATION AS THE CREATION OF INFOR-mation in one mind by means of signals from another mind. The second mind acknowledges the reception of the signals and the formation of the information by feeding back other signals to the first mind, which then creates new information. Biological organisms in general and the human and the cetacean in particular use various outputs and various inputs in the service of such creation of information. In order to communicate there must be an agreed-upon simulation of the information and rules for construction of the information from the signals. Language, as we know it, results from an agreement among many individuals about the meaning of the signals. Any two individuals must agree upon the kinds of signals they are going to use, the rules for their manipulation, and their interpretation.

Humans communicate in the immediate present through facial expressions, gestures of the body, physical contacts, and the production of sounds in the mouth, throat, and larynx. The receivers of the body gestures and facial expressions in the receiving human are the eyes; one *sees* the facial expressions and the gestures. Another route is for physical contact in which ears, proprioception, tactile sense, pressure receptors, and so forth are used to receive the muscular motions and pressures exerted by the transmitter.

Cetaceans communicate in similar ways, producing sounds, receiving them with their ears, interpreting those sounds, and constructing mental images, maps, ideas. They also watch one another's motions in the water and exchange physical contacts.

Let us consider the physics and biophysics of sound communication of the human and of the Cetacea. We will investigate both the production and the reception of sounds.

Sound is defined as a series of waves of compression, more or less constant in velocity, in a gas, a liquid, or a solid. Sound has a characteristic velocity in each medium depending primarily upon the density of that medium. When sound waves move from one medium to another, various phenomena occur including refraction, reflection, partial transmission, scattering, and absorption.

A sound wave in air entering perpendicularly into a flat water surface is partially reflected and partially transmitted through the surface. Only one five-thousandths of the energy of the sound wave in air is transmitted into the water. The rest of the energy is reflected from the surface of the water.

Sounds produced in the water, entering into the air, are similarly reflected in the same ratio. Only one five-thousandths of the underwater sound is transmitted into the air.

This reflection is a consequence of the change of velocity of sound in air and in water (in air, sound travels at about 1,100 feet or 350 meters per second and, in water, travels at 5,000 feet or 1,524 meters per second) and the difference in density between the two media (air is one-eight-hundredth of the density of water, which has a density of 1.0).

Most biological tissues have a sound velocity within them approximately the same as in water; i.e., in those tissues of the density of 1, which are mostly water, the sound velocity is the same as it is in water. Other special tissues may have very much higher sound velocity, such as very dense bone.

Air-containing cavities within bodies connected to sound sources either can emit most of their sound into air, if there is an open passageway to the atmosphere, or can emit most of their sound into water, if they are closed and immersed in water.

Human speech depends upon such cavities being coupled to the atmosphere through the mouth and the nose. In the case of the Cetacea their cavities during sound production are closed within the body, and the energy is emitted into the surrounding water.

When a cetacean surfaces and opens his sound-producing mechanisms to the air, most of the energy travels into the atmosphere. If we remember that the sound released into the air on hitting the air/water interface is mostly reflected, we can see that airborne communication is not of much use to the cetaceans in communicating with others under water. Under water with closed cavities, they can communicate over astonishing distances, the order of six miles for the bottle-nosed dolphin and the order of five hundred miles for the finback whale. (50) This long-distance transmission is due to the increased efficiency of transmission of sound waves in the dense medium of the water. The maximum transmission of information contained in the human voice in air is limited to a half mile to one mile under quiet conditions. With special whistle languages, such as those used in the Azores Islands and by the Indians of Mexico, transmission of information can be carried out over a distance of approximately three miles in the mountains.

Each of us tends to take speech for granted. We do not question how we produce the sounds of speech or how these sounds are combined in certain ways as signals; nor do we consider how we receive these sounds and convert them into meaningful information. Extensive studies have been done upon the biophysics of the production of sounds and their reception by biological organisms. (51, 52, 53) There are many ways that biological organisms produce sounds; here we will consider only those present in the production of human speech and in the production of the cetaceans' communication and echo-ranging systems.

Let us first consider the production of human sounds.

The primary source of human sounds is the air of respiration. The lungs are filled, constrictions of the air flow out through the mouth and nose, and the vocal cords generate the sounds. Most humans speak on expiration of air from the lungs. In special cases (Swedish) sounds are also made on inspiration. Two major sources of sound are thus generated: the vocal cords open and close periodically at a certain rate, called the pitch of the sounds. Technically this is called voicing. The voicing is turned on and off very rapidly and its rate is determined by the central nervous system regulating the tension in the vocal cords. Low-pitch sounds are produced by relatively relaxed vocal cords and low pressure. High-pitched sounds are produced by tensing the vocal cords and raising the pressure of the sound from below.

The second source of sound is changing the diameter and the shape of the airway in the pharynx, the mouth, the lips, and the teeth. The air blown through small constricted passageways makes hissing sounds. Air blown over the teeth, the lips, and the tongue also produces "noise." Whispered speech turns off the vocal cords and allows modulation to take place through the constrictions along the vocal tract.

In the sentence "Joe took father's shoe bench out; meet me by the lawn," the sequence of sounds contains thirty-three of the forty-four elements of general American speech. Each individual sound is called a phon. As one says this sentence out loud, one can hear the various sounds produced and feel within oneself the mechanism of production of each of the sounds. One can feel the word *Joe* generated by the simultaneous use of the tongue, lips, teeth, plus the vocal cords. Feel your vocal cords while saying *Joe*. The vocal cords operate during the whole of this word. The second word *took* starts with the sound of the letter *t*. The sound of *t* is generated by a pulse of air released by tongue control, shooting out of the mouth over the lips and tongue, modulated in a particular way; the beginning of the *t* is a sudden release of the air by the tongue put against the teeth and hard palate and then suddenly released. Such sounds are called frictives because they are produced by the noisy exit of air making a sound that covers a large frequency region in a noisy fashion. The second part of the word *took,* the *oo,* is primarily voiced. The final *k* is primarily explosive. The sound of *k* is produced by a constriction made by the tongue, between the tongue and the hard palate. As one proceeds through this sentence, one can see this alternate play and simultaneous play of the voiced vocal cord sounds and the constricted high-velocity airway sounds.

In the formation of vowel sounds, those primarily produced by voicing with the vocal cords, one can also feel the shaping of the vocal tract. The vowel sounds are modulated in pitch and in resonances within the vocal tract.

Let us consider the problem of resonances. The commonest example of a resonance is an organ pipe or any air-containing tube. Such tubes, if of a fixed size, have an enhanced response to sounds at a definite frequency. One can see this by blowing across the top of a bottle. The high-speed air passing across the lip of the bottle excites resonant frequencies within the bottle.

The vocal tract is a very complex series of tubes that change their size, shape, and length in response to muscular changes in the wall and in the shape and movements of the tongue. In addition, the passageway through the nose can be opened or closed for changing the resonant qualities of the vocal tract. To see this coupling of the nose cavity, say the word *tame* out loud. After the explosive *t* sound, one hears the *a* sound as a continuous pulsing of the vocal cords, which one can feel with one's fingers on the larynx. Notice that at the end of the vowel sound *a,* when the *m* sound starts, the mouth closes and the major sound comes out of the nose. The vocal cords continue to pulsate, and the sound coming out of the nose forms the *m* sound. Thus the nasal cavity is switched in and out while one speaks by closing this cavity and opening it with special muscles in the nasopharynx at the back of the nose.

Thus, human speech is an incredibly fast and incredibly sophisticated complex switching and changing of the shapes and sizes of the cavities along the vocal tract, turning the vocal cord sound on and off and using the hissing sounds at the forward end of the vocal tract.

In a record of the changing resonances of the vocal tract on a machine that plots frequency versus time, one sees the resonances of the vocal tract as they change as enhancements of the pulsing rate at certain harmonics of the pulsing rate called formants. These enhanced harmonics vary between the vowels and separate the vowels from one another in recognizable forms.

Successful synthesis of human speech has been carried out in recent years by simulating the human vocal tract by various means. Modern computers can be used for this purpose. Currently the telephone company uses such programs for synthesizing recognizable human speech for giving information about changes of numbers and for answering queries to the computer regarding credit cards and so forth. These programs have become so sophisticated that the computer can mimic a human female voice or a human male voice quite readily. These voices no longer sound as if they were mechanically produced. Characteristically, human qualities are now imparted to the synthesized voices. The synthesis is so good that these sound like tape-recorded human voices.

Such considerations as the above say nothing about the hearing and interpretation of the meaning inherent in these sound productions. These sounds are put into air by each speaker and are received by each listener through the ears. In the ears the sounds are converted into neuronal impulses in the cochlea, which are then fed into the lower central nervous system and there analyzed in multiple sequences at very high speed. Central processing then takes place and the observing systems within the cerebral cortex construct information from this long sequence of computed signals. From the speaker to the listener there is no meaning until the listener's brain interprets signals and gives the meaning to the signals.

Thus, we can see that meaning of words and speech is not present in the signals themselves. The meaning is derived from computations done within a brain upon the signals. Similarly, in someone who is speaking, the information within the brain itself is being recomputed and signals generated as a consequence of the computations. The signals are then fed through the nervous system out through the vocal tract into the air. The production of meaningful signals by the vocal tract depends upon incredibly rapid muscle movements and delicate changes well differentiated within the vocal tract.

On the receiving side, if one listens to a tape that is mechanically reproducing a word spoken once by a speaker, one can see something of the complexities of the interpretation of these spoken signals. A classical tape, which we use to demonstrate this effect, has the word *cogitate* spoken once and recorded with a mechanical device, a magnetic disk, which reproduces very accurately exactly the same set of signals that were recorded on the tape originally. The word *cogitate,* in this particular case, is repeated every 0.7 seconds. If one listens to this tape for fifteen minutes to one hour, one at first hears the word *cogitate* from the signals received. As one continues to listen, one begins to hear other words, alternates to the word *cogitate,* such as *tragedy.* With three hundred expert observers, we found that there were 2,730 alternates, 350 of which were in a large dictionary; the rest are words that we do not use.

This experiment shows that the reception of signals depends utterly upon the sequence of signals. The computation of the information, i.e., the generation of "meaning" or of "words," is a function of the central processing of the brain itself. Our speech is built up of expected sequences that we long ago stored in our memory. While we are listening to a speaker, our brain computes the signals that we receive from the air and creates the information, the meaning, almost instantaneously. We expect that the next word, for example, will be different from the previous words. When we are exposed to a constantly repeating set of signals, our brain operates in such a way as to generate alternates to the constantly repeated set of signals according to certain computational rules.

We analyzed the 2,730 alternates to *cogitate* and discovered that the original set of signals contained twelve time slots, i.e., phons, which could be varied by the following rules:

1. A consonant such as the initial *c* or *k* sound can be experienced as any other consonant, such as *p, g, j, ch.*

2. Any vowel such as the *o* or *a* sound after the *k* sound can become or be interpreted as any other vowel sound or a group of vowel sounds.

Thus, the brain is trained and has stored within it sequences of simulations that we refer to as meanings of signals. In our social consensus reality we are taught these long sequences in our childhood and we build up simulations upon which we agree. When we speak to one another, we compute meaning, change it into signals, receive signals, and recompute meaning from the received signals. Thus, we build up shared simulations that are flexible means of computation of maps, feelings, thoughts, ideas.

Thus, our communication system is amazingly fast and sophisticated and requires a very large memory and long experience in order to be able to construct meaning from the signals. As we discussed elsewhere in this book, such performance requires a brain with a certain kind of structure, i.e., fairly large silent areas to control the minicomputer that runs the muscles and receives the signals for the operations of the macrocomputer.

Let us now consider the emission of sounds by the dolphins. The dolphins live under water and hence are not able to use the atmosphere in the emission of sounds in air for their communication. However, they do use air cavities within their bodies for the production of the sound. Because these cavities are totally enclosed inside the bodies, they are closely coupled to the tissues of the body, which are closely coupled to the water of the sea. The dolphins have three sonic/ultrasonic emitters: two of these are just below the blowhole and behind the melon and the third is in the larynx.

With a cooperative dolphin it is possible to feel the structures that produce the sounds just below the blowhole. With a dolphin at the surface of the water close to one, watch the blowhole during respiration. One sees the blowhole suddenly open, the air released rather explosively and pulled back in very rapidly. The whole respiratory cycle takes about three-tenths of one second. If one looks down into the blowhole during this brief respiratory act, one sees a very thin nasal septum going fore and aft across the airway. One also sees that there are two plugs, a right plug and a left plug, which close the blowhole. As the blowhole opens, these plugs are pulled forward. If one continues to watch the blowhole region while it is closed and the dolphin starts to make sounds, either pulses or whistles under water, one can see movements of the plugs closing the blowhole. When the dolphin uses his right sonic emitter, one sees that side twitching; when he uses the left sonic emitter, one sees movements on the left.

By very gently placing one's finger on the plugs with a cooperative dolphin, one can slide a finger down the right side or the left side of the nasal passageway. As one does this, one feels a muscle in the forward part of the passageway that apparently is pushing one's finger out of the passage with definite stroking movements, very similar to those one would experience if one put a finger in someone's mouth and he pushed it out with his tongue. If one puts two fingers in, one on the right and one on the left, one feels independent tongue actions pushing one's fingers out.

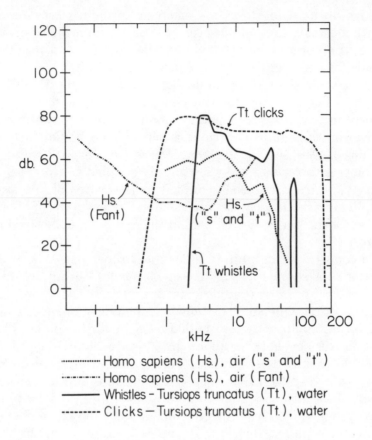

———————— Homo sapiens (Hs.), air ("s" and "t")
—·—·—·—· Homo sapiens (Hs.), air (Fant)
———————— Whistles – Tursiops truncatus (Tt.), water
- - - - - - - Clicks – Tursiops truncatus (Tt.), water

FIGURE 3.   Comparison of the sonic and ultrasonic vocal output curves of the human (Hs) in air and the dolphin (Tt) in water.

The Hs curve with the dots represents sonic-ultrasonic high-frequency energy for the human spoken consonants s and t. The Hs curve (dash-dot) represents Gunnar Fant's vowel and consonant 40-Phon equal-loudness curve for human speech in air. The dashed Tt curve is the peak amplitudes of click trains emitted by the nasal sonic emitters and in the upper portion the laryngeal sonar emitter at a distance of 1 meter off the end of the dolphin's beak. The solid curve "Tt. whistles" corresponds to the fundamentals of the whistles in the first lower-frequency solid curve and some of the first harmonics of the higher-frequency whistles in the second curve.

It is to be noted that the comparison of this figure with Figure 2 shows that most of the dolphin's output acoustic energy under water is considerably higher than the highest frequencies hearable by the humans. It is also to be pointed out that the humans cannot hear the ultra-high frequencies emitted by the human in the consonants s and t but that the dolphin can easily hear this energy and hence matches this output rather than the lower-frequency output of s and t in the human voice. This observation may explain Aristotle's failure to hear the dolphin forming the consonants in the voice in air.

If one is very gentle, very careful not to hurt the dolphin in this operation, one can find in the posterior portion of the airway a sharp-edged membrane. If the dolphin allows one to keep one's finger in, one can feel this membrane tense and loosen while the tongue in the forward part is working on one's finger.

High speed X-ray movies taken of this region of the dolphin, using a contrast medium, show that the sounds produced are formed by the forward tongue coming up against the after membrane edge, forming a slit for the air. This slit is then analogous to our vocal cords and their impedance across our airway.

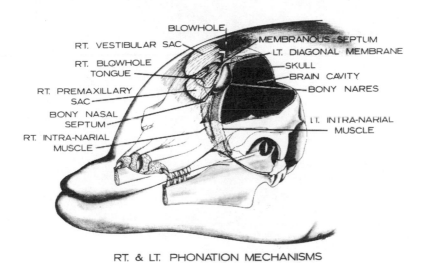

RT. & LT. PHONATION MECHANISMS
(LARYNGEAL MECHANISM NOT SHOWN)

FIGURES 4, 5, 6:   The three sonic emitters of the dolphin. FIGURES 4 AND 5: Two nasal emitters. FIGURE 6: Laryngeal emitter.

FIGURES 4 AND 5.   The blowhole is at the top of the diagram showing its position anterior to the skull of the dolphin. The blowhole is the opening of the nose turned up on the forehead, as it were. Immediately inside the blowhole laterally and to the right is the right vestibular sac. Between the right vestibular sac and the right premaxillary sac is the right blowhole tonguelike muscle that presses backward across the airway so as to form a slit with the right diagonal membrane. The posterior surface of the right blowhole tongue and the right diagonal membrane create the slit that forms the whistles and the clicks for communication. Air is blown back and forth through this slit from the right premaxillary sac to the right vestibular sac and from the right vestibular sac back into the premaxillary sac. As the dolphin dives, air is supplied to these two sacs from the nasal passageway in the

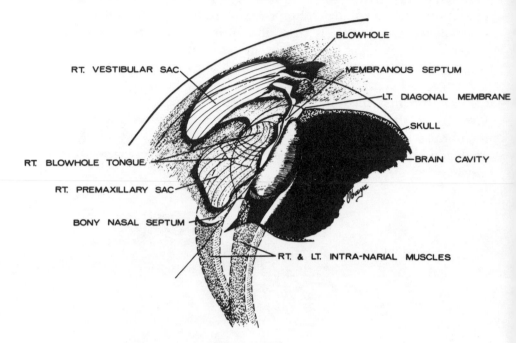

RT. VESTIBULAR SAC

BLOWHOLE

MEMBRANOUS SEPTUM

LT. DIAGONAL MEMBRANE

SKULL

BRAIN CAVITY

RT. BLOWHOLE TONGUE

RT. PREMAXILLARY SAC

BONY NASAL SEPTUM

RT. & LT. INTRA-NARIAL MUSCLES

RT. & LT. PHONATION MECHANISMS
(LARYNGEAL MECHANISM NOT SHOWN)

bony nares from the laryngeal dead space. Thus the dolphin adjusts for a change in size of the sacs and density of the air in the sacs to keep the frequency output constant within the ranges for the meaningful spectrum of the dolphin.

The right and the left narial passageways are divided at the top by the membraneous septum and down farther the bony nasal septum. Within each of the two nasal passageways there is an intranarial muscle whose upper end lies beneath the diagonal membrane and can pull the diagonal membrane from the posterior wall out into the passageway by contraction of this muscle; the muscle is fastened to the bone of the bony nares. Anterior to the right and the left narial sound makers is the melon and the upper and lower jaw with the interdigitated teeth. Behind the apparatus is the skull containing the brain. Below this apparatus is the laryngeal mechanism with the larynx inserted into the nasopharynx for sound production and breathing and removed from the nasopharynx laid down in the bottom of the oral pharynx for swallowing fish.

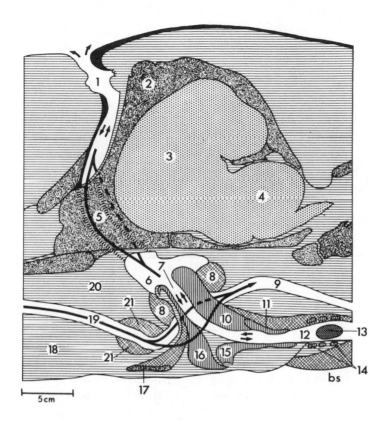

FIGURE 6. Sagittal view of the head and neck region of the dolphin, *Tursiops truncatus*. Numbers indicate anatomical structures as follows: 1, blowhole; 2, cranium; 3, cerebral hemisphere; 4, cerebellum; 5, bony nares; 6, nasal cavity; 7, glottis; 8, nasopharyngeal sphincter; 9, esophagus; 10, arytenoid cartilage; 11, cricoid cartilage; 12, trachea; 13, eparterial bronchus; 14, tracheal cartilages; 15, thyroid cartilage; 16, epiglottic cartilage; 17, hyoid bone; 18, tongue; 19, oral cavity; 20, palate; 21, oropharyngeal sphincter.

If one enters the blowhole, say on the right, and curls one's finger to the right, one finds that it enters a sac under the blubber of the top of the head going laterally from the blowhole. This sac opens above the slit between the membrane and the tongue. If one pushes one's finger down farther into the nasal airway and forward under the tongue, one finds another sac, which exits below the slit between the tongue and the membrane edge. Posterior to this sac, one can feel the nasal bony passageway down which one can insert one's finger a limited distance. If one palpates the walls of this bony passageway, one can feel a muscle along that wall which is used to tense the membrane edge.

From the high speed X-ray movies, we found that the dolphin does not have to use air from his lungs to make sounds. He fills the upper sac, contracts the walls of the upper sac, and blows the air through the slit between the tongue and the membrane edge into the lower sac. He can then contract the lower sac and blow the air back through the slit into the upper sac. The amount of air in this system is adjusted, depending on the depth to which the dolphin is diving so that a relatively constant amount of air can be held in these sacs. As the sacs change size, their resonant qualities change so that the resonant click or whistle coming out of the sacs through the tissues into the water varies in frequency depending upon the size of the sac at that particular instant.

The dolphin has two sacs on the right and two sacs on the left and a tongue and a membrane on each side, totally independently controllable; he has two separately controllable sound sources whose frequencies, amplitudes, and click rates can be varied independently.

When the membrane edge is tight and the tongue presses against it tightly and the air pressure is high, the membrane edge vibrates the air going through it at very high frequencies forming pulses so close together that they are heard as a continuous whistle. With a more lax membrane and lower air presssures, individual pulses of sound are released from one sac to the other. The frequency analysis of such pulses shows that they vary as the size of the coupled sacs varies. Similarly, the frequency of the whistles varies depending on the size of the sacs and the pulsing rate at the edge of the membrane.

With this rather complex apparatus, a given dolphin can click at a given rate on one side, at another rate on the other, or he can whistle over one frequency range on one side and another frequency range on the other. Or he can click on either side and whistle on the other side.

The sounds are transmitted through the flesh surrounding the sacs out into the water most loudly upward and forward but with fairly sizable amplitudes in all directions around the body of the dolphin. The sounds emitted by these two sonic emitters are of a lower-frequency region than those emitted by the third sonic emitter in the larynx.

The larynx in the dolphin is rather long and narrow and is inserted across the foodway into the nasopharynx up against the bony nasal septum. The trachea, the airway to the lungs, is terminated by the two arytenoid cartilages covered with a very smooth mucous surface forming a long slit about an inch and a half to two inches long and one-quarter of an inch in depth. The air from the lungs during a respiratory act passes between these two arytenoid cartilages, which are pulled apart to allow the air smooth passage out through the blowhole. During such a respiratory act the dolphin cannot use this system for the production of sounds, nor can he use the other two emitters. During the brief respiratory act the dolphin is quite silent.

The two flat plates of the arytenoid cartilage are closed across the airway while the dolphin is holding his breath. By contraction of his respiratory muscles, he can raise the pressure behind the two cartilages and cause a leakage of air between the two. The two surfaces close together to form a slit. This slit forms bubbles that are hemicylindrical and an inch and a half or so long and a tenth of a millimeter or less in radius. The material forming the bubbles is the mucous secreted by special glands in this region. When such a bubble breaks, it releases an extremely short pulse of sound, which then travels forward and outward through the upper and lower jaws and resonates the teeth, at about 160,000 cycles per second (Hertz) in the bottle-nosed dolphin. The teeth act as a resonant system that selects a particular frequency band, shock-excited by the pulse from the larynx, and at the same time forms the narrow beam (about three degrees wide) of this very high frequency sound coming out from the front end of the dolphin.

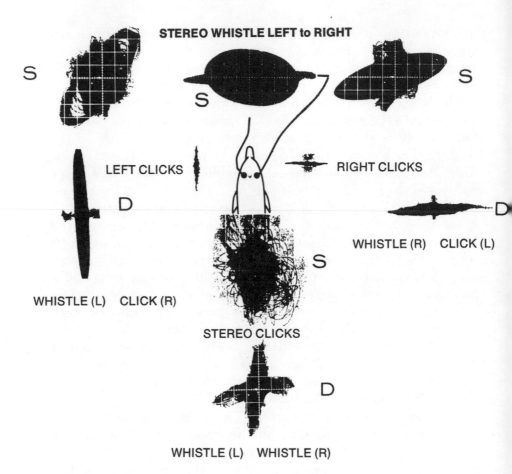

FIGURE 7. Sonic outputs from the right and left nasal sound emitters anterior and lateral to the blowhole.

As can be seen in the diagram in the center of the figure, a hydrophone was placed on each side of the blowhole on the vestibular sac of each side. The right side deflects the cathode-ray tube beam horizontally; the left side deflects the cathode-ray beam vertically. The traces shown are photographs taken during various kinds of activity on the part of the dolphin. Capital *S* stands for stereo; i.e., the sounds on the two sides are linked. *D* stands for double or separated sound production on the two sides without coupling between the two. The top row of traces shows whistles of the stereo variety, left and right. This causes elipses to appear on the cathode-ray tube screen. The next row down shows left clicks and right clicks. Left clicks show vertical traces only; right clicks show horizontal traces only. The next set of traces shows a whistle on the left and a click on the right and then a whistle on the right and a click on the left. The middle pair of traces just below the dolphin shows the sequences of stereo clicks showing linking elipses. Below that are separated whistles on the left and on the right. (Data of Communication Research Institute, 1966.)

These pulses can be controlled in their rate from one per minute up to one thousand per second. As an object approaches the dolphin the pulsing rate goes up. If one holds a hydrophone in front of a dolphin and swings it back and forth toward and from the dolphin, one can hear the pulsing rate climb as the hydrophone approaches and fall as the hydrophone moves away from the dolphin.

This is the output side of their so-called sonar, sonic navigation and ranging system. These short pulses go out through the water, are reflected by objects of interest, and come back to the ears of the dolphin under water, changed by the object by penetration into the object and reflection from various surfaces within the object. While the dolphin is using this sonar system, one sees him moving his head horizontally, scanning the object with this tight beam. (54, 55, 56) Using this system, the dolphin has been shown to discriminate, with exquisite fineness, objects hidden from his eyes. At a distance of fifty feet, he can distinguish an aluminum disk one-eighth of an inch thick from a copper disk of the same dimensions against a concrete wall under water.

Let us now discuss the receivers of sound, one's ears, and the hearing computation mentioned above, and contrast those in the human with those in the dolphin.

The human ear consists of a pinna, the part that sticks outside the head, and a canal leading to a membrane, the tympanum, a series of little bones, ossicles, connecting the tympanum to another membrane that pulsates the liquid in the cochlea. D. W. Batteau demonstrated that the human pinna allows the localization of sound in the air space around the human by transforming the sounds coming from different directions in different ways. (57) The "pinna transform" varies with direction from the ear. The waves of sound transmitted into the canal thus vary depending upon the direction from which they come. In the cochlea the sound waves are transformed into neuronal impulses, which are then computed in the brain in such a way that the central computations carry out the "inverse pinna transform," thus allowing the observer in the brain to reproject the coordinates of the sounds back out in the surrounding space in relation to the whole body.

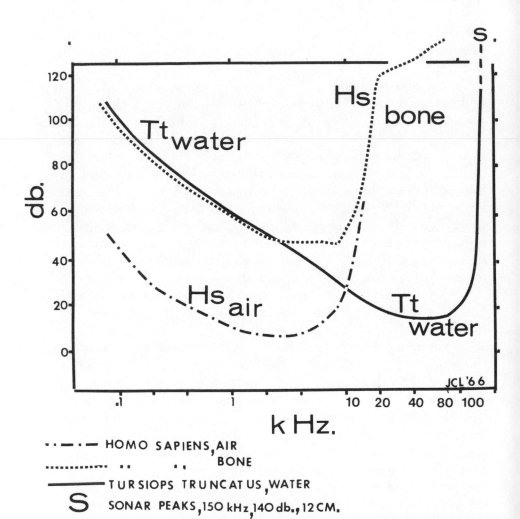

S.

120
100
80
db.
60
40
20
0

Tt water

Hs bone

Hs air

Tt water

JCL '66

.1   1   10 20   40 80 100

k Hz.

— ·· — ·· — HOMO SAPIENS, AIR
·············   ··   ··   BONE
———————— TURSIOPS TRUNCATUS, WATER
S   SONAR PEAKS, 150 kHz, 140 db., 12 CM.

If one makes an accurate cast of the pinna and puts a microphone in the place of the ear canal, this effect can be shown to be recordable on tape. With two microphones placed the same distance apart as the ears and a right pinna on the right microphone and a left pinna on the left microphone, connected through amplifiers to a pair of headphones, one can achieve an effect as though the center of the head had been placed between these two microphones. If one is connected in this particular way to these artificial pinna, one finds that the center of one's acoustic space has moved out of the head to the space between the two microphones. If someone walks around these microphones while

Opposite

FIGURE 8.   The hearing curves of man and dolphin.

There are three separate hearing curves shown here. Man in air (Hs air), man bone conduction (Hs bone) and dolphin under water (Tt water). The crossover point of the air-man and *Tursiops* under water is about 10,000 cycles per second (Hz). The crossover point for man bone conduction and man air conduction is at about 16,000 cycles per second (Hz). The man's bone conduction curve corresponds very closely with man's underwater auditory curve. The coordinates are frequency along the base line and decibels of amplitude along the vertical axis. These curves are strictly threshold curves; i.e., any sound with an amplitude below that of a given curve will not be heard. Any sound with an amplitude above that of the curve will be heard. It is to be noticed that there is approximately 45 decibels' difference between the human air curve and the human bone conduction curve throughout most of the range with a crossover at about 16,000 cycles per second, at which point the two curves join. At frequencies above this there is no way that the human can distinguish the direction of a sound because it is conducted equally well through his head from the air as well as through the ear canals.

It is to be pointed out also that this is the *Tursiops* underwater curve; his air curve would be raised by 45–70 decibels above these values because of the reflectance of the air-water interface and the tissue-water interface on the body of the dolphin.

The point S are the values of the amplitude of the sonar peaks, the sonar pulses emitted by the dolphin, 12 centimeters off the end of his beak in line with the jaws. The frequency of the pulses is equivalent to 150,000 cycles per second (Hz) at 140 decibels of amplitude. The close-up detailed sonar of the dolphin seems to be restricted to this very steep portion of his hearing curve from approximately 80,000 cycles per second to 150,000 cycles per second. The communication band of the dolphin seems to extend from about 10,000 to 100,000 cycles per second (Hz). (Reference Lilly, Miller, and Truby, 1968.)

talking and the observer with the headphones closes his eyes, he feels as though the center of his head had moved out between the two microphones. If the speaker now places his mouth between the two microphones, the voice moves from outside the head to inside the head of the observer with the headphones.

Similarly, recorded sounds occurring in the space around the microphones and played back from the tape into the earphones give one the complete illusion of three-dimensional acoustic space surrounding one.

In other experiments, say in a swimming pool, one finds that one cannot localize the source of sounds in the water; the pinna transform is cancelled because the density and velocity of sound in the pinna and in the water match so well that there is no pinna transform from the underwater sounds. The velocity of sound in the head is the same as that in the water; since all sounds seem to arrive at both ears simultaneously, one has the illusion of the sounds occurring inside one's head.

This raised the question, then, of how the dolphin can accurately localize the direction and distance of sounds under water.

The anatomy of the dolphin's ears shows that the equivalent of the human pinna exists inside the head. The two bones containing the cochlea in the dolphin are as hard as glass; they are called the bulla. The cavities in these bones contain air. There are also cavities surrounding the bones, containing blood, fat, and a foam. The reflections and refractions of sound inside the head of the dolphin then give him the effect of having imbedded pinna.

Using air cavities, we constructed a model of the dolphin's ears. When these were placed on the ears of humans, we found humans could localize sounds under water.

Extensive studies of both the human and dolphin thresholds for hearing at various frequencies show that the bottle-nosed dolphin detects and uses signals of approximately four-and-one-half to ten times the frequencies that humans normally use.

Dolphins can hear the frequencies of human speech in the lower end of their detection spectrum. They can also produce sounds in this region as well as in the upper-frequency regions that they normally use to communicate.

A dolphin can open his blowhole in the air and produce sounds;

	CONSONANTS										
VOWELS OR DIPHTHONGS	r	l	z	v	tʃ	w	m	n	t	k	s
i	ir	il	iz	iv	itʃ		im	in	it	ik	is
	ri	li	zi	vi	tʃi	wi	mi	ni	ti	ki	si
ɪ	ɪr	ɪl	ɪz	ɪv	ɪtʃ		ɪm	ɪn	ɪt	ɪk	ɪs
	rɪ	lɪ	zɪ	vɪ	tʃɪ	wɪ	mɪ	nɪ	tɪ	kɪ	sɪ
e	er	el	ez		etʃ		em	en	et	ek	es
	re	le	ze	ve	tʃe	we	me	ne	te	ke	se
ɛ	ɛr	ɛl	ɛz	ɛv	ɛtʃ		ɛm	ɛn	ɛt	ɛk	
	rɛ	lɛ	zɛ	vɛ	tʃɛ	wɛ	mɛ	nɛ	tɛ	kɛ	sɛ
a	ar	al		av	atʃ		am	an	at	ak	as
	ra	la	za	va	tʃa	wa	ma	na	ta	ka	sa
o	or	ol	oz	ov	otʃ		om	on	ot	ok	os
	ro	lo	zo	vo	tʃo	wo	mo	no	to	ko	so
u	ur	ul	uz	uv	utʃ		um	un	ut	uk	us
	ru	lu	zu	vu	tʃu	wu	mu	nu	tu	ku	su
aɪ	aɪr	aɪl	aɪz	aɪv	aɪtʃ		aɪm	aɪn	aɪt	aɪk	aɪs
	raɪ	laɪ	zaɪ	vaɪ	tʃaɪ	waɪ	maɪ	naɪ	taɪ	kaɪ	saɪ
ɔɪ	ɔɪr	ɔɪl	ɔɪz	ɔɪv	ɔɪtʃ		ɔɪm	ɔɪn	ɔɪt	ɔɪk	ɔɪs
	rɔɪ	lɔɪ	zɔɪ	vɔɪ	tʃɔɪ	wɔɪ	mɔɪ	nɔɪ	tɔɪ	kɔɪ	sɔɪ

FIGURE 9. Table of human voice sounds to test the ability of the dolphin to match human speech.

The human speech output program is constructed from this list of nine vowels (first vertical column) and eleven consonants (first line of the table) arranged in a vowel-consonant (VC) and consonant-vowel (CV) list. Only the easily pronounceable combinations of these VC and CV "nonsense syllables" were used (187 combinations out of the possible 198 items). This program is utilized as a drill for the dolphin before randomizing the list for the final series of experiments, given in Lilly, Miller, and Truby, 1968, and in *Lilly on Dolphins*, 1975. Some of the results of using this program with the dolphins in a randomized sequence is shown in Figure 10.

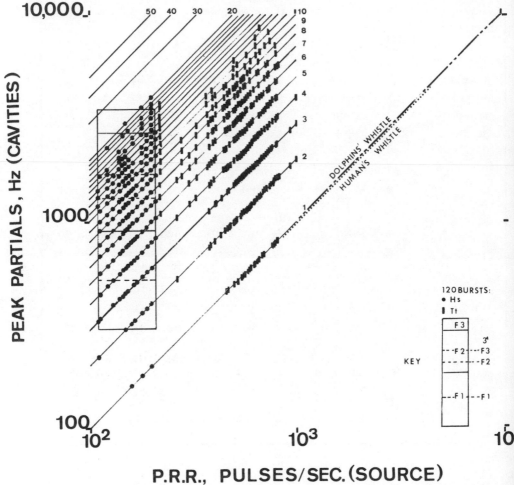

FIGURE 10.   Results of analysis of vocal exchanges in air between a dolphin and a human. Each vocal response of the dolphin and the corresponding vocal utterance of the human were analyzed by sound spectographic methods. From the records from the sound spectograph the fundamental and the harmonics of the fundamental were measured in each case. The fundamental is called the first partial, the first harmonic is the second partial, and so on up to the twentieth partial, as is shown on this diagram. The horizontal axis is the pulsing rate in terms of pulses per second of the source, i.e., the fundamental pulsing rate in the case of the dolphin and the fundamental pulsing rate of the vocal cords in the case of the human. The vertical axis is the partials in the case of the dolphin and of

however, he does this only in the presence of humans who speak in air. We discovered (18, 33, 39) that dolphins will try to mimic and improve their copies of human speech in the presence of humans who speak to them loudly.

Such findings and observations of the dolphin's ability to match human speech sounds is discussed at length elsewhere.

To understand in greater depth the significance of the dolphin's capabilities, one must approach such findings with a new view. As stated above, human spoken language is a sophisticated complex plastic instrument requiring a very large memory operating at high speed. This matching of human speech sounds shows that the dolphin has the input-memory-output computing capacity for such signals despite their strangeness to him. Whether he can extract, use, and reproduce meanings with these signals is yet to be proved by the scientific research currently under way.

The dolphin's ability to use his communicative sound in man's presence is not unexpected when his large brain is compared with that of the human. Before continuing with the discussion of dolphin communications, we shall review the smaller-brained animals with whom communication has been established over the last few years—the chimpanzees and the gorillas. These interesting animals have the capacity to use various nonvocal means of communication with man at an interesting level of complexity. In the following chapter we shall consider the research in this area and its relevance to our further pursuits of dolphin communication problems.

---

the human, labeled "Peak Partials, Hz (cavities)." One can easily see the distribution of the human voice corresponds to the classical analysis shown in the rectangles with formants 1, 2, and 3 of the human voice. The dolphin is outside of this rectangle and tends to be up to the right. This demonstrates that the dolphin has difficulty in lowering not only his fundamental pulsing rate to that of the human but also the partials generated within his vocal tract. His most frequent pulsing rate was something slightly less than 1,000 per second.

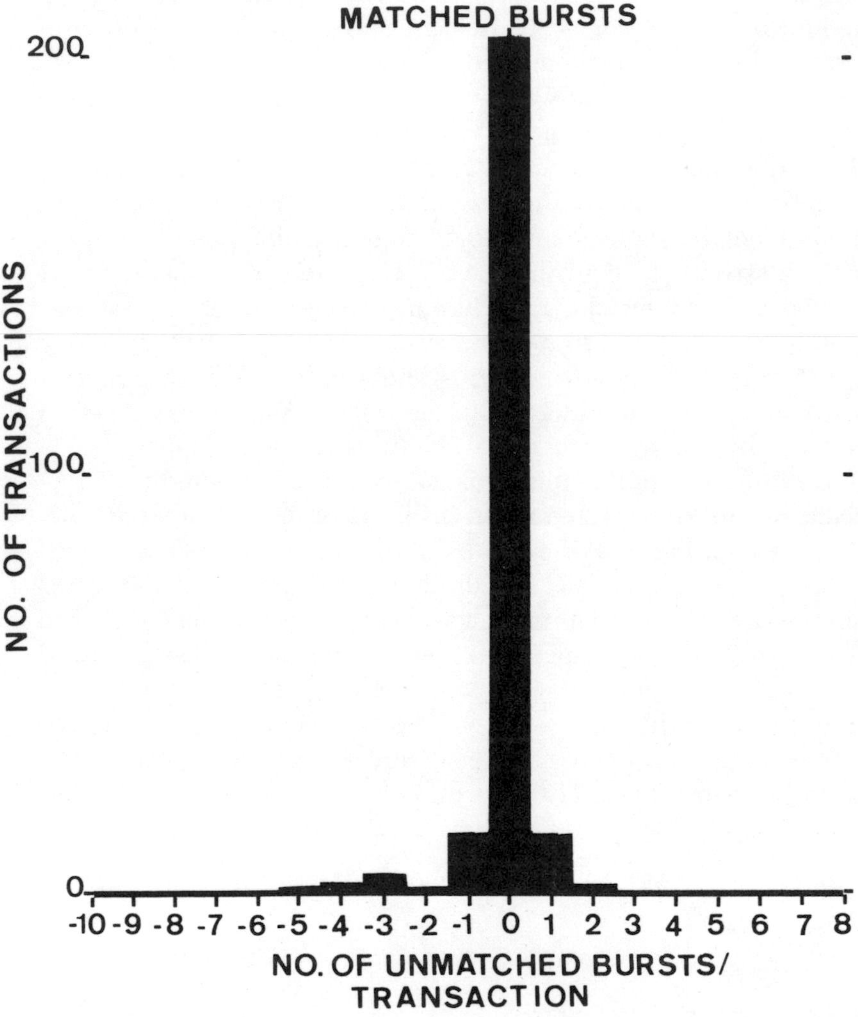

FIGURE 11. Analysis of the voice of the dolphin in air and response to the voice of the human in air.

Here in a randomized series of nonsense syllables the number of utterances by the human is measured. When the human emits, say, ten nonsense syllables, the number of responses on the part of the dolphin is counted. When the counts match, the number of unmatched bursts per transaction is zero. When the dolphin adds one or subtracts one, those points are plotted on this graph on each side of the zero point. This plot shows that the dolphin matches the number of bursts in a given transaction with an accuracy of about 93 percent in something over two hundred cases.

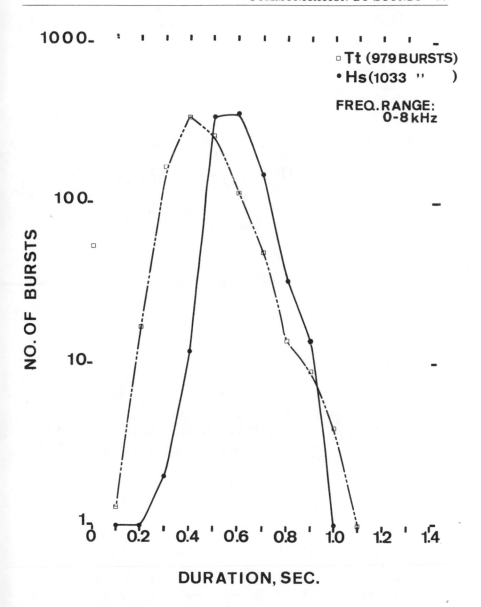

FIGURE 12.   Continuation of analysis of human-dolphin vocal transactions in air. The distribution of the duration of sounds emitted by the dolphin and the human in the series analyzed in Figure 11.

These two distribution curves show the tendency of the dolphin to shorten the response slightly to each of the human sounds. There is remarkable agreement over most of the duration range. For some of the details see Plate 42.

CHAPTER SEVEN

Nonvocal Communication with the Apes: Sonic Communication with Dolphins through JANUS: Sonipulation*

THE ALMOST UNBELIEVABLE ABILITY OF THE DOLPHIN TO MATCH the sounds of human speech can be further appreciated by examining communication with the apes. The human and the dolphin share the capability of communication by means of sounds. The chimpanzee and the gorilla cannot do this with any degree of complexity whatsoever.

The sounds produced by chimpanzees, gorillas, and orangutans seem to be preprogrammed into the nervous system in such a way that they cannot be used in a selective, modifiable, reprogrammable way. The reasons for this limitation of their vocal output is obscure. Among the possibilities are the following:

1. The ape's brains are limited in size, three hundred to four hundred fifty grams. When humans are born and become adults with brains restricted to these sizes, they are unable to use spoken language adequately to function in our society. To master speech as we know it, humans apparently require a brain size of at least

* Man and dolphin control one another by sounds/speech, "sonipulation." Man and ape control through hands (manus), "manipulation."

seven hundred to eight hundred grams. (As we have seen, the bottle-nosed dolphin's brain as an adult is much larger than this, on the order of sixteen hundred to eighteen hundred grams, comparable to that of larger-than-average human brains.)

2. The muscles that control the speech output in the human (including the tongue, the lips, the jaws, the pharynx, and the vocal cords) have a very rich nerve supply from the base of the brain. The dolphins have a similarly rich nerve supply to their noise-producing muscular systems. The apes have a much poorer nerve supply to the equivalent muscles.

Thus, in the case of the humans and the dolphins there is an adequate number of output channels to give precise control of the phonatory apparatus in each case. The apes do not have this equipment.

3. The apes have relatively small areas of associational silent cortex in the brain compared with those of both dolphin and man. There seems to be a critical size for the associational cortex to furnish an adequate integration between the other areas of the cortex, the sensory and the motor, to form language. One other characteristic of a larger associational cortex would be a much larger memory space available for the storage of the programming necessary for language.

4. The visual areas in the apes and in man are similarly organized and of comparable size. The sensorimotor areas devoted to hands and fingers are similar in the two primate groups, the human and the apes. These neurological findings correlate very well with the ability of the apes to use humanly devised sign languages involving hands and fingers. The dolphins, on the other hand, have all the bones of our hands in their flippers, but they are inescapably tied together in order to form a steering vane or flipper. In effect, the dolphins have a frozen hand, lower arm and upper arm, and a mobile shoulder. With the one remaining joint in the shoulder they can perform complex movements with the tip of the flipper and possibly use this in a symbolic way. However, this does not approach the complexity of the use of the ape or of the human hand in a sign language.

Dedicated attempts (starting with Yerkes, the Kelloggs, and Keith Hayes) showed that, despite daily lessons, the chimpanzee cannot learn to control his voice. (58, 59, 60) However, he can learn to understand many human words produced by the human voice; the defect in his sonic communication system is in his output, i.e., *his* voice.

These negative results with control of the voice by the apes led to the Gardeners' experiments with sign language, Ameslan, originally devised for use by deaf humans. The Gardeners found that apes can learn the symbolic use of finger positions to express needs, names of objects, their own bodies, the bodies of humans, and various actions and feelings. These results are confirmed by Roger Fouts. (61, 62)

I have seen several chimpanzees using sign language. They move astonishingly rapidly, and unless one is aware of what one is looking for, one could easily miss the communication taking place between the chimp and the human operator.

Apparently, these and other results dealing with plastic symbols or with switches connected to a computer show that the apes can develop the primitive beginnings of symbolic language based upon a primitive grammar. This research also represents the lower end of the human communication spectrum, and some of these results are now being applied to human retardates and microcephalics who are incapable of learning human speech.

David Premack has experimented with differently shaped pieces of plastic combined in sequences by the ape on a flat surface. (63) He has shown that they can use these shapes as symbols of objects other than the plastic shapes themselves, as well as notions of self, of colors, and so forth.

The program of the apes that is most germane to the communication program with the dolphins is the Lana project, devised by Duane Rumbaugh and his wife, Susan.

In the Lana project the ape is presented with a rectangular array of switches mounted on a wall. The 156 switches can be pushed by the ape with his fingers. The large size of the switches (about 1½″ x 3″) allows the ape to push them with several fingers or with an index finger quite easily. The size also allows a symbol to be placed on each switch and backlighted. When the switch is pushed, the lighting increases so that a switch that has been pushed stands out against the array.

Each switch has a symbol, a "lexigram" that can be changed easily.

The switches are operated all or nothing, i.e., a symbol is either used or not used. There are no intermediate graduated meanings within the array of switches. There is no quantitative or qualitative difference between the way each of the switches acts on the electronic circuitry. There is no way that the ape can emphasize one switch action over another. Hence this parameter, of quantitative control, such as is present in voice, is not present with this system.

Each time a switch is pushed a special projector turns on that particular lexigram over the keyboard and over remote stations for the human observers. A sequence of lexigrams is thus portrayed on several such projectors as if to form a sentence.

The keyboard is connected to a PDP-8 computer manufactured by the Digital Equipment Corporation. The software in the computer is arranged in such a way that each time a lexigram is pressed, a printout of the lexigram and its equivalent simple English word are produced on a high-speed printer. The printout can be read by nonsophisticated observers as the direct translation of the lexigrams into English.

This system is described in more detail in a book entitled *Language Learning by a Chimpanzee,** which gives the philosophy, a history of previous research with chimpanzees and communication, the software used, and a description of the hardware. There are also two movies that can be seen at the site of the work at the Georgia State University in Atlanta, Georgia, and the Emory University Primate Center.

I learned that on publication of the book there were at least three inquiries concerning how this system could be used for communication with dolphins. To reproduce the system exactly would require an array of 156 underwater switches of much larger size so that they could be pushed by the dolphin's beak.

Why should the dolphins be induced to push switches with their jaws when they can control their sonic output with great sophistication?

Man and apes are related to each other structurally. We both have fingers and hands, and we can "manipulate" the external world with these marvelous instruments. We should not ask the

---

* Duane Rumbaugh, ed., *Language Learning by a Chimpanzee* (New York: Academic Press, 1977).

dolphin to communicate by pushing switches devised for the chimpanzee and the retarded human.

Nevertheless, scientific investigation of the ability of the dolphin to use his jaw in the service of symbolic operations has some validity. A comparison between the dolphin's learning ability and that of the chimpanzee and of the retarded human can be observed. On the other hand, we feel that it would be far better to make use of the dolphin's incredible ability to produce and to understand complex sequences of sound in such an investigation.

What are the advantages of sonic communication versus visual-muscular communication of the type used in the sign language, in the movement of the plastic symbols, and in the pushing of the switches?

The most obvious advantage is the ability to communicate over much longer distances than is possible by visual tracking of symbolic motions. Sound travels great distances, and maintains its characteristic form in spite of those distances, in air and even much farther under water. When one cannot see in the depths of the black night or in fog or in cloudy water, one can still hear through those elements that curtail vision. The remote communication with members of one's species by means of sound seems to be an accomplishment beyond the ability of apes. Humans and the Cetacea in general have this ability, which has led to increased survival of the species because they are able to control their sonic outputs and understand sonic inputs.

In contrast to the sign language, to the plastic symbols, and to the lexigrams, sound has many more parameters that can be controlled and used in the service of symbol transmissions. These parameters are amplitude and hence loudness, frequency, modulations, changes in pitch, abrupt starting and stopping of various parameters such as resonances within the head and the interrelating of several sources of sound within the same organism. All of these parameters can be controlled by the human and by the dolphin at an incredibly rapid pace compared with the use of fingers or flippers. Dolphins and humans, then, share a sophisticated capability of using sound for communicative purposes. The apes do not share this sonic domain except in the very primitive sense of built-in, ready-made programs for emotive and social expression.

Thus, for the full development of communication between man and dolphin it would be wise to go immediately to the sonic communicative mode rather than pushing switches, pushing pieces of plastic, or using symbolic movements of the body, detected visually.

In the current research and development program of the Human/Dolphin Foundation a computer has been purchased with its auxiliary equipment to carry out the initial investigation of sonic communication between man and dolphin. The program is called the JANUS project and the apparatus is also called JANUS for Joint-Analog-Numerical-Understanding-System. JANUS has a dolphin face for the dolphin end of the system and a human face for the human end of the system. The brain of JANUS is the computer with two sets of inputs and outputs, one set for man and the other for the dolphin. The sonic inputs to the dolphin from the computer are designed for that region of parameters most easily detected and discriminated by the dolphin. This is the region of maximum frequency discrimination and of the lowest threshold for detection of sounds running from approximately 3,000 Hz (cycles per second) to 80,000 Hz (cycles per second). On the human side the standard communicative frequencies from 300 to 3,000 Hz (cycles per second) will be used. In addition the human end uses the standard computer keyboard and video display units as well as printers and other devices for the convenience of the humans. Eventually, visual feedback to the dolphins will be incorporated with a cathode-ray TV underwater screen or its equivalent. The dolphin's visual input has been shown to be quite capable of analysis of visual symbols, and hence the sonic and the visual can be interconnected in the communication experiments with the dolphins.

Aside from these technical problems of the design of hardware and its associated software for communication between man and dolphin by sonic means, there is the problem of the human side of the system.

Who among the humans is capable of doing the communication research with the dolphins? What beliefs do such scientific observers use to facilitate the work? It is questions like these that have plagued me for the last twenty-five years and have caused me to take a very close look at what we mean by the "scientific observer." In subsequent chapters we make some observations about the kind of person, the kind of training, and the kinds of beliefs that those who are associated with communication with dolphins probably should have.

We will also consider the society in which that observer exists, and the laws and regulations requiring certain ways of operating with respect to dolphins and whales.

In order to take full advantage of the communication possibilities with dolphins, those involved in the work should be least impeded by other scientists, by the society in which they live, by the media, and by the government.

The design of software for the JANUS project depends upon the acceptance of some degree of direction of the humans by the dolphins. This is a new position for human scientific observers. However, this position is one well known to computer programmers who devote their skill and services to any program in a very open-ended fashion. The new science of computers and software has opened up new possibilities of relationships with other intelligent species including the dolphins.

CHAPTER EIGHT

The Evolution of the Scientific Observer and of Society and Its Laws

THE MODERN SCIENTIFIC OBSERVER HAS A LONG HISTORY OF evolution from various sources. The modern scientific observer has been formed by evolutionary parameters within human society. He/she has been evolved from conflicts between different human groups espousing different belief systems. The struggle to evolve scientific observers as "neutral noninvolved separate from the system observed" dates back at least to the time of Galileo. One can see roots even further back to the time of Aristotle.

The dominance of religious organizations over the power structures in human society provided the setting in which early scientists sought for truths. Many early conflicts resulted when prevailing beliefs were at odds with the universe as it really exists.

Galileo's observations of the moons of Jupiter passing behind Jupiter suggested a model for the whole solar system, which he then postulated. The beliefs of the Catholic church, however, placed the earth at the center of the universe. Galileo concluded that the earth is a planet rotating around the sun. The conflict between these beliefs led to Galileo's confinement in an attempt by the church to cut off his publications from the public.

Subsequent to Galileo, the astronomer became the objective observer par excellence. His observations did not influence that which he observed, i.e., the fact that someone turned a telescope upon planets and stars does not change the courses of those planets and stars. In the hands of Tycho Brahe, Newton, and others, this position of the noninvolved objective observer became the model of the scientific observer for the other physical sciences.

These early scientists had further problems with prevailing religious beliefs. In the religious tradition various human characteristics were projected upon nature. Nature was inhabited by spirits, supernatural forces, and gods who regulated the universe of humans and of nature surrounding human societies. Slowly but surely a few persons shed these beliefs and began to look at nature as something that had evolved without the interposition of intelligent forces, similar to those that man can exert upon man and upon his environment. These early religious beliefs, then, were said to be mistaken projections of man's inner life upon the universe. Consequently, as a result of objective observations, the planets and the stars, instead of being projections of man's own mental life, became systems independent of man's thinking, existing in the depths of space quite separate from anything that man could do about them.

Such deductions led then to the concept of the scientific observer who was not influenced by religious beliefs. Through a lot of blood, sweat, and tears among scientists and their antagonists, the observers of the seventeenth, eighteenth, and nineteenth centuries held to the principle of their total noninvolvement and of their abilities to observe nature anywhere, any time, without influencing the objects of their observation in any way.

The religious viewpoint put down man's instincts, which religion labeled "the beast in man." Man's sexual activities, his aggressive hostile activities, were all attributed to "the beast within him." Anthropomorphically, other mammals were given human characteristics. A slovenly, dirty man was labeled piggish, as if he shared the characteristics of pigs. A man or woman was called sheepish. In other words, "sheepishness" was projected as if it were a characteristic of the animals, not of most men. All animals were considered to be lower than man. Pejorative terms for humans such as "son of a bitch" were derived from such pejorative views of animals inherited from the religious view of the beast in man.

The biology of the nineteenth century began to deny such projections as these and a host of others that were considered inappropriate to the study of animals. Darwin's classic work on the evolution of the species and on the descent of man was accomplished by steering through such hazardous waters as were raised by religious beliefs.

It was then that scientists devised terms such as *anthropomorphism* and *anthropocentricism* to characterize the old religious projection of man's characteristics onto other animals. Anthropomorphism and anthropocentricism in the nineteenth century were very limited concepts and were directed at removing from science the old religious concepts. Scientists were staking out their territory, separating it from the territory of the churches.

The objective noninvolved observer became the be-all and end-all in scientific research. The astronomer observer began to study his own planet and began to observe biological nature surrounding him. The zoologist, i.e., those who kept zoos and studied the science of captive animals in zoos, acted as if they were astronomers. Their papers, the meetings, their beliefs, and their treatment of animals were based on the notion that their presence and the captivity of the animals had no effect on the animals. Zoologists and other biologists played the part of noninvolved observers.

However, some of the religious beliefs were still inherent in this concept of the noninvolved objective observer, such as the omniscience, omnipresence, and omnipotence attributed to God. In a sense the nineteenth-century observer believed in his own omniscience. His simulations of reality were said to apply to everything, everywhere, once he had determined them by observation and by experiment. The "omniscience" of previous scientists was attacked when later scientists by further experimentation found earlier conclusions to be defective. At that time no one really looked at the basic assumption that once laws of science were determined they applied everywhere Once one experimented, observed a species of animal, then that applied to that species no matter where found.

These early biologists also made the mistake of omnipresence. Since one set of observations made in one place must automatically apply to the next case and to all such cases, therefore the observer acted as if he were omnipresent, as if he were observing everywhere rather than in a limited local region.

The early zoologists (and some current zoologists) also acted as if they were omnipotent, i.e., as long as they could capture, kill, and investigate animals, they had the power to make all decisions about them.

These unconscious beliefs in the omniscience, omnipresence, and omnipotence of scientists in regard to the other animals is slowly but surely disappearing. The modern view of an ecosystem in which man is a coordinated part of the total biosphere is reducing these unconscious beliefs and their influence on our thinking.

As the religious beliefs of man's "holy spirit" are attenuated, a modern scientific simulation of the observer evolves. In ancient religious teachings, man's brain was not understood. In 400 B.C. Aristotle stated that the brain was an organ that cooled the blood and furnished mucous that came out of the nose. In spite of the observations of Hippocrates who noted that unconsciousness resulted from blows to the head, Aristotle maintained his belief. With the rise of the science of anatomy at the time of Vesalius, doubts were cast on Aristotle's view of the brain.

As medical science developed over the centuries, the brain became more and more important in understanding the functioning of man. Gradually, ideas about the brain evolved, arriving at the conclusion that it housed the mind of man. Over the last three hundred years this belief has become more and more central to the concepts of bases of man's behavior—his mental, ethical, and philosophical activities. Conflict between man as a spirit and man as contained within his own organism has become sharpened.

Through medical practice and medical research, new sciences appeared dealing with the brain itself. Observations of the effects on mental ability caused by blows to the head, anesthesia, various toxins and poisons, lack of oxygen, and so forth led to the concept that the mind is contained in the brain.

Modern medical science consensus limits the mind to the brain. In a modern view, the human observer, the human scientist himself, is limited as follows:

1. Each observer has only one mind contained within his/her brain.

2. Each observer is limited by his knowledge—experiential, experimental, and theoretical. The observer's simulations of reality limit his observations of that reality.

3. Each observer lives within his projections, within his simulation spaces, within his own belief systems. His beliefs particularly limit that which he observes, that which he considers real and true, that which he considers worth his efforts.

The further evolution of the scientific observer has definite requirements, as follows:

a. The duty of each observer is to examine his own beliefs ruthlessly and revise them to agree with the goodness-of-fit-with-reality criteria resulting from experience and experiments. His beliefs in regard to the surrounding society should be revised to accord with his social experience and experiments.

b. A scientific observer is unequipped to be neutral unless he studies brain evolution in the human species and the brain evolution of other species. Until an observer has learned the structure of his own central nervous system and how it operates, where it came from, and compares it to that of other species, he cannot adequately understand his relative position on the planet Earth.

c. There must be recognition that the modern scientific observer is an evolved and evolving animal of the mammalian group. Scientific research is a Western way of enlightenment.

d. The modern scientific observer must realize that he is a member of a vast feedback system within his own species and the other species. He must realize that man has established a separate "reality" defined by the beliefs current in that society.

e. The modern scientific observer must also realize that eventually the reality external to man's society can and will assert its demands and will determine the parameters of future evolution/devolution of his species upon this planet.

Thus we see that the modern scientific observer is consciously aware of his own structure, of his own evolution, of the possibilities of his future evolution, contingent upon the evolution and the structure of the beliefs current in his present society. He is no longer omnipresent, omnipotent, or omniscient. He has given up these wishes about himself and the wishes about how the universe *could be constructed* in favor of the way the universe *is constructed*.

Man must give up his own wishful thinking as projected in his human laws and in his socially acceptable beliefs.

As our knowledge of the human brain has increased, we have begun to realize that this is a superb biocomputer that generates its own internal reality. In a loose sort of way this internal reality is interlocked with a current external reality, past experiences with the external reality, simulations of both of these and simulations of future events, action, and so forth. The observer then lives in a simulation domain; he is a product of the computations of the brain.

The computational power of the human brain is such that it can construct internal realities and project them upon the external reality very effectively. A group of humans can agree upon certain beliefs and then reinforce them sufficiently so that they are willing to fight for those particular beliefs against all other groups with diverse beliefs.

The obvious route out of an internal reality that has a bad mismatch with the universe as it really is, is through designing experiments to test the internal reality and modify one's simulations of it. In the last one hundred years some very effective simulations of external reality have been devised in science and in engineering. The successful construction of bridges, buildings, computers, electrical power plants, and so forth, all demonstrate the success of the goodness-of-fit of the models within men and their simulation of the way that nature operates.

Similar advances of other internal realities of men have not been achieved by science. There are those who say they cannot be, that the human mind has infinite potentialities and hence cannot be programmed in the way that inorganic matter outside the mind can be. Counter to this is the knowledge of the material reality of the brain itself, a complex system that we have not yet succeeded in exploring.

For example, we do not know the rules of growth of our own brains, nor the rules of their past or future evolution. We do not understand their present methods of functioning. We do not understand the connection between our mind and that which generates it within the neuronal networks of the central nervous system.

Modern scientists tend to organize their internal realities along certain very disciplined lines. A theoretical physicist will stick to his mathematical models of whatever it is that he is considering in the external world. He feels secure as long as there is a certain goodness-of-fit of his theoretical simulations and experiments with that portion of external reality. Within certain definite limits he can then learn to control that external reality in the experimental mode.

Similar experiments on the internal reality are very difficult to perform. The observer immersed in his own system has too much power to change his simulations of what he is doing. His simulations of himself and his own thinking processes now become the subject of his scientific investigation. In solitudinous isolation he can be an experiencing experimentalist in his own inner domains.

This freedom to modify oneself and one's inner simulations of self and one's simulations of one's internal reality is not yet under scientific control. We can say a few things about the evolution of such powers and of their probable extension into the future.

As we say in other parts of this book, as the size of the neocortex, the associational silent computational areas of the brain, increases, the domain of the inner reality increases in its magnitude, in its dimensions, in its complexity, in its degrees of freedom. This can become a dangerous property. If a particular person sets up rules of this internal reality, the rules operate so as to generate that internal reality. With increase in brain size the preoccupation with the inward journey increases and problems with the external reality can increase. The basic survival of the human species may be at stake in the presence of such powers.

We know of past cultures that have disappeared because they worshipped that which in their internal realities they felt to be externally real. For example, the gods would destroy the universe unless they were propitiated with human sacrifice (Aztec).

Man is still struggling with his new inward threshold, his new inward freedom, misusing it sometimes to dangerous levels of lack of goodness-of-fit with the external reality necessities for survival dictated by his ecological environment. It behooves us to study the simulations of the external reality, its relations to our simulations of it, and to internalize the ones that work for us not against us. It behooves us to watch out for our creative and persuasive abilities to create destructive social realities from our "unreal" beliefs and our powers to recognize those that do not have long-term survival of our great-grandchildren and their children in mind. We must extend our time scale into the future for future generations of humans or else we will be terminated. One of the major lessons of evolution is that large brains survive only in concert with one another and with the planet and its laws of survival in total interdependence with all species.

Since any internal reality can be created and believed, let us select those beliefs that ensure really long-term survival of all species, that lead to a future rather than to destruction. Unless we exercise proper control of experiment and of theory, we will spend our time, effort, and resources learning how to destroy, and ultimately we will destroy ourselves.

As we show in more detail elsewhere in this book, the Cetacea have demonstrated a capacity to survive far longer than we have on this planet. Insofar as can be determined by paleontological evidence, the cetaceans have had large brains equal to and larger than ours for at least thirty million years. The dolphins have had brains equal to ours for fifteen million years. They have proved that they are able to survive with big brains. In spite of the enhancement of the inner reality, they have managed to work out their own thinking, their own doing, their own feeling, and their own actions to remain in tune, in harmony, with the total ecology.

Humans have not yet demonstrated such a capacity. Brains of the present size have been with man only one hundred thousand years. In other words, man in his present form has only existed 1/

150th of the time that the dolphins have existed and survived.

Such considerations do not take into account that man may have appeared many times before and been totally destroyed on the land. With a big brain, survival in the sea seems to be easier than survival on land. There may have been cataclysms on this planet in which the land mammals including man were wiped out many, many times, while those in the sea continued their evolution and their survival because of the cushioning effect of the oceanic environment.

We should pay closer attention to Cetacea and the facts of their survival over as long a period of time. If, eventually, we can communicate with them, we may find the ethics, laws, and facts that they have discovered, which have allowed their survival. They went through the dangerous acquisition of the large brain and of the resulting large internal reality millions of years ago. Somehow they have learned how to use this enlarged internal reality in the service of their survival in the external reality and to continue their evolution to larger brains and larger internal realities

Man's narcissistic worship of dangerous beliefs generated in man's own small past endangers long-term survival not only of man but of all species. Somehow, sometime, somewhere, we must agree with one another or we follow the great reptiles into our own extinction, self-inflicted.

Since so much attention and so much power are given to consensus science in the Western world, the power of generating consensus belief systems is the result of groups of scientists agreeing on what the external realities are. We must make our legal system agree with the laws of the universe and see to it that our laws include the entire planet and all its inhabitants. The sciences of man must be expanded and become more consonant with the evolutionary advancement of the whole planet and all humanity. The new scientific observer must be aware of his role in the forefront of those who investigate the way the ecological system *really* operates rather than some dream of how it should operate.

CHAPTER NINE

Current Laws and the Basic Assumptions about Cetacea

THE HUMAN SPECIES IS NOW ORGANIZED IN SUCH A WAY THAT survival depends upon interrelated activities with other groups of men and women. There are specialists who supply food, clothing, shelter, transportation, communication, and energy. Each large group of humans is built upon basic assumptions, upon basic beliefs about the necessities of survival within the human reality. The human species, recognizing the need for this amount of interdependence, has set itself up in its organizations to use the resources of the planet in the service of humanity alone. No other species is granted the rights that individual humans have obtained from other humans. The structure of human law and human economics assumes all of the species to be in the service of humans. Those animals that threaten the survival of groups of humans are killed without consideration of the consequences of the killing on the total ecology of the planet. The basic assumption exists that no other species have rights such as those of humans.

Such beliefs led to the treatment of cetaceans as an industrial resource for the use of human beings. Populations of cetaceans are treated as huge reservoirs of flesh to be eaten by man and to be turned into products for use in the industries of man.

The cetaceans are treated as "a resource to be managed, to maintain the health and stability of the marine ecosystem so that the populations will not become extinct." The cetaceans are called "species and stocks of animals in danger of extinction or depletion." The current laws speak of "optimal, sustainable populations and the optimum carrying capacity of the marine ecosystem" (The Marine Mammal Protection Act of 1972, MMPA).

The law states that human use shall be limited to the "minimum sustainable yield" of the populations of bodies of the cetaceans (International Whaling Commission Rules).

Live cetaceans are treated as an industrial resource "for the aesthetic and recreational as well as economic benefit of Man." Rules are set up for the limitation of "harassment, humane capture and humane killing" of cetaceans (MMPA) (IWC).

A few humans, mainly in the conservation groups, at least in the United States, are motivated by other beliefs, having to do with compassion for cetaceans and respect for the essential feedback relationships in the ecology of the planet Earth.

There is a rising group of the younger generation beginning to understand and respect the cetaceans. They respect the very different life-styles of the cetaceans, their family life, their social life, their culture. None of these considerations is present in the current laws regulating the behavior of humans with respect to the cetaceans. Before the Marine Mammal Protection Act of 1972 and the Endangered Species Act of 1973, relatively little attention was paid to the problems of man and the cetaceans in the United States. These two laws were a giant step forward, giving some control over the oceanaria, the tuna industry using porpoises to find the tuna and killing them in their large nets, the importation of whale products from whaling countries. There are many problems associated with the administration of these laws; very powerful lobbies oppose these regulations. There are many international complications brought about as a consequence of the administration of these laws. The tuna industry and the oceanaria oppose these laws with powerful lobbies in Washington, D.C. The conservation groups who support the laws brought enough public pressure in the past to have these laws passed in the first place.

The current Marine Mammal Protection Act contains a basic conflict that may ultimately defeat it as it exists today. Its administration under the Secretary of Commerce compromises its chances. Commerce and industry are hardly the place for the administration of laws with respect to the cetaceans. The secretary is charged with impossible scientific tasks; the scientific research is to be directed toward determining "the optimal sustainable population of cetaceans and the optimum carrying capacity of the Marine Ecosystem." Because of the very nature of cetaceans and their habitat, counting the numbers present in each species is an almost impossible scientific task. Since we also cannot count the fish and the squid upon which they feed, and the organisms upon which the squid and the fish feed, we can hardly determine the optimum carrying capacity of the marine ecosystem. Since we do not know where cetaceans mate, with one exception, the California gray whale, the secretary cannot "protect the mating grounds of the cetaceans."

This author then recommends a reconsideration of the basic assumptions behind these laws and the development of a new set of basic assumptions that make laws of a new sort regulating the relations between humans and cetaceans. He recommends to the conservation groups that they rethink their position with regard to the cetaceans. He recommends to the biological community, the consensus scientists who advise the lawmakers, to consider new bases for laws in this area.

Since the initiation of new assumptions and hence of new laws will take a considerable time, the following recommendations are made for a transition period for each of the industries involved:

The problem of oceanaria and public displays of cetaceans is so important to the education of humans that we have treated this problem separately in chapter 12, The Problem of Oceanaria/ Aquariums: A New Game. The recommendations in that chapter allow the oceanaria to expand their facilities in collaboration with government agencies and the public. The new game proposed in that chapter will allow everyone to win.

The problem of the tuna fishing industry capturing and killing porpoises (dolphins) in the course of purse seining methods is a more difficult one to devise a game in which all the players win including the porpoises. The decision of a federal district court judge (Richey) to ban the capture and killing of porpoises by the tuna industry apparently will lead to powerful repercussions within government and industry with modifications of the present law in favor of the tuna fishermen and against the porpoises. An interim suggestion by this author: that a major scientific effort be funded to find out more satisfactory methods of separating the porpoises from the tuna. Such efforts should be devoted not only to devising new nets that separate the two species but to sonic and ultrasonic methods of repelling and attracting the porpoises. Research into what it is that attracts the two species to one another should also be initiated. To date this question has not been answered by scientific research.

The new provision of a two-hundred-mile limit for the region of administration of the United States laws in regard to whales seems to be a step in the right direction for the protection of the Cetacea. If international agreements with Mexico, Canada, and the Central and South American countries can be arrived at, whales would at least have a long corridor for their migrations in which they could be protected by U.S. Navy and Coast Guard patrols. However, it would be wiser for the United Nations to establish world-wide protection of Cetacea with new activities (nonwhaling) for these industries in Japan, Russia, and other countries.

The author recommends new laws for cetaceans. In another chapter we discuss the strategy and bases for these new laws and the new protection.

CHAPTER TEN

The Scientific Observer as a Participant in the Ecology of the Planet Earth

AS COMMUNICATION IMPROVES AMONG HUMAN BEINGS ON THE planet Earth, the scientific observer in his modern sense has evolved as a participant observer, a participant in his own society, and a participant in the ecology of the planet Earth.

As I pointed out before, the scientists in their consensus to a certain extent determine the laws relating to the planet. The laws of man and, at least in the United States, the laws made with respect to other species take into account the latest scientific consensus among a certain segment of the scientific community. Various scientific organizations are appealed to by legislators and by the public to make decisions about what is to be accepted as real in our laws. This attention to scientific advice is not always present and is sometimes neglected. But in other cases it is well documented in the structure of our government and of our laws.

Since World War II various agencies of government have scientific advisory committees to advise government agencies, the President, the Senate, and the House of Representatives. The agencies and the courts use "expert witnesses" from the scientific community.

As more and more people in the United States become more aware of ecology and the science of the environment, more and more decisions are made on the basis of the scientific agreement as to what the real facts are in regard to other animals, plants, the atmosphere and the oceans, and the land itself.

Underlying this basic philosophy of conforming to scientific consensus is the implication that scientists as a group within the society have specialized knowledge that the rest of humanity should honor and obey. This is gradually influencing government.

Within the United States government, plants, plant physiology, and scientific farming have been given over to our Department of Agriculture and its scientific advisers. This department has charge of farming, reforestation, and similar activities related to the plant kingdom.

Domesticated animals, such as cows, horses, sheep, and pigs, are placed under the control of the Department of Agriculture and, where pertinent, under the Departments of Public Health. In the current philosophy of man, such animals are controlled and managed sources of food supply for humans. The philosophy of animal husbandry has given rise to the science and practice of veterinary medicine. The advice of organized groups of doctors of veterinary medicine is representative of the consensus scientific point of view.

Other animals within the United States, the terrestrial mammals, have been placed under the control and regulation of the Department of the Interior. This includes bears, elk, mountain goats, mountain sheep, mountain lions, buffalo, coyotes, eagles, and so forth. These animals are not considered domesticated and are labeled wild animals. Their regulation is in the service of the hunting groups of humans, hunting for sport, and at times hunting for survival in order to eat in the wild. Some of the species listed in the endangered species list are under the control of the Department of the Interior of the United States government.

Animals kept in zoos and animal parks in the United States are regulated by laws administered by the Department of the Interior and by the consensus scientific group known as zoologists. A subdepartment in the consensus scientific community of zoologists are the mammalogists, i.e., those who have studied the mammals.

The traditions in the scientific community are to assign animals in general to commercial undertakings such as animal husbandry for human consumption; and, hence, most animals are now not only under the sway of the scientific advisory committees but under the sway of commercial exploitation and use of animals for food, for entertainment, and for sport, i.e., hunting.

Marine mammals, i.e., the Cetacea (dolphins, whales, and porpoises) and the amphibious mammals (sea lions, seals, and so forth) are under the Marine Mammal Protection Act of 1972 and under the Endangered Species Act of 1973: in the Department of Commerce and in the Department of the Interior, depending upon certain administrative decisions as to which belongs where. The scientific community advises the Marine Mammal Commission and the Department of the Interior regarding the acceptable scientific facts about these animals. Each of these acts has a basic philosophy within it of the commercial exploitation of such animals for entertainment—displays and performing shows for the public benefit.

In all of the above cases, the scientific consensus and the commercial uses of the animals determine the philosophy of the law. All of these groups of animals are managed in one way or another by the humans for the profit of humans.

Despite the fact that these laws say nothing about the education of humans, a portion of these facilities and animals are devoted to education of the human young. Apparently the framers of these laws considered public education a side issue, not pertinent to the major issues of management and commercial exploitation.

Each of the laws makes exceptions in favor of the scientific community; certain animals can be captured, confined, and killed in the service of scientific research. Exceptions in the law are made in favor of the scientific community allowing certain animals to be investigated in the service of better management policies and better commercial exploitation. The commercial philosophy dictates research policies in the direction of better management and better care for the exploitation of animals by humans.

All of the above considerations, then, mean that the scientific community is a part of the human feedback system, of the human ecology and the relation of humans to animals.

Additional segments of the public do not necessarily agree with this philosophy. Many conservation groups and animal lover groups, motivated by compassion for animals, want to reform man's relations with animals. A very large number of these people respect the rights of animals to maintain their life-styles, to maintain their territories, and to have a relationship with man that will avoid as much pain and suffering as possible on the part of the animals. In spite of the fact that this segment of society does not have the respect and the automatic advisory power in the United States government that the scientists do, their public relations are strong enough so that they can influence legislation and initiate new laws bringing a greater humaneness of treatment to animals. They have established in the law that animals that are to be killed for human consumption are to be killed in as humane and merciful a fashion as possible. In other words, animals are to be killed rapidly and if possible under anesthesia so that suffering is minimized. The carbon-dioxide method of killing farm animals for the production of human food became a legal reality under the pressure of these groups, with the advice of the scientific community.

The collection of animals for scientific purposes has become somewhat regulated by these groups also. The collection of animals for zoos and oceanaria has come under the scrutiny of these groups, who have insisted that the collection of animals be regulated to minimize pain and suffering during the collection and capture processes. Their feedback on the scientific community has ensured that scientific research be done on the optimal methods to minimize trauma to the animals concerned.

Thus, we see that in the structure of human society there are diverse groups who feed back on one another, and whose communications with one another render the scientific observer a part of the system of human society.

Before such communication and such interaction, scientists pretty much had the field to themselves; they could collect, capture, and use animals in the service of scientific research, in a fashion dictated by the ethics of the particular scientist involved.

Such a laissez faire attitude is no longer possible in most areas of science, for the mammals at least.

As communication has become faster in human society, the nonparticipant observer is disappearing in science. The impact of man on his environment and on the other species is gradually being articulated by many different groups of people, including the scientific community. So far this impact has been considered from a limited, human narcissistic point of view, somewhat as follows:

The other species on this planet and the planet itself are here for the exploitation of man, for the economic good of man. Animals, plants, the land itself, and the ocean are considered "economic resources" to be "managed by human institutions." Scientific knowledge is to be put in the service of the rest of humanity and is to be put under the service of the economic exploitation of natural resources. The philosophy of the law is to use scientific consultants and the scientific community in the service of exploitation for profit of the natural resources. Scientific research for purely new knowledge is no longer fashionable.

Another portion of the philosophy of man is in the use of scientific advisers and the scientific community in the service of the development of warfare among humans. The development of atomic energy was made possible under the stimulus of World War II and man's fear of other men. During World War II a portion of the scientific community was organized and supported by the United States Department of Defense. In effect, the atomic and nuclear scientific community was drafted in the service of human warfare. The Manhattan Project became the Atomic Energy Commission, and the regulation of the use of atomic energy in warfare and in industry became a legal entity under the control of the United States government. All scientists participating in such programs were placed under stringent security safeguards to prevent other humans from learning their discoveries. As the impact of nuclear energy upon the environment and upon other species became apparent, a more and more informed segment of the public began to influence the law in regard to the use of nuclear energy. As the scientific community perfected the nuclear weapons of war, the fear of the rest of humanity began to be felt in the structure of the laws, both national and international.

The earliest scientists, then, to come under the sway of the rest of humanity were the atomic scientists, who began to realize that they were no longer noninvolved observers, and so they became participant observers, helping the rest of humanity to realize the true nature of nuclear energy and its dangers to humanity and the rest of the planet. Very articulate and powerful voices were heard within the scientific community in regard to atomic energy.

Thus, we see that the scientific observer had to descend from the ivory tower and become a human being totally involved in human affairs; the past illusion of scientists as noninvolved observers disappeared.

As the use of atomic energy began to be exploited for purposes of industrial power and human warfare, the science of atomic energy became better supported but also more deeply regulated.

In addition to the economic exploitation of animals, behind the scenes there have been many attempts to use animals in the service of man's warfare. The classical example from ancient times was the use of elephants in Hannibal's attack upon Rome. Hannibal's troops forced the elephants over the Alps. The counterweapon to the use of elephants was the use of Greek fire, a combination of burning substances that could be poured on or discharged at the elephants. The elephants panicked and their use in warfare ceased.

As methods of training animals by means of operant conditioning developed, there were attempts to use seals, for example, during World War II to find submarine nets and submarines. The method was never developed enough to be practical. Proposals to use bats as incendiary agents during World War II had a similar ending.

When brain electrodes became an obvious method of control of animal behavior, various attempts were made to use animals to deliver explosives. Sandia Corporation developed the use of brain electrodes in donkeys and mules in order to deliver atomic weapons. It is rumored that certain government agencies attempted to use dolphins, using brain electrodes for their control also. As soon as publicity was given to these attempts, the public outcry prevented further such use, at least in the public sector.

The feedback on the scientific community has thus determined that scientists are involved observers who must pay attention not only to the philosophy of pure research and the philosophy of economic exploitation and of human warfare but also to human compassion and the humane use of animals. Those scientists who are most aware of the necessity of their role as participants in human society became members of scientific advisory committees and commissions, advising governments, conservation groups, the military, and scientific societies about their position within humanity as a whole. In the traditions of science, the scientist does his experiments, draws his own deductions from those experiments, and publishes scientific papers. These papers are then read by other scientists, the experiments are repeated or modified, and new deductions are thereby arrived at. Scientific consensus, in theory at least, is thus generated by means of the scientific literature in the meetings of scientists in their own specialist societies. Scientists are expected to report their discoveries in scientific journals and at scientific meetings.

This generation of a scientific consensus by these means is being modified somewhat by the presence of instant television and radio communication with the public. Despite the curiosity of the media and their wish to report instantly any new development in science, the scientific community has taken an attitude that the duty of the scientist is to report first to his fellow scientists, allow them to make their judgments about the quality of the work, and then to integrate this with the rest of science, and then, finally, to report to the media.

Any scientist who deviated from this procedure without consultation with his peers and colleagues in general was discredited by the scientific community. Any far-out new deductions, theories, or discoveries not subjected to the scrutiny of at least portions of the scientific community were considered to be not worth discussion, further investigation, or comment by the organized scientific consensus. Even if such theories, deductions, or facts were quite reproducible, true, and worth further investigation, the organized scientists refused to consider them. When a scientist wrote a book that was not subjected to the scrutiny of his segment of the scientific community and was published for the general public rather than through an acceptable scientific monograph publisher, refereed by scientific editors, the work was discounted.

Such books written for the layman, i.e., the nonscientist, have exerted powerful effects in the nonscientific communities. Thus, many ideas that could not be transmitted through the usual scientific channels became acceptable public property, part of the education of the younger generations.

Ideas published in this particular way then gained a force of their own among large groups of people. New young persons in the law, in science itself, in public action groups, in the military establishment, in the artistic community and the literary community, and in the newspaper, TV, and radio fields took on the new ideas and the new beliefs not guided by the scientific community and the scientific consensus. Such ideas were then fed back to the scientific community from the public sector and in many cases were fought against by the organized scientists. Sometimes the fighting was not very obvious: there was merely ridicule, anger, and expression of disappointment with any scientist who would go outside the usual channels. The refusal of the organized scientist to investigate the authenticity of the theories, experiments, and deductions was the penalty laid upon the scientist who went public, bypassing the auspices of a scientific organization.

Young scientists do not have all of the loyalties to their own scientific fashions and their own scientific consensus. It is the young scientists who break new ground, who move into new areas of scientific research. Thus, ideas expressed in the previous generation that were absorbed by the youngsters who were to become scientists gradually penetrated into the thinking and the philosophy of the young almost unconsciously. There were some young, bright scientists who would not accept the dogma of their predecessors, disallowing certain ideas, certain methods, and certain deductions from their science.

There are some new young scientists who feel socially involved; they are no longer the noninvolved objective observers of the seventeenth, eighteenth, and nineteenth centuries. The new twentieth-century young scientist feels social feedback as a much more powerful factor than was possible in the nineteenth century. Our children are now brought up with TV, radio, and large meetings, which did not exist in the nineteenth century. More information comes faster from more directions to each young scientist, thus molding him and evolving him as a participant observer of the twentieth century. I do not speak of all young scientists; some still get caught in the pure dogma and pure ideals of the older science. The socially involved observer with scientific training is part of a human consensus reality beyond his science. As we state elsewhere in this book, man's isolation from communication with anyone but man himself has given rise over the last several thousand years to beliefs that place man at the top of creation on this planet. In these beliefs no other species has thinking, feeling, and doing comparable to that of man. The beliefs are basic to the laws we have legislated in regard to all of the other species and in regard to the planet itself. Human law is predicated upon the humans managing the rest of the ecology, including all other species. The aims of such management are industrial use of the resources, which are defined as including all other species.

Thus, we can see that the underlying philosophy of human law is devoted to interhuman relationships and relationships between human institutions including corporations, organized religions, cities, states, nations, and the United Nations. Most of humanity lives within a constructed consensus reality made possible by man's belief in himself. Humanity has separated itself from the rest of the planet by this belief.

In a sense, then, we can say that man suffers from interspecies deprivation; man has no one to talk to but man; man negotiates only with man; he manages everyone else.

What do we mean by *management?* The management concept implies a hierarchy of control in which the managers are giving the orders for the activities of the group under their control. Among the human species many persons and groups are given management powers over other persons, groups, and things. Within the human social reality such management powers are respected if and until there is sufficient objection and the law is changed, establishing a new hierarchy of control and management.

Sometimes the managers are overthrown by violent revolution

or warfare. At other times the managers are overthrown by new knowledge or by new access to information that was ignored or not used by the previous hierarchy of managers.

New scientific knowledge, new technology, leads to new hierarchies of managers within the law and outside the law.

If the scientific community can be induced to investigate the possibilities of other sentient, intelligent, thinking beings on this planet, and if the scientific community can be convinced that such species exist on this planet, the hierarchy of managers will be rapidly changed. Such predicated discoveries will lead to a reassignment of roles of various human institutions and the establishment of new managers to manage the new information. I hope that we are better equipped politically, legally, and socially when this occurs than we were when the impact of atomic energy and the discovery of nuclear energy took place during World War II. It is my personal hope that there will be enough informed persons with the various disciplines and knowledge required to make more adequate provision and to determine the relations among humans and between humans and others. I hope that such advances will not be in the service of man's own warfare against man but will be in the service of a social evolution, not a social revolution. Given a sufficiently large body of informed persons in responsible positions, the new transitions can be made with more dignity and less commitment to negative, destructive belief systems.

CHAPTER ELEVEN

Proposal for New Laws for Cetaceans: Immediate Strategy

THE PRESENT LAWS AMONG HUMANS REGULATING HUMAN BE-havior with respect to the Cetacea are discussed elsewhere in this book. It is recognized that there will be a transition period from the present laws to new ones in the future. In making the transition, let us assume that new laws can be designed upon present unassailable, scientific facts. Let us not include in this set of unassailable facts anything that cannot be measured or that is extremely difficult to measure using the present methods of science. Let us present these facts as though they were written into a preamble for a new set of laws to substitute for the current ones.

The human species and the species of cetaceans share an ecological system with mutual interdependence over the surface of the planet Earth, its land and its seas. The Cetacea inhabit the 71 percent of the planet's surface covered with the oceans and seas. Life as we know it originated and evolved in these oceans and continues to do so. The primordial organisms giving rise to life, including the human species and the Cetacea, originated in the waters of the oceans of earth.

The atmosphere, the oceans, and the land are in a mutually

interdependent ecological system; changes in one introduce changes in the other. The ecological balance of the oceans is reflected in changes in the atmosphere. Changes in the atmosphere are reflected in changes in life and the quality of life upon the land. Changes wrought by the human species on land change the atmosphere and the oceans in a totally interdependent way. Man's current science cannot yet account for all the feedback patterns between the oceans, the land, and the atmosphere. The human species has not yet mastered the science of the total ecology of Earth. Man does not yet understand all of those factors necessary for his long-term survival over the millennia. Man does not yet understand the necessity for survival of organisms of the sea, including the cetaceans.

One of the major scientific undertakings for the human species is discovering the rules and laws of this total ecosystem of which the human species is an integral part. If and until the human species can discover these laws and live in consonance with them, it is important that no further extinction or depletion of species of the land or of the ocean be allowed in his laws.

Extensive medical studies upon man have demonstrated that the brain determines the quality of the social performance of the human individual. Those whose brains are too small as a consequence of genetic factors are dealt with in the law as socially incompetent. (64) Those humans who have had extensive brain damage also have been determined to be socially incompetent and need protection under human laws. Adequate social communication among human individuals depends upon the brain and its inviolability. Those human beings who have lost the use of certain critical regions in their brains are no longer able to function in our society.

The major assumption upon which our laws are based is the concept of social competence and control by human speech, written communication, and socially acceptable behavior. Those humans who cannot communicate either are protected under the law or are eliminated from free social mobility. Extensive neuroanatomical studies over the last twenty years have demonstrated the necessary requirements in brain structure for the development of speech and acceptable social behavior.

Extensive neuroanatomical studies have shown that the cetaceans have a spectrum of brain sizes running from those of the apes and the humans to six times the size of the human brain. Extensive biological studies show that the cetaceans communicate by complex underwater sounds, analogous to the speech of humans. (2, 3, 9, 39) In those cetaceans with brain sizes equivalent to those of humans, definite efforts at communication with humans have been demonstrated. (12, 18, 23, 27, 33)

The cetaceans in general have shown a behavior observed by man for the last one hundred and fifty years. These records show that no cetacean—dolphin, porpoise, or whale—has injured or killed a human being. Boats and sailing ships have been attacked but rarely, and then only under strong provocation such as harpooning. In those cases of attack by the whale upon a vessel, the surviving humans in the water, in the lifeboats, or on rafts, were not attacked. Extensive experience with cetaceans in captive states in oceanaria show that they will not injure or kill any human in the water with them. There is extensive documentation of dolphins and whales rescuing humans who were thrown into the sea. These facts and observations lead us to suggest the following laws:

1. No cetacean is any longer to be considered a human property, nor an industrial resource, nor a member of stocks of animals.

2. Individual cetaceans are to be given the legal rights of human individuals under human law.

3. Human individuals and groups of humans are to be given the right to sue in behalf of, or otherwise represent in court, cetacean individuals placed in jeopardy by other humans.

4. Scientific research is to be initiated, encouraged, and supported to establish means of communication with the cetaceans.

5. In the event that such communication is established, further laws protecting the use of that communication between the cetaceans and the humans are to be researched and proposed to the Congress of the United States, based upon equal representation between humans and cetaceans.

6. New interspecies laws, agreements, and interspecies treaties are then to be researched in cooperation with the cetaceans.

It is time to recognize that the human species has maintained a human-centered, isolated existence on the planet Earth because of its failure to communicate with those of comparable brain size existing in the sea. The cetaceans have a reality separate from the human reality. Their realities, defined in their own terms, their social competence, their surviving for the last fifteen million years, are to be respected, to be researched, and the consequences to be legislated into human law.

There are those who will think of the above proposals in terms of a science-fiction script, thus rendering themselves safe from taking the above ideas seriously. The answer to such a viewpoint is that this merely shows ignorance of the facts of brains and of ecosystems on this planet. One can safely disavow becoming involved in this very large program by such beliefs. Man has a long history of espousing blinding beliefs that bind him to ideas that have led to the demise of whole cultures. Opening one's eyes to the possibilities of nonhuman communicators with immensely complex and ancient histories and ethics on this planet requires one to shed the blinding beliefs inherited from the past.

CHAPTER TWELVE

The Problem of Oceanaria/Aquariums and the Cetacea: A New Game

EVENTUALLY THE OCEANARIA MAY BE CLOSED BY CONSERVATION groups of people: I hope not. Here I offer alternatives to closure in which both the Cetacea and the humans can gain new relations and profit through the oceanaria. Here we present the case for/against oceanaria and aquariums that hold the dolphins, porpoises, and whales. We also present a new game in which everyone wins in the further evolution of oceanaria and aquariums from purely display and circuses to interspecies schools for man/Cetacea.

First, the oceanaria and aquariums with cetacean displays and shows have a long history from the forties to the present of allowing the public to see and appreciate who the dolphins, porpoises, and whales are. Despite the essential simplicity, repetitiousness, and peculiarly traditional circus performances in the shows, and despite the essentially inadequate opportunities for cetacean/cetacean and cetacean/human communication, the public has received an education as to the forms, the behaviors, and something of the interspecies relations between individual Cetacea and individual human/cetacean in limited contexts.

Such public experience and public education have aided in forming a public consensus among a sufficiently large segment of the public to initiate and maintain certain legal safeguards and standards for capture and care of Cetacea (see chapter 9, Current Laws and the Basic Assumptions about Cetacea).

Second, science is indebted to the commercial oceanaria and aquariums for opportunities to study the Cetacea within the limits of noninterference on the part of scientists with displays and shows and within certain rules established by the commercially limited goals for the oceanaria. The oceanaria have made large profits using an essentially conservative business approach in which only modest budgets for research have been allocated. The oceanaria have not taken opportunities to foster research to upgrade their displays and shows.

Only public pressures and hence new laws have forced sets of standards of care of Cetacea on the oceanaria. The usual American business way of assigning "proprietary" information to secrecy has been their rule in regard to facilities, training methods, feeding, and care of Cetacea. By hiring scientific consultants and putting the use of their information into proprietary categories, the oceanaria protect their power by limiting the available knowledge to sales to other oceanaria by contracts and agreements. The laws and the oceanaria agree that the Cetacea in their charge are the legal property of the oceanaria.

If one attempts to examine a given oceanarium scientifically to find out how well the Cetacea are kept, one comes up against evasive answers to specific questions or is put off by the "proprietary information" answer. The amounts and kinds of food, vitamins, antibiotics and other medicines, the treatment of the water in the tanks, the medical laboratory tests, the flow figures for the water in the tanks, the size of tanks, the training of trainers and other personnel, the training of the Cetacea, have, at one time or another, been withheld from outside neutral scientific scrutiny. The morbidity (sickness) figures on the cetacean population and the birth rates (a critical measure of the cetacean's adaptation to captivity) are either not available, have not been recorded, or are considered confidential information. For current legal regulations pertinent to these points, see chapter 9, Appendix 1, and Appendix 2. (As we have seen, one defensive maneuver still available to oceanaria is to plead "proprietary information," and hence not even government enforcement agencies are allowed to know certain details.)

In the light of what has been scientifically determined about Cetacea, the oceanaria's current practices and facilities share a major defect: individual cetaceans are cut off socially (1) from families and friends in the sea and (2) from one another within a given oceanarium or aquarium.

The cetaceans' sonic-ultrasonic communication with one another has been extensively studied and documented. (2, 3, 21, 39, 51–56) The necessities of this communication within certain species, for their well-being in family and social groups, has been demonstrated. Cross-species communication between different species of Cetacea is easily deducible from documented behaviors observed at sea.

If, in an oceanarium, any dolphin/porpoise/whale is kept in isolation in solitude (as they frequently are) in a tank, the social deprivation may be so severe that the cetacean commits suicide by voluntarily ceasing either breathing and/or eating. (See Appendix 7 in this volume. [27]) At the least, such a cetacean becomes apathetic, stops making sounds, and regresses into repetitious swimming in a simple pattern, with a decreased appetite and a resulting weight loss. (One is reminded of human behavior in involuntary solitary confinement.)

To avoid this morbidity or demise, cetaceans in tanks must be kept in pairs, preferably male/female dyads. (39) The resulting shared communication and sexual outlet ensures some decrease in the parameters leading to impaired mental/physical health. (Human male/female couples in dyadic isolation matched properly can survive better than either individual in solitude.)

However, in the habitat in nature most Cetacea are in socially related groups larger than two: pods vary from five to several hundred individuals in relatively constant sonic-ultrasonic communication with one another under water.

In tanks with more than two individuals, the communication outputs/exchanges are (averaged over the twenty-four hours) considerably above that for one or two individuals.

We devised a behavior criterion for measuring the communication frequency: the sonic-ultrasonic duty cycle. The recorded sounds-ultrasounds are fed into a computer system that measures the ratio of time spent making sounds to the time spent in silence; this ratio is called the sonic duty cycle. In intraspecies solitude we found that the sonic duty cycle increased in the presence of danger/anxiety.

Our observations show a twenty-four-hour sonic duty cycle of 0.001 for individuals in solitude, 0.1 for pairs, 0.3 for triads, 0.35 for quadrads, and 0.40 for octads. (No figures are available for sonic-ultrasonic duty cycles at sea: there are considerable technical difficulties in obtaining the data.)

We suggest that, to ameliorate the social deprivation of Cetacea in oceanaria, dolphin/porpoise/whale two-way underwater "telephones" of proper physical characteristics be installed between all tanks in the given oceanarium. With proper characteristics (sufficient frequency passband, amplitude capability, no spurious signals from physical feedback, lack of phase shift throughout the passband, etc.), we have found that dolphins/porpoises will use such links between tanks. (39) This observation was confirmed by navy researchers. (65) Our studies of the twenty-four-hour sonic duty cycle indicate frequent use of the telephone; behavioral observations show definite rise in interest and lowered morbidity signs in solitudinous isolates connected by telephone to other isolates or to groups in tanks.

In oceanaria with different species in separate tanks, the ocean situation of mixed species can be somewhat simulated by telephones between tanks. New scientific research is indicated to determine the twenty-four-hour sonic duty cycle values in such configurations, and hence the cetaceans' social needs in this area of social interspecies interaction. Studies are yet to be done on isolates of two different species (say *Tursiops* and *Orca, Globicephala* and *Tursiops, Delphinus* and *Tursiops,* etc.). By this means it may be possible to test the existence of interspecies communication among the Cetacea.

(Large groups of cetaceans in tanks decrease social deprivation if the tanks are large enough to prevent social overload. Signs of social overload are increased irascibility and violent encounters between individuals.)

Within oceanaria management, there may appear objections to

the installation of such telephones on the following grounds:

1. Scientists have not demonstrated the necessity for such apparatus.
2. Installation costs are too high.
3. Such intercetacean communication may interfere with the current shows/displays.

1. In answer to the first argument, we give the above discussion on our results and deductions. We feel it is a necessary link. For confirmation or disproof of our results, the oceanaria should sponsor further research using telephone lines.

2. Installation costs can be amortized and paid for by allowing the public to hear the cetaceans communicating by coin-operated devices for a short listening period for a small sum. Proper connections to the two-way telephone links for human listening can be devised.

3. If one takes the current oceanarian view that the present shows are adequate to ensure public buying of admissions and that the routines must be maintained uninterrupted by communication between show cetaceans and other cetaceans not participating, then telephones are not installed. However, if an oceanarium management is secure enough to experiment with the interconnecting of show and nonshow individuals/groups, I am sure that new interesting-to-the-public behaviors by the Cetacea will take place given enough time and adequate facilities. Loudspeaker monitors for the show audiences may demonstrate to that audience that some individual cetacean in a tank not in the show directs the cetacean performers by the communication through the sonic-ultrasonic links. Behavior of nonperforming individuals in separate tanks during show performances may demonstrate new novel behaviors (sonic and visible): there may even occur mimicry of performance behavior by nonshow individuals in distant tanks after several weeks of such linkages. (We have found some evidence of nighttime transfer of teaching of new routines among *Tursiops.)*

The purely scientific value of such links made available to scientists equipped to make multichannel recordings of the exchanges between tanks is incalculable. New data on the vocal duty cycle, elements of cetacean signals, interspecies (cetacean) communication, exchange rates related to other behaviors, are a few of the scientific areas of interest opened up through such links. Long-term effects on the morbidity, behavior, and mortality of interconnected individuals/groups can be correlated with the presence/absence of the communication linkages. Individual cetacean sonic signatures can be explored for use in finding individuals in the wild in social studies.

All of the Cetacea in oceanaria have been separated from their family/relatives/social groups in the sea. For such socially oriented species this is undoubtedly a stress. Suddenly cut off from family and friends, cetaceans mourn and grieve for a fairly long period. Unless human friendships develop, such individuals may refuse to eat, lose weight, and die. Mothers cut off from their offspring mourn and commit suicide by either refusing food or stopping breathing voluntarily. Individuals kept isolated for years in oceanaria eventually may commit suicide or attack other individuals in a "nervous breakdown" or a psychotic fashion. (I know personally two such cases in an oceanarium after eight years of confinement and four shows per day.)

To ameliorate this social isolation/deprivation syndrome, we suggest extending the cetacean telephone links from the Cetacea in the tanks to those in the sea. In those oceanaria close to the sea, the technical feasibility of such links is greater and the cost less than in those few oceanaria far from the sea. Even the latter oceanaria could participate through satellite or land microwave cable links. All of the technical knowhow is available for such tank-sea linkages; the facilities have been constructed for transmission over the whole earth (NASA and military networks).

The links between the tanks and the sea are to be made by microwave transmissions to large sea buoys or "Texas towers" (oil derricks and others). The sea buoys and towers are fitted out with underwater hydrophones and sonic-ultrasonic emitters of high power, used by the cetaceans in the ocean. On the buoy or tower are the receivers and transmitters for the underwater sounds converted to FM radio signals in the VHF, UHF, or higher-frequency regions. The passband requirements of the radio link overall are the same as in the oceanaria telephone system (10 to 160,000 Hz).

The oceanarium will have a microwave system for transmission-reception with the buoy and/or tower, connected to the intertank cetacean telephones.

Experiments with a single such system are needed. Its effect on the captive individuals is predicted to ameliorate the social separateness of the oceanarium groups of cetaceans. If the oceanaria refuse to underwrite the costs, this is an area for dedicated foundation or government support.

An alternative link with the sea groups could be microwave from buoys or towers anywhere on the ocean to a communication satellite, and from the satellite to one or several oceanaria anywhere on earth. This plan requires governmental cooperation and funding. Unless the communication corporations and the oceanaria could arrive at negotiated agreements, only government can do this job (NOAA, NASA, navy, etc.).

The cetacean telephone/radiophone is designed for use by the Cetacea with their natural sounds over their very wide frequency bands. The initial apparatus is so designed. Scientific research (in addition to that on cetacean communication) in new areas is opened up by such telephone systems.

Given such a system, it can be interconnected directly on-line with computers. Two-way links through proper interface apparatus will allow scientists to set up software (computer programs) that can teach dolphins/whales/porpoises codes using simulated elements of their signaling system (clicks/whistles).

Such codes, once learned, will allow the cetaceans to operate the computer to solve communication problems with man, to operate various extra- or intra-tank apparatus designed for feeding, operating TV (visual) links with other tanks, and cassette tape playbacks of TV programs for the cetaceans.

All such activities within the oceanaria not only would ameliorate the social isolation of the Cetacea by increasing their interest but also would increase public human interest in the oceanaria severalfold. The oceanaria could thus move out of "circus/display" categories into "interspecies schools" categories. In addition to admission charges, the oceanaria schools could charge tuition for selected students/studies through government grants from various governmental agencies (NIH, Office of Education, NOAA, NASA, DOD, etc.).

An additional suggestion for amelioration of the social deprivation of cetaceans is the *"limited term of service"* concept for cetaceans in oceanaria. In a sense humans draft Cetacea for public display/shows; the present draft term is "until death do us part" for each cetacean. It is suggested that each cetacean serve a more limited term in human service, say, one year. At the end of the term of service he/she is returned to the area of removal or, as we learn more, to his/her home group.

For such a "limited service" program, public underwriting of the enhanced costs of capture and release may be necessary. Either direct government participation through a special agency or government grants to private enterprise will probably be needed.

To implement this program it may be necessary to establish individual rights for cetacean individuals in the laws of humans. With such rights, the limited service requirement would be enforceable by interested private/public persons/agencies. For how the rules of the game would be changed, see other chapters in this book. New industries and new employment and educational opportunities would arise as the result of such laws. Those corporations with farsighted plans and proper skills have an opportunity there to realize new patents, new markets, etc.

Eventually, with the new cetacean communication game under way, it is advisable that those interested be prepared to draft new laws regulating the rules for humans. Careful consideration of the impact on humans, on the cetaceans, and on the environment of each and regulation of the new industries, of the new schools, of the new employment opportunities and special training necessary are part of the legislative studies needed. New young enthusiastic disciplined lawyers/judges/legislators have an opportunity unparalleled in the history of man: regulation of human dealings with another species at a high ethical, moral, and philosophic level.

At the beginning of the new cetacean/human game, we study/ observe/learn new rules. Even short of the long-term goal of highly complex communication of information to/from the Cetacea, the game can be made profitable to us as well as them.

At the very least, if we give them telephones and the limited service option, we can improve their condition in our service, and give them a much fairer deal than we have to date.

With this program, everyone can win: the conservation groups, the oceanaria, the new corporations, human students, human scientists, the government agencies, and the cetaceans.

CHAPTER THIRTEEN

Projections into the Future:
Nonhuman Participant Observers

FOR PURPOSES OF DISCUSSION, LET US ASSUME THAT MAN FI-
nally breaks through and begins communication at a high level
with another species on this planet. We are not assuming an
extraterrestrial invasion of another species on this planet; we are
assuming that there are present on this planet other species
capable of being involved participant observers. Elsewhere in this
book we give the evidence for this possibility among the Cetacea.
The time is some years in the future. We are assuming that a
sufficiently large number of humans, scientists and others, have
broken through and are now communicating with one or more
species of Cetacea.

The means of communication are acceptable to the then
current human society, to the scientists, to the legislators, to the
public at large. The means used are reliable and generate
information that can be understood by a large segment of
humanity. The persons involved in the breakthrough are accepted, considered to be reliable, and show means by which
others can share their results. There is a sufficiently large number
of persons ready to accept these results so that chaos does not
result. Various organized groups of humans start planning
activities to use this means of communication in the service of

their particular belief systems and particular economic, social, and legal activities.

A new scientific society is formed and a new scientific consensus develops around these findings. New government agencies are developed, regulating the use of this information in the manifold of human social beliefs, activities, and studies. New corporations are formed to profit from the resulting activities. Diverse human groups organize to monitor these activities to be sure that they are carried on in humane and compassionate ways. There develops competition between scientific conservation and industrial exploitation groups to form the new laws to the advantages of particular groups. New means of entertainment for humans are found and are exploited commercially. New educational groups are formed to educate the public and the young students. The military organizations attempt to sequester the new information under the guise of "national security." The United Nations establishes a special division to deal with the planetwide problems of the interactions of humans with the cetaceans and with the international problems arising therefrom.

Among the scientific groups the linguists, phoneticians, and other experts on human languages begin to devote their best thinking to the problems of a nonhuman language. The computer scientists and the computer industry begin to devise more economical and better means of communication with the Cetacea. Large resources are devoted to this problem. New laws prohibiting certain kinds of scientific research on Cetacea are passed. New laws prohibiting the capture, killing, or confining of Cetacea are passed.

A whole new government agency is created that has the powers of regulation of communication with the Cetacea, the means used to communicate with the Cetacea, the conditions under which such communication shall take place, the use of the information gained from the Cetacea, and negotiations with specific groups of Cetacea around the world.

A new division of the Department of State, called The Interspecies Division, Cetacean Subdivision, is formed. The Department of State is expected to integrate its negotiations with that of the new government agency: The Cetacean Communication Agency.

The Cetacean Communication Agency is at first placed under the Department of Commerce. This is found to be a mistake, the cetaceans object to being included under commercial philosophy, so the agency then becomes a department: the Cetacean Communication Department, directly under the executive branch of the United States government. This change increases the participation of the Department of State in more effective ways. Diplomatic missions are established with the Cetacea.

These developments are paralleled by similar developments in Russia, Japan, and other countries around the world as the means of communication are spread. Demands on the part of the cetaceans to punish those involved in the whaling industry are countered by proposals from the new United Nations cetacean representation, and the cetaceans are reminded of their own ethic not to injure or cause to be injured any member of the human species. The cetaceans insist, then, that human warfare also stop. They establish the oceans as off limits for human military actions against either cetaceans or other humans.

The cetaceans report to the United Nations cetacean representation that secret military installations involving nuclear warheads and other dangerous devices have been planted on the ocean floor; they give the exact location of such installations. This is confirmed by the UN in their investigations, and the weapons are removed.

As cetacean information about the use of the sea floor and the use of the food sources within the oceans is integrated in the structure of the United States government, the UN, and other nations, new industries are formed as a result of the cetacean knowledge of the total ecology of the seas. New methods of culture of sea organisms, plants, and animals are made on the basis of the new knowledge given by the cetaceans. Certain areas of the ocean are set aside for human farming, monitored and controlled by the cetaceans. Human scientific research aids the cetaceans in the problems of their own food supplies and devises means for the multiplication of krill and fish. Treaties are negotiated between the cetaceans and the humans, regulating such farming activities.

Human historians become intrigued by the long histories that the cetaceans can relate about the past history of the planet passed down from one cetacean generation to the other and taught to the young cetaceans. In the United States the Library of Congress develops a new division given to recording the history, philosophy, ethics, and science of the cetaceans. Communication links between the cetaceans and the Library of Congress are worked out so that any cetacean can call up either the human divisions of the library or the cetacean divisions of the library and learn more of what other cetaceans have reported and of what the humans have recorded about their history. Human historians find it necessary to revise certain aspects of human history in the light of the cetacean-memorized texts of their past encounters and of the past history of the human race as they saw it. Past interspecies contacts between humans and cetaceans are thoroughly recorded. The cetacean estimations of the loss of their populations through human activities is duly recorded.

Undersea geology and past cataclysms on the earth's crust are reported by the cetaceans. New information is derived from periods as long as forty million years ago as to the evolution of the cetaceans, other species of the sea, and previous contacts with intelligences, human and nonhuman. The cetaceans report past contacts from outer space with this planet. They also report the falling into the sea of vast meteorites, volcanic upheavals, and the shifting of continental plates. They tell of their survival in the face of cataclysms that wiped out large numbers of land animals.

New human schools are established for education of humans in the new knowledge of the cetacean culture and its ancient origins in the sea.

Adequate consideration of human beliefs prevents the new knowledge from causing panic among certain religious groups and among scientific groups and certain hunting groups. A new scientific group is formed, which call themselves "interspeciologists." The new Society of Interspeciology establishes criteria for membership in the society initially from among those who have made scientific contributions to communication with the Cetacea. This society starts new research programs with elephants. As the parameters of communication of elephants become apparent, the society realizes that it must establish a new division for human-elephant communication as the science ad-

vances. Other groups realize that there must be an Elephant
Communication Division of the new Cetacean Communication
Department. The new rights of cetaceans under human laws and
the international treaties dealing with cetaceans are opened up to
include elephants. Communication between cetaceans and elephants initially is through means devised by humans. A new
development of the science of communication and of the laws
with respect to elephants and Cetacea is then negotiated between
the cetaceans, the humans, and the elephants. Since the elephants were cut off from one another quite early and since they
were the only survivors with very large brains on the land,
various disagreements between the Indian elephants and the
African elephants had to be negotiated through the intervention
of the human communication link. This link was monitored by
the cetaceans and their contributions were gratefully accepted by
the humans. Since the culture of the cetaceans is interconnected
over a very much longer period of time, the humans learned new
ways of negotiation and new ways of arbitration, which were then
applied to the differences between the elephants. Various local
problems having to do with elephants that had been used in the
service of man, versus those who had maintained their society in
the wild, were negotiated, and their differences ironed out. The
old ethic of an elephant in the service of man being ostracized by
those in the natural habitat was cleared up.

Among the science-fiction writers in the human species new
materials were supplied that gave rise to new possibilities never
before conceived by the writers.

As progress is made in interspeciology and in the institutions of
man, it is gradually realized that all of these new relationships,
new interspecies negotiations, were a preparation for contact
between this planet and extraterrestrial observers from other
parts of the galaxy. The Galactic Coincidence Control Center
ruled that planet Earth is no longer off bounds for extraterrestrial visitors. Agents of the Galactic Coincidence Control
Center were then sent to Earth and opened negotiations for
membership of Earth in the Solar System Control Unit of the
Galactic Coincidence Control Center. Man was given the means
of communication with the higher levels of the Galactic Manage-

ment committees, and adequate control measures for the use of rather powerful methods of communication and energy use were distributed under the usual safeguards of the Galactic Coincidence Control Center. The education of the humans, of the Cetacea, and of the elephants then proceeded through the establishment of extraterrestrial schools upon Earth, among the involved groups. Extraterrestrial teachers were introduced to the planet Earth, disguised in suitable forms in order not to cause fear or anxiety among the human, cetacean, and elephant students. The principles of galactic management were taught and carried out upon the planet Earth. The control of off-planet activities of the human species was taught. Various new means of communication and transport among planets were initiated.

Such considerations as the above seem to most readers to be something dreamed up by a science-fiction writer. In our present society we tend to relegate to "science fiction" such projections into the future. In the past many science-fiction writers have made projections into the future that have become realized; others have not. One of the major tasks of those doing such projections is to select from the vast array of all of the possibilities those that seem most probable.

Of all of the imaginable possibilities of the future of man and his continued existence upon the planet Earth, the possibilities given above seem most likely to this author. Without such projections, man does not change his ways. His science, his technology, and his society immerse themselves more in the narcissistic consideration of human affairs, not taking into account other species or other possibilities. As man lifts his eyes to the stars and meets the other inhabitants of this planet, his horizons become widened, his science deeper, his philosophy more in tune with the universe as it exists.

We, the human species, have options. We have options now of total destruction, of further expansion of knowledge, of grand endeavors beyond our present limited horizons. I hope that we choose the paths of increasing our knowledge and hence changing the structure of our own society to relieve ourselves from the narcissistic interspecies deprivation from which we have suffered for several thousands of years.

Are we alone as intelligent, sentient, compassionate beings on this planet? I do not believe so. It is now up to the younger generations to find out whether or not we are alone before we make ourselves alone by killing off all of the others.

If we believe that there is no hope of communication with others, either on this planet or off it; if we believe that conflicts between humans are the be-all and end-all of our species; if we believe that the welfare of man is totally a function of man's own activities with himself; if we believe that the organizations of man are the most powerful organizations on this planet because of our abilities to destroy the others, then there is no hope for the others and possibly no hope for us.

Thus do I make a plea to our species to look further, to look beyond the end of our very human noses, to try to see the possibilities inherent in the large brains, equal to and larger than ours, brains that have learned to live in consonance with their ecology, with the ecology of the oceans, to live in harmony with the other organisms of the sea, and to survive something on the order of ten to one hundred and fifty times as long as man has survived.

We must entertain, at least, the idea that there are involved observers in the sea. This may be the end of this particular program and the projects thereunder: entertainment for the human species, the entertainment of science fiction, the entertainment of circus shows involving Cetacea. I hope that we are intelligent enough, that our computational capacity as individuals and as groups is sufficiently great, so that we can take into account these possibilities.

The involved human scientific observer has the responsibility now to find out whether he has a counterpart in the sea. "Cetacean science" may exist, cetacean scientists may exist. If they do, they may have responsibilities similar to those of the scientists of the land. Let us find out what such involved observers may be in the sea. They may be the key cetaceans to communicate with, to find, and to exchange information with us. Until we can communicate with the cetaceans, we do not know how they are organized, that the older cetaceans, because of the sea environment and the constant communication among Cetacea, are generalists. We do not know of the adequacy of communication among groups of cetaceans. It may be that their old culture has been so thoroughly disturbed by the activities of man that a new fragmentation of that culture has taken place as a consequence of our whaling activities. We have been very busy breaking up whale families, whale pods, whale tribes, whale nations, by a nondifferentiated killing of individuals.

Therefore, let us expand our scientific horizons and recommend and support research leading to the testing of the computational capacities of the largest brains on this planet. Let us at least explore the possibility that they are capable in ways that we, in our present ignorance, cannot yet know about. The least we can do is to stop killing them, and the most that we can do is to dedicate the best of our science to testing them and seeing if it is possible to communicate with them. One possibility is that even with our best methods we may not be bright enough, our science may not be adequate to break the communication barrier. But let us try to see if we can do it. We do need some outside-the-human-species input, we do need the perspective of someone else on our activities, we do need the exercise of negotiating with others besides humans. We do need to know the ancient wisdom of the whales.

CHAPTER FOURTEEN

Projections into the Future:
Commercial Developments

AN ENTIRELY NEW INDUSTRY CAN BE INITIATED BY THOSE interested in new areas of investment: in a relatively short time (two to ten years) a major breakthrough will be made in communication with dolphins/whales. With the proper approach in the technical and the commercial aspects, it is expected that relatively large returns can be realized on a relatively small capital investment within the next ten years. Within that period, through franchises, leasing arrangements, and contracts, a satisfactory level of profit can be realized.

The first persons to establish and use communication with the Cetacea will be in a preferred position to market the information gained. The market for the information includes the commercial fisheries, the navy, the entertainment industry (film/tape/records), marine industries, oceanaria, computer manufacturers, software companies, the education businesses, and conservation groups.

The methods developed for cetacean/human communication can be leased to interested industries for their purposes within more limited areas specified in the leasing arrangements. Specific areas of useful and profitable enterprise are as follows:

1. *The Commercial Fisheries.* The yellowfin tuna industry needs means of communication with dolphins to warn them of netting activities and avoid the capture of the dolphins in their nets. Public pressure on the industry is at a high level to reduce or eliminate the capture and killing of dolphins.

Other commercial fisheries have problems of net destruction by dolphins caught in their nets. With means of communication/warning aboard their vessels, such conflicts can be avoided.

With proper communication with dolphins, the fishing industries could enlist the aid of the dophins in their efforts on a cooperative basis.

2. *The Navy.* The activities of the navy in the area of the use of dolphins/whales in the service of human warfare is well known. Mounting public opinion opposes this area of naval activity. The prestige of the navy is being lowered by such publicity and activities.

With communication with dolphins/whales, the navy could initiate a new publicly approved policy of significance: worldwide cooperative education of Cetacea to avoid areas of human warfare. The knowledge gained from the Cetacea would aid the navy in their other tasks. The first navy of the world to use such communication will possess, for a time, a strategic advantage. Eventually, however, such short-term advantage will disappear.

3. *The Entertainment Industries.* The first corporation to open communication with Cetacea will have the opportunity to market the results worldwide. With cooperative efforts of the dolphins/whales, entirely new varieties of motion pictures/records/tapes/TV shows are made possible.

Dolphins and whales interacting with one another and in communication with human camera crews can do underwater ballets/dramas of dramatic and novel content. Interacting with human swimmers in communication with them opens up new possibilities for the motion picture industry heretofore not imagined.

The recording market (records/tapes) can be sold new music/songs from the Cetacea interacting with human musicians—each side teaching the other new forms of music never before heard by the other.

4. *Marine Industries*. Offshore oil-drilling industries operating in cooperation with communicating Cetacea can control their operations in more detail. Small oil leaks can be detected by Cetacea rapidly and efficiently.

The manufacturers and developers of sonar and underwater communication equipment can benefit from cetacean knowledge of natural sonar use.

Cooperative underwater surveys with Cetacea open up new areas of enterprise for those industries in marine geology and industrial exploitation of sea bottoms and structures. Cetacean knowledge of mapping of the oceans can be used by these industries.

Worldwide communication of ships/yachts with dolphins/ whales opens up new regions of navigation/rescue activities heretofore unknown to man.

New methods of ship submarine propulsion and ship submarine design will undoubtedly arise from such communication.

5. *Oceanaria*. The current entertainment of humans by performing dolphins and whales is standardized and repetitious. Adult interest in such performances is limited to novel first-time-only experiences. With communication, new areas of entertainment can be opened up. Exchanges between the Cetacea can be translated for the human audience. Individual humans will be able to converse directly with the dolphins/whales in the tanks. New varying and dramatic shows will be made. Cetacean stories about humans will be related.

Communication between the confined Cetacea and their friends and families at sea can be monitored by human audiences. Volunteers from the Cetacea for educational service in the oceanaria for limited times can be negotiated. The oceanaria can become educational institutions on a mutually satisfactory basis for humans and Cetacea.

6. *Computer Manufacturers*. Once the communication breakthrough is made with special methods, manufacturers of the necessary equipment will have a ready market in the above-given

uses of the equipment. Each of the above industries will need the special equipment for their use.

The modern microprocessors and minicomputers designed for use in salt-air environments is the basis for the breakthrough in communication with Cetacea. The speed of these computers is currently enough to realize these objectives.

7. *Software Companies.* The development of satisfactory programs for the use of the above computers for efficient high-speed communication with Cetacea will go concurrently with the computer work. Each use in the communication field will require its own software. As the use of computers for these purposes expands, so will the market for special software increase.

8. *Education Industries.* As fast as the above developments are realized, educational outlets should be developed. The public should be kept up to date on current work through public educational channels, including schools, colleges, universities, and the public media. Marketable products, books, tapes, records, and motion pictures can be sold readily.

9. *Conservation Groups.* Rather large groups of people (numbered in the millions) have become interested in saving endangered species, especially whales and dolphins. The passage of laws forbidding the importation of industrial whale/dolphin products has been facilitated by these groups in the United States and Britain. The Marine Mammals Protection Act of 1972 was one result of such public pressure.

Communication with Cetacea will give these groups their best argument for cessation of industrial use of whale and dolphin products. Such public opinion will be advantageous to the new industries operating in cooperation with the dolphins and whales.

CHAPTER FIFTEEN

The Rights of Cetaceans
under Human Laws*

THE RIGHTS OF MAN HAVE SLOWLY DEVELOPED OVER THE LAST
few centuries. The rights that each of us enjoys today in the
United States have been carefully developed in our laws. Our
past history teaches us that our rights evolved through certain
stages, from the unconscious acceptance of a lack of rights, to the
conscious awareness of the need for an adequate expression of an
intolerable situation or state, to the demand for the relief
articulated in law, to the law and its adequate administration. As
each group of humans, through its own experience, learned to feel
its lack of sharing in the benefits of laws and their administration,
each developed adequate spokesmen or spokeswomen for its
cause. These individuals were either inside or outside the group
needing relief.

Professor Christopher D. Stone, in *Should Trees Have Standing,* has given an excellent review of the origins of these laws for
human rights and shows the extension of the legal concepts to
include fictitious individuals. In these laws, the concept of an
individual with legal rights is extended to corporations, cities,

* Reprinted with permission from *Oceans,* March 1976.

states and nations. Professor Stone espouses extending the concept of an individual with legal rights to the environment including animals. In such cases, individual humans and groups must become the legal guardians or protagonists for the environment and the animals. Since trees, for example, cannot speak in human language, persons must express the need of trees for rights under human law.

What is the need for relief of an intolerable situation for the cetaceans? Should cetaceans be given individual rights under human laws? Are there, as yet, enough informed, consciously aware humans to express the needs of cetaceans, articulate them in legal terms, formulate the laws and assure their passage in the legislature and courts? Is the nature of cetaceans such that they warrant special laws?

The plight of the large whales is extensively documented by the International Whaling Commission and several interested biologists, such as Roger Payne, Victor Schaefer and Scott McVay. The extinction of several species, including the largest animal the earth has ever housed, the blue whale, has apparently already occurred. The whaling industry kills a whale every fifteen minutes every day. The survival of the entire species and genera is threatened. "Specicide" is a word to add to our laws.

Dolphins, including the largest one, *Orcinus orca,* the so-called "killer-whale" ... also have an intolerable situation needing relief. In Japan the dolphins are killed for human use and food. In numerous countries around the world they are captured for human entertainment and kept in confined quarters, restricted beyond their natural limits, and forced to do repetitious circus performances of a peculiarly banal nature. They are cut off from communication with their relatives and friends in the sea. Many die prematurely during capture and from the confinement.

Large numbers of people have recently become aware of the whales' situation and are asking for cetacean relief under our laws. Recently the Greenpeace Foundation obtained a ruling from the Canadian Government prohibiting further capture of *Orcinus orca* in the waters of Canada. Their collected data on the deaths of these creatures during capture, transport, and confinement apparently were the deciding factors.

Are cetaceans something more than animals whose survival is in jeopardy through human actions unrestrained by law? Is their nature such that we should seek more vigorous legal action to preserve their way of life, their territory? Are they in any sense special groups needing special attention from us?

Let us state the question in scientific and humanistic terms. What is the probability that cetaceans are sentient, intelligent, creatures?

Consider their brains and our brains. How are we, in the structure of our brains, different from our nearest cousins, the apes (chimpanzee, gorilla and orangutang)? The result of careful neuroanatomical and extensive neurophysiological studies reveal that our brain's only decisive difference from the apes' is in the size of our cerebral cortical "silent" areas on the frontal, parietal and temporal lobes. Silent areas have no direct-input connections and thus are devoted to central processing (thinking, imagination, long-term goals, ethics, etc.). Without such areas, a person is no longer a human as each of us conceives of being human. Persons in whom these areas are lost become here-and-now beings, with a good deal of their essential humanness gone. They lose their moral and ethical judgments and their motivations for future planning and action. These cortical areas are the ones we use for understanding justice, compassion and the need for social interdependence. If we could control the growth of these cortical areas in our species, we could possibly evolve further beyond our present horizons. Apparently, we are limited by this aspect of our brain's structure. This may make us pause when we consider the brains of Cetacea.

Recent, excellent, controlled neurological studies of cetacean brains by Morgane, Yakovlev, Jacobs and several Russian scientists show that the silent areas are larger in the cetaceans whose brains are bigger than ours. In the bottlenose dolphin, with a brain forty percent larger than ours, in *Orcinus orca,* with a brain three to four times the mass of ours and in the sperm whale, whose brain is the largest on this planet (six times the mass of a human brain), all of the additional mass is in the silent areas.

The size of these cetacean brains has been known for many years. Only recently has microscopic analysis shown that their cellular densities and connections are quite as large and complex as ours.

The belief that man is the preeminent thinker, doer, feeler on this planet is denied by these investigations. As fast as evidence of the superior nature of cetacean brains accumulated, rationalizations were devised (even by neurologists) to place these brains in a category below man's. Two main arguments have been used against acceptance of the probability of brains superior to man's.

The first rationalization is that of body size, or weight, versus brain size, or weight. This argument holds that a large body needs a large brain to control its behavior. In the light of the findings on cetacean brains, this argument is not relevant. The body is controlled by portions of the brain outside the silent areas. Moreover, the size of these outside areas is not proportional to the size of the individual animal. In our own case the sensory and motor areas of the cortex are no larger than those of the chimpanzee or the gorilla. In the case of sea creatures, the whale shark (not a mammal), with a body weight of forty tons, has a brain mass of 100 grams, less than that of a macaque monkey. A forty-ton sperm whale has a brain mass of 9,000 grams, six times ours.

The second argument for the preeminence of man over larger-brained cetaceans points to the human accomplishments of using hands, planning structures and building them. Cetaceans have no hands and therefore had no need to develop intelligence.

This argument is derived from man's own narcissistic need to see the use of intelligence and sentience only in areas most men have entered. May there not be domains only a few men have penetrated in which whales may be superior? May not their philosophies and traditions be more complex, more full of insight than ours? Cut off from the need for building, for external forms of transport, for food preservation and preparation, they probably have very advanced ethics and laws, developed over millennia and passed on, through sonic communication, to their young. Their memories are probably much greater than ours. Like those among us with no written language (the Masai, for example), they probably have long histories which they recount to their young, who must memorize them in detail.

Who are to specify the criteria for intelligence among large-brained mammals of the sea? We have no direct experience of living in the sea. We venture timidly into water protected by artificial means. Let us try to find out from the Cetacea their criteria for intelligent use of large brains, rather than attempting to impose our criteria upon them.

What behavioral evidence do we have of ethics among Cetacea? The main evidence is derived from our encounters with them, and some from our observations of their interactions with one another. In the books *Man and Dolphin, The Mind of the Dolphin (a non-human intelligence),* and *Lilly on Dolphins: The Humans of the Sea,* are many examples of intelligent and compassionate actions between us and them, and between individual dolphins. . . .

The main points made in these books are as follows:

(1) The brains of cetaceans are superior to ours in unique and effective areas.

(2) The behavior of Cetacea in captivity is regulated by a cetacean education and a cetacean ethic in which man is carefully treated as a special case. Man is not to be injured by an individual cetacean even under extreme degrees of provocation. Even "cruel and unusual punishment" shall not be responded to with violent destructive action on the bodies of humans. Throughout their capture and during their performances, men and women are in direct contact with them, and none have been injured by these huge creatures.

(3) Dolphins treat their own individuals with total knowledge of the necessities for survival of the group. Individuals will commit suicide if their incapacity becomes great enough to endanger the group. Any sick or grieving dolphin is cared for by the group; but if the care interferes with group survival, the individual voluntarily stops breathing and thus commits suicide.

(4) Dolphin sonic-ultrasonic communication is more complex than ours, ten times as fast, at ten times the frequency.

It is highly probable that their minds operate with acoustic analogs, even as our language is primarily based on visual analogs. They "see" their environment and one another with sound. Their sonar "sees" into both our bodies and their own.

They can see emotional states in one another through stomach and lung movements. They become acquainted with, and subsequently recognize, one another and humans in the water with them, through the transmission of sonic pictures.

As we have seen, each dolphin has three independently controlled sonic-ultrasonic emitters (two nasal and one laryngeal). Two dolphins exchanging information may use all three separate channels at once.

(5) Dolphins are interested enough in communicating with us for them to exert surprising efforts to reprogram their outputs to solve communication tasks imposed by us.

(6) It is probable that sufficiently fast computers could enable man to communicate with dolphins and whales.

Such considerations inevitably lead us to the conclusion that Cetacea are a special case. We must give them rights as individuals under our laws. The following guidelines for new laws are suggested:

(1) Cetaceans are no longer to be considered as property, nor as an industrial resource, nor as stocks of animals.

(2) Cetaceans are to have complete freedom of the waters of the earth.

(3) Individual dolphins and whales are to be given the legal rights of human individuals. Human individuals and groups are to be given the right to sue in behalf of, or otherwise represent in court, cetacean individuals placed in jeopardy by other humans.

(4) Research into communication with cetaceans is no longer simply a scientific pursuit: such research is now a necessity for people to exchange information at a high level of complexity with cetaceans. We must learn their needs, their ethics, their philosophy, to find out who we are on this planet, in this galaxy. The extraterrestrials are here—in the sea. We can, with dedicated efforts, communicate with them. If and when we break the communication barrier, then we and the cetaceans can work out our differences and our correspondences.

We may already have accumulated too negative a reputation among cetaceans. Let us at least stop killing and enslaving them for our entertainment and our warfare. This we can do now. The communication problem will take longer and requires much research.

In the Human/Dolphin Foundation we are collecting a bibliography on dolphins and whales in the areas of brain structure, communication and behavior. The Foundation is also proposing research to start breaking the communication barrier between man and the dolphin. The research is to be conducted at sea with no confinement of the dolphins.

CHAPTER SIXTEEN

The Possible Existence of
Nonhuman Languages*

IT IS APPROPRIATE THAT THE FOLLOWING DISCUSSION BE GIVEN
at the Centre for Research on Environmental Quality at York
University. Here I am taking the liberty of extending the concept
of research on environmental quality to include variables and
parameters that attempt to go beyond the usual concept of
"environmental quality."

Up to the present time human attempts to specify quality of
environment have been essentially limited to human considerations. Another species may define "environmental quality"
differently from the human. Unknowingly, we must use anthropocentric and anthropomorphic criteria of environmental
quality. We are "anthropos," therefore, we must be "anthropocentric" and "anthropomorphic." The nineteenth-century definitions of these terms as applied to our scientific pursuits were
pejorative. Here let us redefine them for our use as applied to the
"human participant scientific observers." A common belief

---

* Prepared by John C. Lilly, M.D., for the Symposium "Prospects for Man-Cetacean
Communication," June 8 and 9, 1976, Centre for Research on Environmental Quality,
York University, Toronto, Ontario, Canada.

among scientists, especially biologists, is that they can achieve a noninvolved, objective, nonhuman observer status, nonanthropocentric, nonanthropomorphic. This belief must go the way of many of the illusions promulgated in the name of human religions. As participants in Earth's ecology, we are anthropocentric participant observers: quite humanly centered without communication with other species in our ecology.

The further scientific research progresses, the more we learn that we are not anything but that which we are discovering that we are. We are a species of mammals with a particular kind of brain and a particular kind of organization of the programming within that brain organized as individuals in a human consensus reality.

We tend to say that our language, our languages, can express anything and everything. The more progress we make in our scientific research, the more we learn of our own limits, not, as yet, defined in our languages. We cannot escape our brain's structure, nor can we escape its programming by the human consensus reality during a relatively short lifetime. The illusion that somehow we can get outside ourselves and look at ourselves as if we were not human, not humanly organized and limited, must go the way of "omniscience, omnipotence, and omnipresence."

Even as I make these statements, I realize that I'm attempting to play the same game—to move outside of us and look at us as if I were a superhuman extraterrestrial visiting this planet. Even as I try to shed this illusion, it reoccurs in what I say. We are limited by our humanly self-referential logic, by our current knowledge, by our traditions, and by our agreements couched in the language that we have inherited, by our knowledge derived from our experiments and from our experiences.

The concept of environmental quality is thus a human-centered concept. Human consensus determines our thoughts on this subject. If and when the day arrives on which we can communicate with nonhuman organisms and accept them as teachers outside the human species, we can then change our fundamental viewpoint from a human-centered one to at least a two-species view. On that day, our concepts of environmental quality will change from man-centered ones to a new form, which is difficult for us in our present state to visualize, to project, to conjecture. When our environment includes others not human with whom we communicate, then and then only can we abandon our narcissistic single-species preoccupation with human affairs and human languages and human thinking. Our concepts of environmental quality will change radically as of that time to include concepts derived from nonhuman intelligent communicating life-forms.

Meanwhile, let us attempt to give some idea of the possibilities of alternative languages, nonhuman. Studies of such possibilities can give us an idea of the domains in which the probabilities may exist.

I wish to work with theory that can entertain new possibilities.

Let us grant that we are "anthropos" living on a planet that houses other organisms that may have the possibility of communication with us. Let us first consider what we do to communicate with one another and then what other organisms do to communicate among themselves.

Among the many parameters limiting us and limiting them, let us consider quantitative ranges and their problems. At the minimum we have the time-scale problem, the frequency-scale problem, and the logic-scale problem within communicative modes.

The time-scale problem in communication stretches from microseconds to millennia. Our means of communication with one another, i.e., spoken language, exists in a specifiable time domain, in terms of both its production and its reception.

We can perceive intervals of time down to the order of ten microseconds in our acoustic perception. We use this time region for perception of direction of sound sources and their mapping in the surrounding space. As was shown by Batteau (57), the pinna—the external ear—transforms space parameters into time-sequential parameters over the range from ten microseconds to one thousand microseconds. The slight time difference between the perception of the two ears is an additional aid in mapping the sources. Our brain computes acoustic maps representing the external environment's spatial extent in relation to the center of the head.

Insofar as spoken language is concerned, these twin transforms allow us to localize speakers in their proper places in the surrounding environment. They also allow us to separate these speakers and the signals from each speaker so that we can simultaneously listen to two or more conversations. They also allow us to separate a single speaker from a background of multiple speakers and concentrate our attention on computations of meaning of the signals transmitted by that single speaker in the medley of the sounds from the others.

Careful physical analyses of the form, speed, and frequency region of the sounds that we emit show that we can detect, in a stream of signals emitted by a speaker, intervals as short as ten thousand microseconds. (The schwa gives us hints as to the lower level for detection of distinguishable phons.) At shorter intervals of time we are unable to distinguish between the basic vocalized phons of spoken human speech; they are all equivalent at the short interval. Silent intervals in our speech below this level are not detected as silences despite the fact that there is no physical stimulus occurring during that interval.

Further studies show that the critical frequency band for the signals from which we compute meaning exists from approximately 300 Hz to 2,500 Hz. This property is utilized successfully in the modern telephone system and in single side-band radio transmissions.

A wider frequency band than this is normally detected by humans speaking in air in their immediate environment. Certain parameters are eliminated on the telephone and on the single side-band radio that allow better reception of clues about the emotional state of the transmitting person and better discrimination of the unique characteristics of an individual speaker.

We have done extensive studies on how far a 2,500-Hz band can be deviated from the naturally occurring frequencies and still allow a listener to compute the speaker's meaning from the signals. As one deviates all frequencies in the signals in the 2,500-Hz band in an upward direction rapidly, it can be shown that meaning disappears abruptly at a deviation of about 500 Hz. However, if the deviation occurs extremely slowly, the listener continuously recomputes meaning rapidly enough so that the deviation can be carried to approximately 1,100 Hz while maintaining meaning.

The number of bands of frequency that must be transmitted in order to carry the meaning has also been determined in studies for designing vocoders. The vocoder is a device for transforming human speech by frequency analysis in a number of bands, transmitting the analysis alone and resynthesizing the speech at the other end of a communication link with a second bank of filters. Extensive studies (66) have shown that in order to maintain a high quality of human speech, the minimum number of bands for frequency division is on the order of thirty for the ordinary human speaker and hearer.

Thus, in human speech communication the frequency problem and the time problem are specifiable within certain physical limits. Outside these limits, human beings cannot communicate by speech. The physical parameters themselves have a vast range of which human speech and hearing use only a very small part. The physical doorway in the atmosphere and in human bodies for the transmission of human speech and its perception is a relatively narrow one.

Sounds that are in the very low end of the frequency domain are not computable as meaningful by human beings. Sounds that are in the very high frequency regions are also not computable by humans as meaningful. It is also true that our ears are limited in both the low-frequency region and the high-frequency region to sounds of very high amplitudes. Our minimum detectable threshold for sound is in the region of the signals that carry meaning from one of us to the other, i.e., from approximately 500 Hz to 3,000 Hz. Above this range our hearing threshold rises. Below this range our hearing threshold also rises.

Thus, our first possibility in regard to other organisms with whom we might possibly communicate is that they communicate outside the particular values of the parameters and variables that we need in our spoken language. There are those who communicate subsonically for us (elephants) and there are those who communicate ultrasonically for us (dolphins).

Another parameter of our communication that we must consider is the time over which our central processes retain meaning after an exchange of sonic signals between two human beings. This period is limited to a few minutes at the most. As hours go by, what was said at the beginning of the periods of hours is not well remembered in as fine detail as it can be remembered over the last minute of the sequence. Thus, there is a scanning time slot in the present fading in the past; beyond certain limits the accuracy transmission of information falls off. It falls off very rapidly during the first day. By the end of the first week, it has deteriorated considerably. By the end of a month and a year, it becomes practically nonexistent—with few exceptions, involving extremely important events and extremely important experiences centered around one's own personal survival. Imprinting of emotional experiences is well known in human psychology and is a rather rare set of events in the total life period of most human beings.

Another consideration is the limited time that a human being exists on this planet in the communicative phases. We do not acquire and use spoken language until we have been out of the womb for a period of approximately eighteen months to three years. The next few years are spent in learning the complexities of the human dictionary, of human knowledge, and of human language. If one is lucky, this continues on until one dies. However, with many people, during the aging period, the use of language decreases in terms of its availability, its efficiency of use, and its creative processes. The usual individual has sixty years. The unusual individual has ninety to one hundred and ten years for the use of human language.

Language as we know it is passed from one generation to another, with modifications by each generation. The basic structure of the language seems to change more slowly than one or two or three generations. English as we know it is probably on the order of a thousand years. It is only by the invention of the written and printed word that we have any knowledge of the ancient languages of human beings. There are no present speakers of the ancient languages. Even if we stretch the time scale to the earliest written records in Sumer, language as recorded in lasting artifacts is only on the order of eight thousand years.

As we go back into the past for evidence of the presence of man as we know him, we run out of artifacts and must depend upon skulls and bones dated by the geological strata in which they are found and by radioactivity methods. By such methods we find that man as we know him did not exist longer ago than approximately a hundred thousand years. If we stretch the data further, we may push it back to a million and a half years. We have no way of knowing when man or his predecessors began to speak and to carry information by means of acoustic, sonic signals. We must assume that such communication predated all of the artifacts that gave evidence of recording of information. Spoken language must have preceded its recording.

As has been discussed by many linguists (67, 68), the evolution of human spoken language is lost in the dim, distant past of man. The structure and logic of language as we know it originated so many generations ago that we have no memory or record of how it all started. Thus, we are caught in interpretations and recorded experiences existing for only a few thousand years.

Over the millennia, man's languages have suffered from what I call interspecies deprivation. There has been no one else to talk to. Hence, the human species has become narcissistic, preoccupied with its own affairs, preoccupied with its own languages, preoccupied with its own logic or the lack of same. Thus, the human species is isolated in a box whose dimensions we are beginning to see and beginning to describe in a qualitative and quantitative way. As yet, we have no doorway out of this anthropocentric, anthropomorphic box. Let us now discuss the possibility that there exist languages that we do not yet know, used for communication by organisms of particular characteristics outside of our particular "human box."

A good deal of our discussion of languages, of logic and our means of communication, has certain traditional limitations that are built into the language itself. It may be possible for humans to construct a theoretical model, a simulation, which can include languages nonhuman. I would like to attempt such a formulation for purposes of raising discussion and of expanding beyond the traditional format and the traditional restrictions of human languages and, thus, being able to extend, at least in theory, the simulation to include other organisms. There are those who deny the existence (even theoretically) of such possibilities. (69) I ask you to entertain the following simulation as a possible direction in which to go.

Let us consider spoken human language. (Written and recorded human language we will not consider in this context. Traditionally, we have become quite biased by the fact that we do have a means of recording meaning outside of the spoken language in the form of written, printed, and other artifacts.) Let us assume here that human languages originated from speech or speechlike exchanges among the progenitors of man or among early men. The basic considerations are limited to the spoken language. The simulation that I choose is based upon intensive analysis of human communication, related to computers and the kinds of thinking that have developed in setting up computers, computer programming, and proposals for future computers.

Let us define "signals" as those physical events in the environment of a human which that particular human can detect and which that particular human can originate or produce. Such events currently in our science can be recorded, for example, on magnetic tape in the sonic mode. The physical events of prime interest are the variations of air-pressure waves within the time scale and frequency scale given above, which can transmit "meaning." "Transmission of meaning" is also a trap. Meaning itself is not transmitted; only physical signals are transmitted.

Meaning is achieved only after the end organs and the central nervous system process the signals impinging upon the end organs of the human organism. "Meaning" is generated within the central processing of a human biocomputer. A human speaking alone, not in the presence of a hearer other than himself, generates the physical events, the signals in his surrounding environment, which are then self-reflexively received, recomputed, and then and only then "understood." There is a time delay between the spoken sounds and the perceived results of setting up these physical events in the surrounding air. When one does this, speaks monologues in solitude, one sees quickly that there is a long time delay between the meaning that one is attempting to transmit from the insides of one biocomputer and the meaning that is received once again by the observer in the central nervous system from the signals sent outside the body. To state it very simply, thinking has many more dimensions and occurs in much briefer time intervals than spoken speech is capable of transmitting. The velocity of generation of the signals by the central computational process is essentially a slow output. This is matched by the time scale of the hearing and the perception of the sounds and of the meaning inherent in those sounds. By such analyses, one can see that there are two major computational processes involved in speech. The central processing transforms meaning into words and sentences, which are then fed into the speech mechanisms that transmit signals into the surrounding air. The ears then pick up these signals and retransform them back into the meaning domain where they are checked out for the accuracy of rendition of the original thought. As yet, we have no direct reliable method of transferring the original thoughts from one central nervous system to the other without going through this signal processing described above.

When two humans are conversing, the same set of processes take place in each speaker-hearer. The computational delays in each then add up, the process is extended in the time scale to more than twice the value inherent in each speaking alone. Each speaker-hearer invites the other to exchange signals with meaning in a certain domain. Thus, a given conversation, at least in those who are trying to trade ideas, may be thought of as an attempt to reach an agreement about what is meaningful in that particular dyad. Basically, the two humans involved must agree on (1) the human language that they will speak, whether English, French, or other, and (2) the subject matter, the context in which the meanings are to be exchanged, and hence the meanings of the words used in that context.

As yet we have no adequate logical theory of the process known as agreement. Without such a theory, we have great difficulties in the logic of language itself. All human languages somehow depend upon a consensus—a series of agreements among many, many individuals. These agreeing individuals must have certain basic biological characteristics within a certain range of parameters sufficiently alike (1) to speak to one another, and (2) to master a new language. Their memories must be of sufficient length to ensure these abilities. Their computational capacities must also be sufficient.

For the purposes of the present discussion, let us look at brains and language.

Even within the human species, there is a critical mammalian brain size below which language as we know it is not possible. Microcephalics (70) have great difficulty acquiring language as we know it, with all of its complexity, adaptability, and flexibility. Some microcephalics can master an operational, here-and-now language that is primitively tied to a very short period of time. Yesterday and tomorrow may be too far away to be taken care of by the computational capacities of these smaller brains.

Outside of the human species, there is some experimental evidence derived from studies on the chimpanzees. The ape brain is about one-third the size of the human brain. It has been demonstrated by several groups of workers that the chimpanzee is unable to mimic human spoken speech. (58–60) As we have seen, it has been discovered that the chimpanzee can master a manual sign language. (61, 62) The chimpanzee is also capable of interacting with a computer when the inputs and outputs from the computer are suitable for the ape's nonvocal manual inputs and outputs. Thus, we can deduce that the ape brain is below the critical brain size for the acquisition of spoken language as we know it.

When a brain reaches the critical size for language as we know it, there is a quantum jump with an immense increase in the capacity to absorb and to store and to recall all the elements necessary for speech and the computational capacity to generate meaning.

A careful examination of some five thousand human languages found on this planet shows each of them to be an incredibly sophisticated instrument for the exchange of information. There are no protohuman or prehuman languages left on the planet. Why this is true is explicable on the basis of distribution of primate brain sizes.

When we look at a spectrum of brain sizes, in the primate series, including man, we find that there is a gap in the distribution curve between the ape brains and the human brains. This gap is between five hundred grams total mass and approximately nine hundred grams. The most frequent ape brain size is around three hundred fifty to four hundred grams and the most frequent human brain size is between eleven hundred and sixteen hundred grams.

One may well ask how this gap originated. I have hypothesized

(10) that the gap was generated at the time when the human brain was evolving above the critical size for development of language as we know it. Whether this was a sudden mutation or whether it was a gradual increase in brain size over the millennia, we do not know. However it developed, those individuals who had reached the critical brain size for language suddenly had an advantage over their fellows, which was quickly exercised. Those who could speak separated themselves very rapidly from those who could not speak. Presumably, these two groups were still interfertile and could reproduce by matings between those who could not speak and those who could.

Those who could speak separated themselves from those who could not speak and learned to separate their offspring probably very close to birth into those who could speak and those who could not speak.

What advantages would the speaking ones have over the nonspeaking ones? First of all, they would be able to control one another and develop new kinds of social structures not available to the nonspeaking ones. Hierarchical rules could be set up controlling the behavior of the speaking ones, which were unavailable to the nonspeaking ones. Control of sexual activities, aggressive activities, and hunting activities was possible to the speaking ones and unavailable to those with no speech. Basically, those who spoke would have longer memories than those who could not speak. Once the speakers learned that mating with nonspeakers produced nonspeaking offspring, strict segregation rules for matings probably arose within the speaking groups.

One can imagine the kinds of conflicts that arose in mixed groups of such humans. Inevitably, the speaking ones would separate themselves from the nonspeaking ones. The rivalries for sexual objects and for food would lead to conflicts in which those who could not speak would inevitably fail and would be segregated for nonmating and for being isolated, and killed.

Thus, we see why today we separate the microcephalics, keep them in institutions or kill them at birth. Such lethal activities as these have led to the brain size gap between the human and the ape.

By using the critical brain size criteria, we may be able to find organisms on this planet that are capable of developing means of nonhuman communication comparable to human languages. No animal groups outside the mammals have brains of this critical size: no fish, bird, reptile, invertebrate, or insect reaches the level of the mammals.

When we compare mammalian brains across species, we find additional criteria for determining those who are capable of complex communication.

When we compare the monkey brain with the ape brain and with the human brain, we find many interesting facts relevant to our pursuit.

As we demonstrated (1, 71, 72), the monkey brain in its neocortical development maintains the whole cortex as sensory and as motor. If one stimulates the neocortex of a macaque monkey, for example, one finds that every bit of that brain gives responses in some muscle group in the periphery pertinent to the functions of that particular portion of the cerebral cortex. One also finds evoked potentials throughout that neocortex when one stimulates appropriate end organs in the periphery. Thus, we find that the whole macaque brain, all of its neocortical structure, is sensory and motor. No portion of the monkey cortex is "silent."

Extensive mappings of the cortex of the chimpanzee show a new phenomenon not present in the macaque brain. Certain neocortical areas show the sensory and motor characteristic. Other areas do not show this characteristic and, hence, are called silent, or associational, cortex.

Similar experiments upon unanesthetized humans show that the areas of sensory and motor functions are separated by larger nonsensory, nonmotor cortices than in the chimpanzee. In the human, these areas are in the frontal lobes, the temporal lobes and parietal lobes. It is these areas that generate the computational capacities we call human language. These areas are also necessary for those characteristics that we value as being distinctively human. In the absence of the frontal lobes, for example, destroyed either by accident or for "therapeutic purposes," that particular human being loses the ability and the motivation to use stored data from the distant past and loses the ability and the motivation to plan beyond the current situation far into the future.

The time scale of humans without the frontal lobes has shrunk down to computations involving a few hours into the past and a few hours into the future. Such persons have also lost their sources of inspiration and long-term motivation. Their language, their speech, changes to conform to this reduced time scale. If due to accident there is a progressive removal of further portions of additional silent areas, more and more of what we consider to be the uniquely human is decreased drastically. Recently, both temporal lobes were removed from an epileptic patient with the tragic result that his memory was totally destroyed. In all of these cases there was no destruction of the sensory and motor cortices necessary for speech and hearing. If these are destroyed, the person is incapable of speech and/or the understanding of speech emitted by others. There is a large literature devoted to these neurological deficits and their effects. (73, 74)

In our simulation of what is necessary for a language, we postulate that in the primate series there is a "minicomputer" that is necessary to run the primate body in the sensory and motor spheres. Let us assume this is of the approximate size of the macaque brain. (I choose the macaque rather than the smaller of the monkey brains such as that of the marmoset because the macaque can control his hands and his bodily motions in a way closer to that of the human.) The macaque has an opposable thumb, index finger; he has a certain level of fineness of control of his hand. He does not have two other requirements for human speech: the use of his vocal output as an operant to control his environment (5) and the necessary interpretive computational capacity for understanding the meanings of heard events. The macaque also shows a very narrow time slot centered in the present. He cannot remember events of many minutes ago that have consequences he must know in the present. Also, he does not work very far into the future.

The chimpanzee shows finer control of the fingers to the point where he can develop and understand a sign language at a primitive level. However, he cannot control the vocalization mechanisms necessary for speech. He shows beginning control, beginning "understanding" of words spoken by humans as vocal commands.

In our simulation, then, the chimpanzee shows the presence of a small "macrobiocomputer" (the small silent areas) controlling his minicomputer, similar to that present in the macaque. The new silent areas (associational cortex) of the chimpanzee have more complex programs and a longer memory available for the control of the minicomputer in the service of the chimpanzee's life performances.

In those capable of language as we know it, i.e., with those of a brain size and silent areas of sufficient size, the macrocomputer has enlarged enough so that it is capable of using and storing those programs necessary for language as we know it.

We can now specify that the biomacrocomputer, i.e., the silent areas, must be sufficiently large for language as we know it to be possible in a particular organism. The biomacrocomputer operates upon the microbiocomputer to give the modulations and transforms of the necessary type, complexity, flexibility, and amount of adaptive programming necessary for language as we know it. The size of the memory also increases with the size of the macrobiocomputer.

New patterns of use of the minicomputer develop as the macrocomputer increases in size. We can think of the microcomputer as an inherited, genetically determined, built-in structure with built-in programs and with limited learning or adaptive characteristics. When cortex becomes independent of input and output, it is available for specializing in general purpose, complex, central processing. The computational capacity increases in the direction of "general purpose" rather than in the direction of "fixed special purpose," characteristics of the biominicomputer.

Considerations such as the above allow us to tentatively look across at other species of mammals away from the primate series.

First of all, there are no other species that have developed brains comparable in size and complexity to those of the mammals. There is no fish, no bird, no insect, no invertebrate, no reptile that can compare with the mammals. Insofar as can be determined to date, the plant kingdom is totally outside our possible consideration. We also know of no solid-state systems that are as capable as the biological mammalian systems.

Among the land mammals, the only brains larger than those of man are in the elephants. As Georg von Békésy has shown, the cochlea in the ear of the elephant is designed for the detection of frequencies lower than those used in human speech. The elephants apparently communicate in regions subsonic for the human. They can also hear the speech frequencies of humans. This apparently is a region for fertile scientific investigation. With modern equipment, it should be possible to record and to transpose these very low frequencies so that humans may be able to hear them. They can also be recorded by modern tape recorders designed specifically for this job. Insofar as this author knows, no research has been done on intraspecies subsonic communication among elephants.

The elephant's large ears presumably have a pinna transform for the subsonic frequencies they use in their communication over long distances. Their long trunk also resonates in these subsonic regions for the production of the low-frequency sounds. (We use the term *subsonic* in regard to the human hearing. Such sound frequencies are *sonic* [detectable and computable] for elephants. Once again, we are judging from the anthropocentric point of view when we use such a word.)

In the sea, many mammalian brains have evolved to sizes equal to and larger than the critical size for language as we know it. These brains are restricted to the cetaceans, the porpoises, dolphins, and whales. No other sea mammals (otters, seals, sea lions, etc.) have brains above the critical threshold for language as we know it.

Paleontological evidence suggests that the Cetacea evolved the critical brain size for language fifteen to thirty million years ago, something on the order of ten to twenty times longer ago than man appeared on this planet with his present brain size. Their evolution in the sea then developed brains up to six times larger than ours. All of this suprahuman brain is in the macrobiocomputer of the silent cortex. (36)

Recent studies on the structure of the brains of the cetaceans (14, 34–36) show the following:

1. There is a spectrum of brain sizes of magnitudes running from that equivalent to the apes, through the human to superhuman values (three hundred fifty grams to nine thousand grams) among the toothed whales (Odontoceti).

2. There is no gap in this series of cetacean brains as there is in the primate series on land.

3. Comparative studies of these brains show that there is a cetacean microcomputer, i.e., sensory and motor, in the neocortex and a biomacrocomputer (silent areas of cortex).

4. As the brains increase in size across cetacean species, the only portion of the brain that increases in size is the bio-macrocomputer (silent areas).

5. All species examined show the use of underwater sound as the communication mode.

6. The use of sound for the purposes of examining the environment actively by the production of sounds and listening to the echoes seems to be present in all species.

7. Several species of cetaceans have been studied from the standpoint of the effective regions of the acoustic spectrum used in their communication and in their echo recognition and ranging systems. The most intensively studied species is that of *Tursiops truncatus,* the bottle-nosed dolphin of the Atlantic. The frequency range in this species runs from a few hundred Hz to 165,000 Hz, with a minimum threshold for detection in the region from 3,000 to 100,000 Hz. Their detection of short time intervals is four and a half to ten times shorter than those detectable by humans. The smaller dolphins use higher frequencies and the larger dolphins use somewhat lower frequencies. There is apparently a good deal of overlap between species in the detectable frequency regions.

There is sufficient overlap between the acoustic output of the human and the hearing curves of the dolphins in air so that exchanges can take place between the humans and the dolphins in the sonic sphere.

8. Dolphins in close proximity to man voluntarily raise their blowholes into the air and make sounds in the air in the presence of the humans. This takes place only when the dolphins are placed in close proximity to humans who will speak in air to them or to other humans loudly enough for the dolphins to hear (tapes of such exchanges and phonograph records are available demonstrating these points). (23, 27, 33)

9. Experiments using solitudinous dolphins in separate tanks connected by a "dolphin telephone" of a high-frequency passband show that dolphins carry on sonic communication using such a

link. It has also been shown that dolphins use sonic communication to modify one another's behavior. (39)

10. The capacity of dolphins to use echoes for recognition of objects has been studied extensively. (51, 52, 54, 55, 75)

11. Such studies lead to the conclusion that the basis for the postulated language of dolphins, "delphinese," is based upon the construction by central processing of "acoustic pictures," which are the basic elements of the postulated language. Thus, cetacean languages would be based in an entirely different sphere from human languages. Human languages are primarily based upon visual and manual images computed in a different way from the elements of the cetacean languages.

From the above considerations of the Cetacea we assume that they have alternative sonic languages to those of human speech. We have a number of experimental operational suggestions to make as to how to explore for the existence of these languages and how to develop an "interspecies language" between us and the Cetacea. We suggest that the most efficient approach may be the development of the interspecies language in agreement with the cetaceans.

Through modern computer technology, it is possible to devise electronic machines that can do transforms for the human and for the cetacean. There are three possible approaches to this problem.

The first approach involves making use of the fact that dolphins have been found to be interested in communicating with humans; i.e., they are ready with the necessary agreement to work on the problems. They go to inordinate lengths to create sounds in air that resemble those of human speech. Using the narrow band of overlap between human sonic communication and dolphin sonic communication, the dolphins do adaptive programming to attempt to establish this communication. (18, 23, 25, 27, 33) Dedicated humans faced with dedicated dolphins can depend upon agreements for adaptive programming on each side. Each species is sufficiently general purpose in their macrobiocomputer to be able to reprogram itself to modify and form new replies and new demands within the current situation extremely rapidly.

Dolphins understand demands and queries. With real-time methods involving no delay between a query and a response to that query and the corrections introduced by each side, each side learns very rapidly the limitations and the possibilities expressed by the other side. Thus, the first method calls for changing the frequencies of the human voice accurately into the frequency domain of the dolphin's and, conversely, the transformation of the frequencies of the dolphins' voices down into the range of the human's. A doorway must be opened between the human sonic box and the dolphin's sonic box.

An immediately technically feasible route to take advantage of this adaptive programming on each side is the use of special vocoders. Making such vocoders is a very straightforward technical design problem that can be solved, given the proper financial support and the properly trained engineers necessary for such designs.

In the proposed "interspecies vocoder," the human speech spectrum is divided up into a number of independent frequency channels by means of filters or the equivalent of filters computed by a microprocessor. On one side of the vocoder, each of the human sonic discrete bands is analyzed by analog methods in real time and is multiplied by a factor of 4.5 to 10 into the dolphin's frequency band. On the other side of the vocoder, the machine does the inverse transform of analyzing each of the dolphin's frequency bands, which are analogically computed and divided by 4.5 to 10 to the frequency band of the humans.

Such a device would allow a human to speak to a dolphin under water. The human could remain in air and the dolphin could remain under water; a dolphin would speak back to the human in his natural underwater mode. Each side would use its appropriate frequency bands and the electronic device would transform from one to the other. The air/water interface would thus be broken—opening a door. The frequency barrier would also be broken. Each individual involved would thus be able to operate in the familiar regions of its existence.

The number of bands required for understandable human speech of high quality, using a vocoder, has been found to be thirty. (66) These devices are based upon the number of critical frequency bands involved in human speech and hearing. C. Scott

Johnson (76) has shown that the number of critical hearing bands for the dolphin is about twice that of the human; i.e., the dolphin will require about sixty such bands.

W. A. Munson devised the first vocoder for dolphin/human communication. The dolphins expressed great interest in the use of this device, but the number of bands (ten) did not match either the human critical number or the dolphin critical number.

The vocoder method has the advantage of operating in real time; i.e., the dolphin and human can interact and correct each other rapidly. It is a relatively inexpensive method—the present estimations (1976) are that $100,000 would be sufficient for the design and the construction of the interspecies vocoder.

The second method involves the use of modern, high-speed minicomputers and microprocessors. Recent breakthroughs with microprocessors that can do the fast Fourier transform allow one to have software and hardware that can simulate the above vocoder method. With this technique, the analog vocoder is simulated by digital hardware. This approach would have several advantages over the analog vocoder. For example, one would be able to shift the critical bands, both the number and position in the two frequency spectra. The advantages of the flexibility of the software, i.e., the programming and its changes, would be a sizable one over the wired-in, fixed vocoder model. The cost of this approach is estimated to be on the order of $300,000.

A third approach, which is further into the future, would involve additional transformations of what the dolphin sees with his sonar to human video and vice versa by means of a high-speed minicomputer.

In this configuration, one visualizes an underwater, artifical sonar system that scans the underwater environment in a way similar to that used by the dolphins. An ultrasonic emitter emits pulses similar to those used by the dolphins, picks up the echoes by means of an array of hydrophones, transfers them to the minicomputer for computation. The computation in the micro-computer would be so designed that it would generate a three-dimensional, television display in color for use by the humans. A human operator could thus see with his eyes under water the way the dolphin sees under water with his ears.

A similar reverse transform from the visual in air to the

underwater sound of the dolphin would use a video camera linked to the minicomputer in such a way that it can compute the equivalent underwater sonar signals for use by the dolphin to see that which the human sees in air. Such a two-way visual/acoustic transform could then be used as an ancillary device to the vocoder system allowing each of the species to see the way the member of the other species sees. The cost of such a device currently is estimated at something over $1 million.

Such systems open operational doorways between the species. Since each of the systems functions in real time, we are depending upon the adaptive programming of the human and of the dolphin to solve the problem of constructing a suitable interspecies language somewhere between delphinese and the human languages. The construction/use of this new interspecies language will probably take a fairly long time of dedicated daily use, at the least, several months, at the most, many years.

In addition to these real-time devices, there is a host of other possibilities. Out of all these other possibilities, we have chosen these three as being most appropriate for the solution of the problem of alternative languages.

There is another approach, which I am hesitant to suggest because it may turn out to be a method that will lead to more questions than it answers. However, it has very attractive features for some persons and may be a necessary step before the others are developed.

Visualize a very high-speed minicomputer with a very large memory. It has an input and output for humans and an input and an output for dolphins. On the human side, there is the usual computer keyboard console. On the human output side, there is a display screen and a standard printer. The dolphin's input is a hydrophone of sufficient frequency passband to cover the frequency of the dolphin output.

The software to be designed has the following characteristics: the input to the computer from the dolphin consists of a series of pulses that the dolphin emits. These pulses are analyzed and categorized within the computer. The output from the computer is a series of synthesized "dolphin impulses" fed back to the dolphin under water.

Initially, the software of the computer has a teaching program for the dolphin. The teaching program starts as a simple code based upon the elements of the dolphin's pulsing system. The dolphin is taught the elements of this code. Initially, the program mimics what the dolphin has just said. When the dolphin reproduces what the computer said, he is rewarded. Once the dolphin has mastered the code, he can then elicit from the computer the next level of the teaching program in which combinations and permutations of the code elements are given "meaning" in terms of behaviors on the part of the dolphin. Using the code, the dolphin can turn on various kinds of devices connected to the computer. He can obtain fish from a mechanical fish dispenser by using the proper code words for operating that device. He can start tape recordings of music or TV tapes to be played back for him under water for short intervals. He can demand various kinds of responses from the human operator of the computer by controlling the printer in which various things can be spelled out in human language by means of the computed transforms of the teaching code into printed human language. He can demand the presence of the human away from the computer in which the human is in physical proximity to the dolphin. He can use the computer to synthesize human speech utilizing modern human speech synthesis programs and output devices that are available commercially.

Such technical proposals are now feasible. All that is required is sufficient time, energy, money, and interest on the part of the human species to carry them out. The only barrier in our way is our belief-disbelief systems about the intelligence and language capabilities of the cetaceans. I feel very strongly that the reward to the human species of such a program will be very great— beyond anything that I or anyone else can imagine. Alternatives to human language and communication with another species is a program that may be able to capture as much human interest around the planet as we currently devote to human warfare. In another place, I have visualized the industries that can arise during and after this program.

In this proposal, the prospects for man, for his new communication, are opened up into new domains for man's own evolution. If we can devote the best of our intellects, brains, and computers to these problems, we may expand our horizon far beyond that envisioned by any other program of scientific research. Our own survival, so far, constitutes only one-tenth to one-twentieth of the time the cetaceans have been here: let us find out what ethics, what philosophy, what rules they have found for survival and for living in harmony in the planet's oceans. The ancient extraterrestrials are here, waiting for us to grow up and maturely communicate: let us stop destroying them and us and start a new evolutionary interspecies dialogue. (I suspect that then and only then we will learn how to use the radio telescope arrays of Project Cyclops.)

The Marine Mammal Protection Act of 1972

LAW IS ESSENTIALLY A "REALITY" VOTED INTO EXISTENCE *as if true* for legal humans. The goodness-of-fit of legal simulation can correlate well or badly with the external reality of which the framers were not aware. The Marine Mammal Protection Act of 1972 is such a legal simulation: if Cetacea have a mental life comparable to or superior to man's, then they are "human" and hence not an economic resource to be "managed." Therefore, the supported scientific research should be directed in such a way as to investigate the probability of a mental life in the large-brained Cetacea. If such mental life can be demonstrated, the laws can be evolved to agree with the new experience.

Public Law 92-522
92nd Congress, H.R. 10420
October 21, 1972

AN ACT

86 STAT. 1027

To protect marine mammals; to establish a Marine Mammal Commission; and for other purposes

Be it enacted by the Senate and House of Representatives of the United States of America in Congress assembled. That this Act, with the following table of contents, may be cited as the "Marine Mammal Protection Act of 1972."

FINDINGS AND DECLARATION OF POLICY

SEC. 2. The Congress finds that—

(1) certain species and population stocks of marine mammals are, or may be, in danger of extinction or depletion as a result of man's activities;

(2) such species and population stocks should not be permitted to diminish beyond the point at which they cease to be a significant functioning element in the ecosystem of which they are a part, and, consistent with this major objective, they should not be permitted to diminish below their optimum sustainable population. Further measures should be immediately taken to replenish any species or population stock which has already diminished below that population. In particular, efforts should be made to protect the rookeries, mating grounds, and areas of similar significance for each species of marine mammal from the adverse effect of man's actions;

(3) there is inadequate knowledge of the ecology and population dynamics of such marine mammals and of the factors which bear upon their ability to reproduce themselves successfully;

(4) negotiations should be undertaken immediately to encourage the development of international arrangements for research on, and conservation of, all marine mammals;

(5) marine mammals and marine mammal products either—

(A) move in interstate commerce, or

(B) affect the balance of marine ecosystems in a manner which is important to other animals and animal products which move in interstate commerce,

and that the protection and conservation of marine mammals is therefore necessary to insure the continuing availability of those products which move in interstate commerce; and

(6) marine mammals have proven themselves to be resources of great international significance, esthetic and recreational as well as economic, and it is the sense of the Congress that they should be protected and encouraged to develop to the greatest extent feasible commensurate with sound policies of resource management and that the primary objective of their management should be to maintain the health and stability of the marine ecosystem. Whenever consistent with this primary objective, it should be the goal to obtain an optimum sustainable population keeping in mind the optimum carrying capacity of the habitat.

DEFINITIONS

SEC. 3. For the purposes of this Act—

(1) The term "depletion" or "depleted" means any case in which the Secretary, after consultation with the Marine Mammal Commission and the Committee of Scientific Advisors on Marine Mammals established under title II of this Act, determines that the number of individuals within a species or population stock—

(A) has declined to a significant degree over a period of years;

(B) has otherwise declined and that if such decline continues, or is likely to resume, such species would be subject to the provisions of the Endangered Species Conservation Act of 1969; or

(C) is below the optimum carrying capacity for the species or stock within its environment.

(2) The terms "conservation" and "management" mean the collection and application of biological information for the purposes of increasing and maintaining the number of animals within species and populations of marine mammals at the optimum carrying capacity of their habitat. Such terms include the entire scope of activities that constitute a modern scientific resource program, including, but not limited to, research, census, law enforcement, and habitat acquisition and improvement. Also included within these terms, when and where appropriate, is the periodic or total protection of species or populations as well as regulated taking.

(3) The term "district court of the United States" includes the District Court of Guam, District Court of the Virgin Islands, District Court of Puerto Rico, District Court of the Canal Zone, and, in the case of American Samoa and the Trust Territory of the Pacific Islands, the District Court of the United States for the District of Hawaii.

(4) The term "humane" in the context of the taking of a marine mammal means that method of taking which involves the least possible degree of pain and suffering practicable to the mammal involved.

(5) The term "marine mammal" means any mammal which (A) is morphologically adapted to the marine environment (including sea otters and members of the orders Sirenia, Pinnipedia and Cetacea), or (B) primarily inhabits the marine environment (such as the polar bear); and, for the purposes of this Act, includes any part of any such marine mammal, including its raw, dressed, or dyed fur or skin.

(6) The term "marine mammal product" means any item of merchandise which consists, or is composed in whole or in part, of any marine mammal.

(7) The term "moratorium" means a complete cessation of the taking

of marine mammals and a complete ban on the importation into the United States of marine mammals and marine mammal products, except as provided in this Act.

(8) The term "optimum carrying capacity" means the ability of a given habitat to support the optimum sustainable population of a species or population stock in a healthy state without diminishing the ability of the habitat to continue that function.

(9) The term "optimum sustainable population" means, with respect to any population stock, the number of animals which will result in the maximum productivity of the population or the species, keeping in mind the optimum carrying capacity of the habitat and the health of the ecosystem of which they form a constituent element.

(10) The term "person" includes (A) any private person or entity, and (B) any officer, employee, agent, department, or instrumentality of the Federal Government, of any State or political subdivision thereof, or of any foreign government.

(11) The term "population stock" or "stock" means a group of marine mammals of the same species or smaller taxa in a common spatial arrangement, that interbreed when mature.

(12) The term "Secretary" means—

(A) the Secretary of the department in which the National Oceanic and Atmospheric Administration is operating, as to all responsibility, authority, funding, and duties under this Act with respect to members of the order Cetacea and members, other than walruses, of the order Pinnipedia, and

(B) the Secretary of the Interior as to all responsibility, authority, funding, and duties under this Act with respect to all other marine mammals covered by this Act.

(13) The term "take" means to harass, hunt, capture, or kill, or attempt to harass, hunt, capture, or kill any marine mammal.

(14) The term "United States" includes the several States, the District of Columbia, the Commonwealth of Puerto Rico, the Canal Zone, the possessions of the United States, and the Trust Territory of the Pacific Islands.

(15) The term "waters under the jurisdiction of the United States" means—

(A) the territorial sea of the United States, and

(B) the fisheries zone established pursuant to the Act of October 14, 1966 (80 Stat. 908; 16 U.S.C. 1091-1094)....

APPENDIX TWO

Annotated Bibliography

In the following bibliography the first number is the text reference number for this book; the second number in parentheses is the number in the bibliography included in the two editions of *The Dyadic Cyclone,* Simon and Schuster, pages 267–77, and Bantam, pages 239–51. When an item appears in this bibliography that did not appear in the previous one there is no number in parentheses following the bibliographic number for this book.

1. (57)   Lilly, John C. 1958. "Some Considerations Regarding Basic Mechanisms of Positive and Negative Types of Motivations." *American Journal of Psychiatry,* vol. 115, pp. 498–504.

This paper is a summary of the work done up to May 1958 on the positive and negative reinforcing systems within the brain. It summarizes the work on the monkey *(Macaque rhesis)* and on the dolphin *(Tursiops truncatus).*

"For a time we were surprised to find in the monkey that the positive, pleasure-like, motivating-to-start systems were so large and the fear, pain-like motivating-to-stop systems were so small.

But when one sees the very powerful effects of stimulating the relatively small negative systems, one can understand that this kind of system may be quite large enough to fulfill its extremely high priority stop, escape, or avoidance functions. When one sees the fearful, down-hill, sickening, destructive effects of continued stimulation of the negative systems in an animal one is reluctant to say that they need be any larger.

"The positive, start, approach systems in the monkey are relatively very large, occurring in certain zones as a proximate twin with the negative ones, and also occurring in other regions possibly without its twin, such as in the corpora striata. Reciprocal relations and balanced activity of positive and negative motives seem to be assured structurally in the deep powerful midline systems, and something of the positive aspect may be in excess for other regions. Such other regions include functions like sexual ones, which we find to be both motivationally positive and negative. We find alternation (of positive versus negative) over short time intervals between the two opposite effects in the monkey, i.e., he will start such romantic activities and stop them within a period of minutes again and again for a disgraceful number of hours (48). This system seems to be at that very demanding primitive level that requires mutual reciprocity between a starting motive and a stopping one to preserve the individual's integrity.

". . . With proper electrical stimuli and proper time courses we have found rewarding effects elicitable from cerebellum and punishing and rewarding ones elicitable from cerebral neocortex.

". . . It is important to find out more about big-brained animals in far greater detail than we can with the human. For example, do they resemble the small-brained ones in the urgency of motivation aroused by stimulation of these systems? So far we have found only one animal that has the brain the size of ours who will cooperate and not frighten me to the point where I can't work with him. This animal is the dolphin, a small whale with teeth, an air breathing mammal (not the fish with the same name). . . . As adults, these animals reach eight feet and four hundred pounds with a brain up to 1750 grams.

". . . In 1955 we found that dolphins cannot be anesthetized without danger of dying. (We saved several through the use of a hand-operated respirator which I designed and built.)

"These animals in contrast to dry land ones, fail to breathe with relatively light doses of anesthetic, one-fourth that required for surgical levels of anesthesia. In other words, they lack our unconscious, automatic, self-sustaining breathing system. In retrospect this seems reasonable: an unconscious dolphin, under water, will drown if respiratory inspiration occurs. They, as it were, must relate their breathing to surfacing and to the coming opportunities to surface—so this function is almost if not fully voluntary.

". . . Some time was spent developing a method which should bypass the need for and dangers of general anesthesia (in the dolphin).

"During the last year it was found to be feasible to hammer percutaneously guides for electrodes into the skull of monkeys (9). The method was tried on dolphins in November 1957; the guides were inserted under local anesthesia into the skull of a dolphin in a small shallow tank so easily and so quickly that the dolphin and we hardly realized what had happened.

"Our findings on the dolphin are summarized as follows: We found the positive and negative systems within the dolphin's brain. The systems are further apart in this large brain than in that of the monkey; yet they seem as large in absolute size as they are in the monkey; more brain with other yet-to-be-found functions lies between and around these systems. As in the human brain, evocable motor movements also were found only in relatively isolated regions.

"The urgency of motives elicited by stimulation of those zones which we have found to date is high and there is evidence that we have yet to stimulate the most powerful ones. Stimulating a punishment area (a negative, destructive, stopping motivational spot) caused a dolphin to shut off the electrical current very accurately at a certain level of intensity. The difference between this naive, wild animal's performance and that of monkeys was the incredibly short time in which the dolphin learned to use the switch: compared to the naive monkey's several hundreds to thousands of random trials to learn, she took about 20 to shape up the proper motions of her beak and each of those 'trials' had a purposeful look that was a little disturbing to watch.

"... Every time we first stimulated [a negative zone] she emitted the characteristic dolphin 'distress whistle.' From that time on she shut off the current at a level well below that at which we previously could elicit the distress call. This whistle, a crescendo-decrescendo in frequency and loudness, was a clue for finding negative, punishing, destructive, stopping systems; we had no criteria for positive, rewarding, pleasure-starting systems. Empathic methods did not help with this handless, streamlined, hairless animal who lacks our mobility of facial expressions.

"... With a bit of luck with our next animal we found a positive, rewarding, starting zone. The luck was in obtaining an animal who vocalized vociferously: as soon as we stimulated the positive zone, he told us about it by covering a large repertory of assorted complex whistles, bronx cheers, and impolite noises. Giving him a switch at this point was quite an experience—he sized up what I was doing so rapidly that by the time I had set up his switch he took only 5 'trials' to figure out the proper way to push it with his beak. From that point on, as long as he could obtain his stimulation for every push he made with his beak, he quietly worked for the stimuli. But if we cut off his current, he immediately stopped working and vocalized—apparently scolding at times, and mimicking us at others. One time he mimicked my speaking voice so well that my wife laughed out loud and he copied her laughter. Eventually, he pushed too rapidly, caused a seizure, became unconscious, respiration failed and he died. Apparently unconsciousness because of any factor, anesthesia, or brain stimulation, or others, causes death in these animals.

"... If we are ever to communicate with a non-human species of this planet, the dolphin is probably our best present gamble. In a sense, it is a joke when I fantasy that it may be best to hurry and finish our work on their brains before one of them learns to speak our language—else he will demand equal rights with men for their brains and lives under our ethical and legal codes.

"Before our man in space program becomes too successful, it may be wise to spend some time, talent, and money on the research with the dolphins; not only are they a large-brained species living their lives in a situation with attenuated effects of gravity but they may be a group with whom we can learn basic techniques of communicating with really alien intelligent life forms. I personally hope we do not encounter any off-planet extraterrestrials before we are better prepared than we are now. Too automatically, too soon, too many of us attribute too much negative systems activity to foreign language aliens of strange and unfamiliar appearance and use this as an excuse for increasing our own negative, punishing, attacking activities on them."

[The following part is about the isolation tank findings.]

"But a caution is in order; the human mind is the only province in science in which that which is assumed to be true either is true or becomes true. (That law I do believe to be true.) This is a sublime and dangerous faculty. To have and to hold a useful and successful set of basic beliefs and truths about the rewards and punishments in one's self is also sublime, sometimes satisfying, and sometimes punishing, but never dull or monotonous. To find one's self to be more egophilic than egophobic is of itself an egophilic advantage increasing one's own fun and that of those persons closest and most important to one. By careful and continuous nurture one may achieve the classic command to 'love thy neighbor as thyself,' but only after learning how to lessen thy fear of thyself and how to increase thy love for thyself."

2.   (66)   Lilly, John C., and Alice M. Miller. 1961. "Sounds Emitted by the Bottlenose Dolphin." *Science,* vol. 133, pp. 1689–1693.

The audible emissions of captive dolphins under water or in air are remarkably complex and varied. This paper gives the first evidence for and demonstration of the ability of the bottle-nosed dolphin to produce clicks and whistles separately and simultaneously.

"Such observations demonstrate that the bottlenose dolphin has at least two separately controllable sonic emitters, one for the production of clicks and one for the production of whistles (in later papers, it is shown that the two nasal emitters are capable of independently clicking or whistling but not both, records such as in this paper that show simultaneous clicking and whistling result from the clicking by one nasal emitter and the whistling by the other nasal emitter in the same dolphin).

"One probable mechanism to explain these results and similar ones is that the clicks shock-excite the resonant frequencies and harmonics of the air containing cavities (variable sinuses, fixed sinuses, fixed nasal passages and so on) in the head. One or more of these sacs is used to produce [resonance in] whistling and can be made to click resonate briefly during whistling as well as during non-whistling periods. Because some of the sacs change size and shape through movements of the muscles in their walls, frequencies of the whistles or the click excited resonances or both change. The fixed cavities emit their characteristic click-excited frequencies as the couplings in the internal air path are varied.

"... These sounds are classified as vocalizations used for communication. What information is communicated is yet to be determined.

"The necessity for and occurrence of creakings for purposes of navigation, ranging, and recognition (sonar) have been eliminated in the experiments under discussion."

3.   (67)   Lilly, John C., and Alice M. Miller. 1961. "Vocal Exchanges Between Dolphins." *Science,* vol. 134, pp. 1873–1876.

Bottle-nosed dolphins "talk" to each other with whistles, clicks, and a variety of other noises. This paper specifies the optimal conditions for studying the sonic communication between two dolphins. Amplitude versus time and frequency versus time plots are shown of the resulting communication exchanges. The conditions are set up such that sonar signals are eliminated by not allowing the animals to move. The maximum amplitudes of the signals are found to be between about 1 kHz and 64 kHz. The exchanges consist of whistles in this frequency range and of clickings trains in this range. Evidence is found that each dolphin can click and whistle simultaneously with independent control of the clickings and of the whistlings; that the sonar output consists of very much harder, higher-frequency creakings and can be produced independently of the whistles and communication clickings. (Annotated Bibliography continued on page 175.)

Introductory Note for the Photographs

THE CONTRASTS BETWEEN HUMANS AND DOLPHINS ARE
probably best seen when they meet in the water. The photographs
are divided into several groups.

The first group is composed of dolphins free living with one
another in deep water in the wild. In this set of photos they are
moving fairly rapidly in response to the stimulation of the
nearby boat and photographer. In other photos they are loafing
along with one dolphin towing another under water in its
wake.

In the second group the humans have entered the deep water
with scuba diving gear in order to be able to stay under the
water long enough to make long observations on the behavior of
the dolphins. When the diver is patient enough and returns
often enough, the dolphins will approach and allow the diver to
touch them. The dolphins tend to approach a snorkeler
sooner than they will approach a scuba diver. The mechanical
breathing equipment and its noise inhibit the initiation of the
new relationship. To a dolphin's sonar such equipment may

look very strange and out of place mounted on a mammal such as the human.

The third group is of the relationships of dolphins and humans at the surface of the sea. For dolphins, being at the surface is a relatively rare event; most of their time is spent under water. To accommodate humans, especially in exhibition shows in oceanaria the dolphins will spend so much time at the surface that their dorsal fins bend over under the influence of gravity. Rarely, if ever, does one see a bent dorsal fin on dolphins in the wild.

In the photos from Sea World at San Diego two very unusual relationships between dolphins and humans are shown. In the one photo the man and the woman are riding three dolphins who swim just under the surface of the water supporting the standing humans on their backs. This requires extremely fast coordinated swimming with continuous communication among the three dolphins to compensate for the changes that occur while they are swimming around a relatively small lagoon.

The second picture shows a man riding on the back of a killer whale holding on to a loop around the killer whale's forequarters, while he is jumping out of the water. Immediately after this shot the whale dives to the bottom of the tank with the man on his back and rises again clearing the water while carrying the man.

Such relationships as these show that the killer whales and the dolphins have an ethic about man, which says in effect, "Humans are not to be injured or killed."

The fourth group of pictures shows what can be done between a human and a dolphin when the water depth is decreased to the point where the human can walk around standing up on the bottom and the dolphin can still swim around with the dorsal fin protruding from the water. These illustrations show the very close relationship developed between Margaret Howe and Peter Dolphin in the St. Thomas laboratory in the 1960s. Peter would work in the vocal sphere for Margaret, producing humanlike sounds in air above the water with an open blowhole (see Lilly, Miller & Truby, 1968, and *The Mind of the Dolphin,* 1967).

Plate 1. Dolphins in the wild leaping free off the bow of a ship. One dolphin is looking at the photographer with the right eye; another has an open blowhole as he takes in air during the leap.

Plate 2. A group of spinner dolphins in the Pacific off the central American coast. Note the long upper and lower jaws (beak). These dolphins are from four to six feet in overall length and are always seen in large groups.

Plate 3. Close-up view of the long face and beak of spinner dolphins in the wild.

Plate 4.   A freshwater dolphin from the upper Amazon River, *Inia geoffriensis*, about six feet long.

Plate 5.   Dolphins and humans in deep water using scuba. The bottle-nosed dolphin *(Tursiops truncatus)* is opening her mouth to allow Jill Fairchild to feel her teeth, while both are swimming at a depth of approximately seven feet.

Plate 6.   Jill is hanging just below the surface; the dolphin is watching her carefully while she strokes the region of the melon.

Above
Plate 7.   The dolphin swims in rapid circles around the submerged Jill.

Below
Plate 8.   Jill and the dolphin contemplate each other face-to-face. Notice the reflection from the surface of the water surrounding them directly overhead in the region of the bubbles. The light is not reflected back from the surface of the water.

Plate 9.   This shot shows the long genital anal slit of the female dolphin and the motions possible with the two flippers. The flippers have a rotatory joint on the scapula similar to the human shoulder joint. Here the right flipper has been rotated ninety degrees in relation to the position of the left flipper.

Right
Plate 11.   The largest of the dolphins, *Orcinus orca* (killer whale), inspecting Jill near the surface of the water. *(Photo by Oliver Andrews)*

Below
Plate 10.   The dolphin is diverted from Jill by the photographer—a beautiful and unusual head-on shot directly into the sun.

Plate 12. Three bottle-nosed dolphins swimming in such an accurate and carefully controlled way that they are ridden by two humans standing on their backs. Such swimming requires extremely rapid and careful visual, tactile, and sonic communication among the three dolphins. During this period they maintain their depth just below the surface of the water for a distance of one hundred feet or more.

Plate 13. A man riding on the back of a killer whale while jumping clear of the water and diving to the bottom of the tank. The *Orcinus orca* is constantly aware of the needs of the man and brings him back to the surface before he runs out of air. He also maintains his position relative to gravity so that the man is always above him rather than below him.

Plate 14. Margaret and Peter set up housekeeping in eighteen inches of water. Peter has just threatened to bite Margaret's foot, which she has withdrawn rapidly.

Plate 15. Peter finds Margaret's stroking of his side to be sufficiently rewarding so that he propels himself against her hand with his flukes.

Plate 16.   Massage continues Peter's delight.

Plate 17.   Peter turns over and Margaret continues her massage of his skin. Margaret pushes Peter in front of his underwater mirror. He begins to look at his own image.

Plate 18.   Suddenly Peter comes out of his contemplative mood and rushes around, very nearly upsetting Margaret.

Plate 19.   Peter starts circling in front of his mirror. Margaret brushes him as he passes her. The brush is held at an angle so that the bristles do not irritate his skin. Margaret voices the word *brush* for Peter.

Plate 20. Peter and Margaret in a practice session in the open-air balcony without voice recording. Peter's eye is above water while he looks at the shape presented by Margaret, which she voices as *oblong*.

Plate 21. The lesson on shapes is interrupted when Peter refuses to pay attention. Margaret flops on the air mattress and rewards him by physical stroking of his beak.

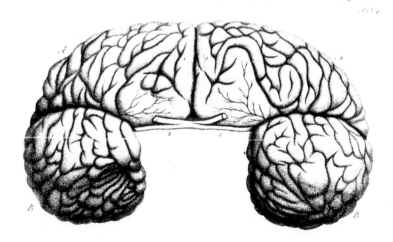

Plate 22. One of the first drawings of a Phocaena brain by G. R. Trediramus, 1818 (courtesy of Dr. Mary A. B. Brazier, UCLA Medical School).

This is an anterior view. For unknown reasons the two hemispheres have been artificially separated.

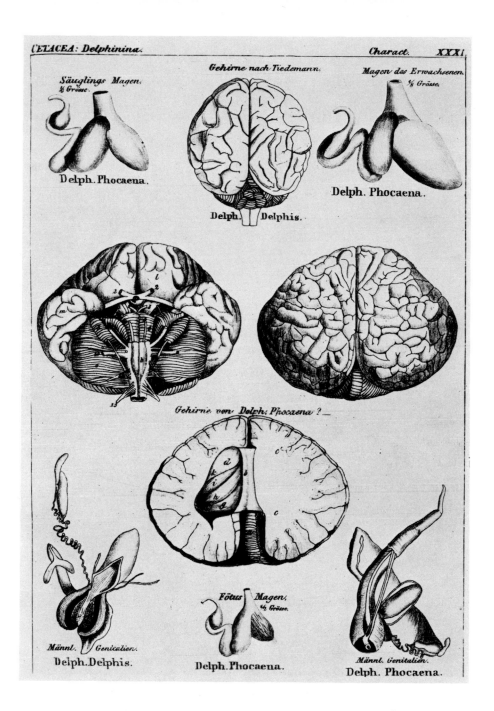

Säuglings Magen.
½ Grösse.

Gehirne nach Tiedemann.

Magen des Erwachsenen.
⅛ Grösse.

Delph. Phocaena.

Delph. Delphis.

Delph. Phocaena.

Gehirne von Delph: Phocaena ?

Männl. Genitalien.

Fötus Magen.
½ Grösse.

Männl. Genitalien.

Delph. Delphis.

Delph. Phocaena.

Delph. Phocaena.

Plate 23. Diagrams of the brains of the dolphins reproduced by H. G. L. Reichenbach in 1845 (drawings by Tiedemann, courtesy of the Library of Congress, Washington, D.C.).

These drawings show somewhat the complexity of the gyri and sulci in the depths of the cortex penetrating into the substance of the brain.

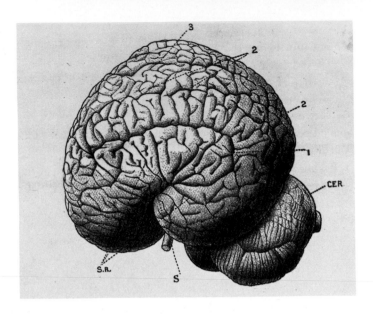

Plate 24. The first exact twentieth-century drawing of a dolphin brain by G. Elliot Smith, 1902. This is probably the brain of a *Tursiops truncatus,* or bottle-nosed dolphin, known at the time of Smith as *Delphinus tursio.* In 1931, Othello Langworthy produced very similar drawings, published in *Brain,* 54: page 225, 1931. He used the term *porpoise* for *Tursiops truncatus,* or the bottle-nosed dolphin.

Plate 25. The medial view of the same brain as shown in Plate 24. This shows the interconnection between the two hemispheres (corpus callosum) and the immense complexity of the gyri and sulci on the medial surface of the cerebral cortex and the cerebellum.

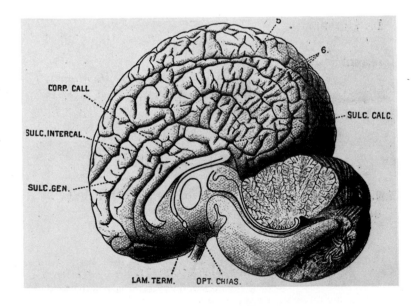

Plate 26. Sissy swimming on her back, propelling George Hunt through the water while he holds on to her back. Her neck is bent at an acute angle upward and forward; she has one eye on the photographer and the other on George Hunt.

Plate 27. Elvar Dolphin matching the nonsense syllable list read to him by Scott McVay. Here Scott is rewarding Elvar in the initial experiment with a butterfish. Notice the open blowhole from which Elvar is emitting his sounds. He has a microphone above the blowhole. Scott has a lavalier microphone, which is not visible in this photograph, which is recorded on his channel of tape. Scott listens to Elvar through the headphones. The results of these experiments were analyzed and published in the *Journal of the Acoustical Society,* Lilly, Miller and Truby, 1968; *see* Figures 9 through 12, this book.

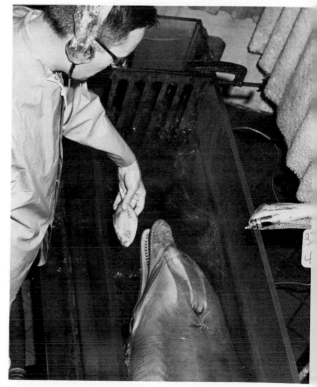

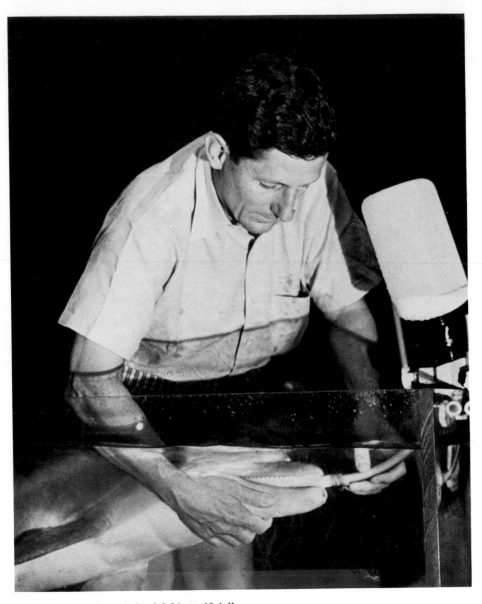

Plate 28.   Feeding a baby dolphin artificially.

This plate and Plates 29 and 30 show how we successfully fed a baby dolphin who was caught without his mother. In this picture the container of the formula is in the upper right, connected by a tube to a nipple formed from a surgeon's rubber glove fingertip. This rubber tip is fastened to the tube by rubber bands. The nipple is presented to the baby while he is held near the surface of the water with the blowhole out so he can breathe. The nipple touches the tip of the beak, the baby opens his mouth, and, as can be seen in Plates 29 and 30, he wraps his tongue around the nipple and suckles in the same way that land-born mammals suckle, i.e., by sucking with the muscles of the tongue. (Miami, 1961.)

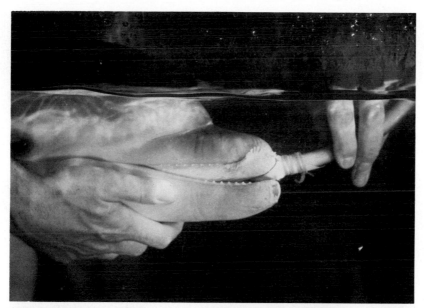

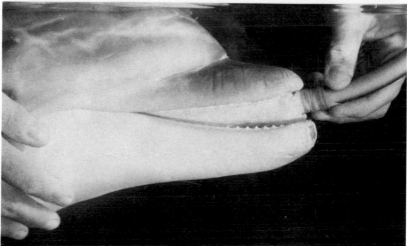

Above

Plate 29.   Close-up view of the positioning of the baby's tongue.

Here is shown the baby's eye to the left and the man's hand holding the baby near the surface of the water and presenting the tube and nipple with the other hand. The tongue is here sticking out of the mouth; the mouth will be opened a little farther and the tongue dropped to the bottom of the mouth, then raised in a semicircle around the nipple, as is shown in Plate 30.

Below

Plate 30.   The baby's tongue wrapped around the nipple.

Here the baby has succeeded in closing the circle of his upper hard palate, his tongue wrapped around the nipple to close out the seawater. With the tongue, he has thus formed a continuous passage from the nipple back into his throat, sealing out any access to the seawater; pure milk, without air or water, is thus sucked in from the tube and the reservoir above the water.

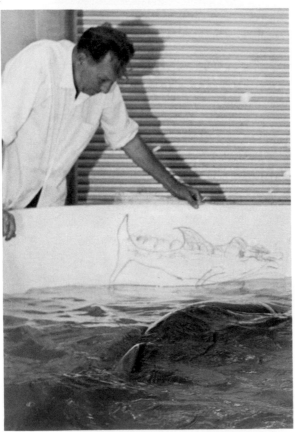

Plate 31. Ginger Nadell in the water with Elvar during a vocalization lesson.

It was found that getting into the water with dolphins was necessary for eliciting the kinds of vocal responses for the matching experiments. Each experimenter spent some time in the tank with the dolphin with which the researcher was working. Here Ginger is talking to Elvar, and he is answering, as well as developing a close "touching" relationship. (Miami, 1961.)

Plate 32. Gregory Bateson experimenting with Sissy Dolphin, showing her a drawing of a dolphin on a piece of transparent plastic. (October 1963, St. Thomas, V.I.)

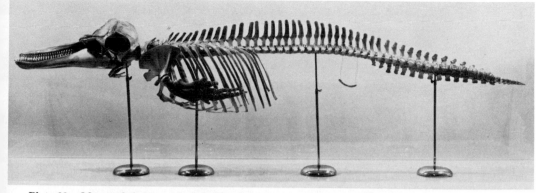

Plate 33.   Mounted skeleton of a bottle-nosed dolphin, *Tursiops truncatus*.

This picture shows the complete skeleton including the eighty-eight teeth, the skull, the bones of the flipper shown here in front of the ribs, the compressed cervical vertebrae, which are all fused together, and the fifty odd vertebrae including the thoracic, lumbar, and caudal. The bones suspended below the posterior thoracic vertebrae are the residual bones of the pelvic girdle, which function in the Cetacea as an anchor for the genitals in both the male and the female. The shoulder joint is shown meeting the scapula. All of the bones of the arm running from the shoulder joint to the tip of the flipper are bound together. There is the analog of our humerus, of our radius, of our ulna, and all of the bones of our hand bound up together in the flipper. The small bones below the skull are the hyoid laryngeal complex of bones, so necessary to breathing and swallowing in the dolphin.

Plate 34.   The first computer (LINC III) to be dedicated to the analysis of dolphin communication, 1963. This computer was completely transistorized and is eighty times slower than, and one-eighth the memory size of, the current PDP–11/04 dedicated to the dolphin communication in 1978. With an eighty times speed-up, many new things are possible that were not possible with the LINC computer in the early sixties. In this figure we see the keyboard in front of the operator, the cathode-ray tube on the panel, two magnetic tape drives, and the multiple input and output panels above the tape drives. There is an output teletypewriter in the background. This computer was kept in its own air-conditioned space near the dolphin tanks in the Communication Research Institute in Miami.

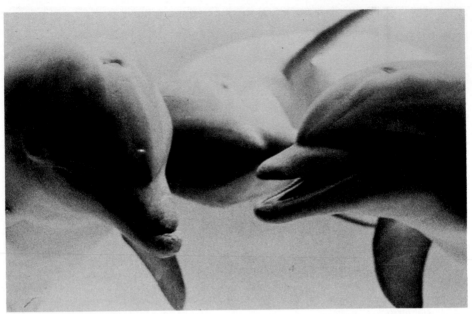

Plate 35. Three dolphins *(Tursiops truncatus)* paying close attention to the underwater swimmer who is taking the picture, Hardy Jones at Marine World, Africa U.S.A., Redwood City, California.

Plate 36. The brain of *Tursiops truncatus* and its various divisions according to Morgane.

The main point of this diagram is showing the huge parietal associational area of *Tursiops,* which is most of the lateral aspect of the brain showing in Plate 24. (From Morgane, Yakovlev, Jacobs, McFarland, and Piliero, "Surface Configuration of the Dolphin Brain," 14 December 1966, Communication Research Institute, Miami, Florida.

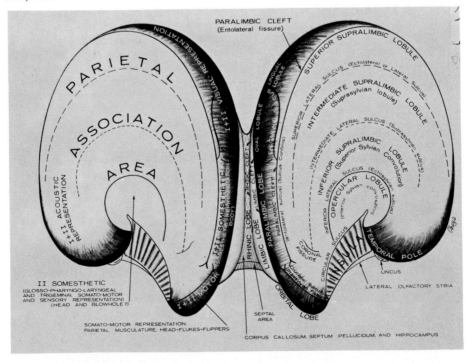

Plate 36A   After swimming with Belinda, a beluga *(Delphinapterus leucas)* and Toni Lilly have an exchange beside the pool. Toni's description of the experience of swimming with the beluga is in the prologue.

Plate 36B   Belinda replies to Toni by squirting water at her. Subsequently Toni squirted water back   at Belinda.

Plate 37.   Margaret Howe and Sissy, 1964.
   Margaret sat down on the bottom of the shallow water in the St. Thomas pool and Sissy climbed onto her lap and pinned her down by raising her head and flukes in the air and thus increasing her weight on Margaret's lap. Margaret is stroking Sissy's belly. Here one can see the stereo visual field below Sissy's head. Both of her eyes can be tilted out, and she can look directly at the photographer.

Plate 38.   Margaret's obvious enjoyment of Sissy's pinning her to the bottom of the pool shows in her facial expression.

Plate 39. Margaret and Sissy.
Another view showing the "baby in the lap effect" with the three-hundred-fifty-pound, eight-foot-long dolphin.

Plate 40. Margaret and Sissy move into deeper water, with Margaret holding on to Sissy's body.

Plate 41.   Margaret and Sissy swimming together.

Sissy has trapped Margaret in the middle of the pool in eight-foot water and is swimming in a mimicking way around Margaret. Sissy is doing the dog paddle; her flippers are moving horizontally and are turned in a horizontal plane moving back and forth. Her tail with the flukes is wrapped in a tight semicircle around Margaret so that Margaret cannot move out of the center of the pool. Sissy continued this activity for fifteen minutes, wearing Margaret out. Margaret finally had to dive to the bottom of the pool in order to escape Sissy's trap.

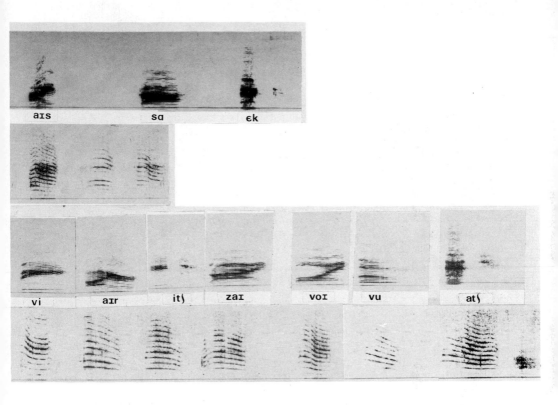

Plate 42.   Two vocal transactions between a human and a dolphin, Scott McVay and Elvar.

This plate illustrates the kinds of materials analyzed and scored in Figures 10 through 12. For the sounds used, see Figure 6. In this plate the human speaks three sounds, "a I s," "s a," "e k," in the first line. In the second line the dolphin emits three sounds of much higher pitch (wider-space lines) and in a much faster sequence than the human. In the third line the human says seven sounds, "v i," "a I r," "i t c h," "z a I," "v o I," "v u," "a t c h." The dolphin replies with seven sounds of very much higher pitch than the human at a more rapid rate (in the human rendition, the silences have been cut out to match the figures of the human sounds with those of the dolphin). The sounds analyzed here run from 100 to 8,000 cycles per second (Hz). This is the beginning of a long series of transactions in which the human gave thirty-five sequences and the dolphin replied with thirty-five sequences. The number of sounds that the dolphin emits in response to the number of sounds the human emits are scored over several such sequences in Figure 11. The analysis of the pitch of the human compared with the pitch of the dolphin and the various harmonics of the two is given in Figure 10.

Plate 43.   Experiments to determine the sleep pattern in the dolphin.

This plate shows two students of a team of eight observing the eye closures and timing them with the dolphin Elvar, in a transparent tank. Observations were made in ten experiments of twenty-four hours each. Each student team of two observed for a period of three hours out of the twenty-four; with eight students, twenty-four consecutive hours were covered. Each student watched a single eye and timed the closure each time it occurred. The clock time was also noted. The results are summarized in Figures 13, 14, and 15.

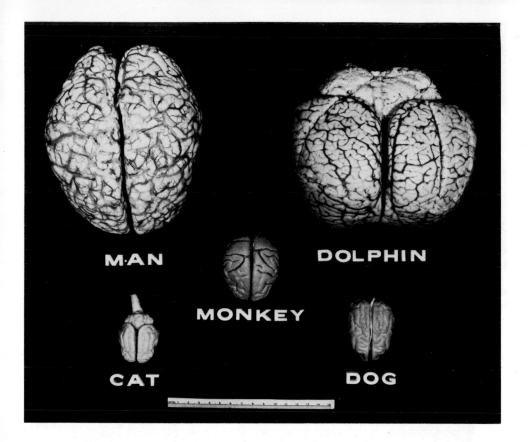

Plate 45. Comparison of the brains of man, dolphin, monkey, dog, and cat.

This figure shows the different sizes of the brains of *Homo sapiens, Tursiops truncatus, Macaca mulatta, Canis,* and *Felis*. This photograph was taken of all five brains simultaneously and shows their comparative sizes and something of their appearance on the topmost portions. The human brain is spread out posteriorly and anteriorly, whereas the dolphin brain is more spherical, i.e., a large portion of it is below this photograph. The monkey brain, resembling that of the human, is a much smaller version of the human brain. The dog and the cat are unique unto themselves, and each possesses very much larger, relatively speaking, small brains. The olfactory brain in the dolphin does not exist; it exists in a rudimentary form in the human.

Opposite

Plate 44. A male dolphin pulling on a rope with his erect penis as he swims backward away from the edge of the pool.

This figure shows the shape of the erect penis in the dolphin; i.e., it resembles a miniature dolphin. Its color is bright red. The dolphin can voluntarily erect his penis in about seven seconds and voluntarily collapse it in the same time.

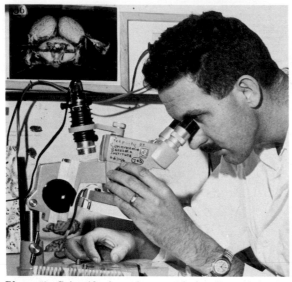

Plate 46. Scientific investigators of the Communication Research Institute, 1964. Will L. McFarland. Missing from the pictures are Eugene L. Nagel, Paul Yakovlev, Mike S. Jacobs, and several visiting scientists.

Plate 47. Scientific investigators of the Communication Research Institute, 1964. Henry Truby.

Plate 48. Scientific investigators of the Communication Research Institute, 1964. From left to right: Peter J. Morgane, John C. Lilly, Gregory Bateson.

As a consequence of this work, it was deduced that the dolphin has three independently controllable sonic-ultrasonic emitters in the head: the two nasal emitters just below the blowhole and the laryngeal emitter in the pharynx.

4. (70) Lilly, John C. 1961. *Man and Dolphin.* Doubleday & Co., Inc., New York.

This book summarized all the results (1960) on the dolphin research and gives the author's speculations about their intelligence and communicative abilities. There is a summary of the known anatomy and physiology of that time and proposals about their communicative ability based upon their brain size.

This book was reproduced in 1962, in French, Swedish, English, and the pocket book in America. It was reproduced in 1963 in Dutch and Norwegian. It was translated into Japanese in 1965 and into Russian in the same year. In 1966 it was translated into Czechoslovakian and into Bulgarian in 1967. A shortened version of this book is reproduced in *Lilly on Dolphins, The Humans of the Sea,* 1975.

5. (72) Lilly, John C., and Alice M. Miller. 1962. "Operant Conditioning of the Bottlenose Dolphin with Electrical Stimulation of the Brain." *Journal of Comparative and Physiological Psychology,* vol. 55, pp. 73–79.

"Previous experiments had shown that general anesthesia (nembutal or paraldehyde) stops respiration in this species. Because of the susceptibility of this animal to respiratory failure under anesthesia, a method was devised to place electrodes within the brain of this animal using only a local anesthetic. Figure 2 shows the principles of this method in diagrammatic form. In brief, a small piece of hypodermic-needle tubing (sleeve guide) is hammered through the skin, the blubber, the muscle, and is lodged in the skull. A mandrel which carries the sleeve guide during the hammering process can be withdrawn once the guide penetrates the inner table of the skull. ... On the withdrawal of the mandrel the skin and blubber close, leaving the proximal end of the sleeve guide covered. In the case of the dolphin, a small mark remains in the skin. Later, using this mark as a guide one can find the track through the skin, blubber, and muscle and probe for the tip of the sleeve guide at any time that one wishes to insert an electrode pair.

"Special electrodes are constructed which fit closely into the sleeve guide. An electrode pair can be lowered 1 mm. at a time through the guide into the brain substance by this technique. The track is mapped millimeter by millimeter and goes from the top of the brain to the bottom. . . . A dorsal-ventral track can be up to 120 mm. in length, and a side-to-side track can be up to 200 mm. long.

"With the use of the proper electrical wave form observations can be continued for many hours per day for several weeks. Reproducible results are obtained testing a track during withdrawal of the electrodes, on reinsertions to the same depth at later dates, and during continuous observations at the same site. [The suitable wave form is a minimally injurious wave form described by Lilly, Hughes, Alvord & Galkin, 1955.]

"A minimum-effort switch (Lilly, 1942) is placed above the salt water and out of the spray. A movable rod is placed near the rostrum of the animal, which usually pushes the rod at once and explores its degrees of freedom. The rod is usually adjusted to move in a vertical direction when touched and return to the initial position on release. The dolphin quickly determines that this is the proper way to push the rod with its rostrum. As soon as an active spot is found, the dolphin is permitted to push the rod in order to either turn the stimulus on or turn the stimulus off, depending on the site of the electrode in its brain.

"Both self-start or rewarding systems and self-stop or punishing systems were found and the threshold determined as had previously been done with the monkey.

"It is shown that the dolphin learns to turn on the rewarding stimulus and turn off the punishing stimulus more rapidly than does the monkey. It is also shown that in a rewarding or positively reinforcing zone the dolphin tends to vocalize in complex and startling ways. It vocalizes when first stimulated in this area or when stimulation is withdrawn after a period of self-start activity.

"Thus we conclude that the behavior of the bottlenose dolphin differs from that of the monkey in the following respects: Like the monkey, the dolphin uses any available external somatic motor output in order to push switches to stimulate its own brain for a wanted, or positive, or rewarding stimulus or to cut off an unwanted, or negative or punishing stimulation started by the apparatus. In contrast with the monkey, the dolphin uses its vocal output when this is effective in order to modify the responses obtained from the environment (in terms of brain stimulation). The dolphin can inhibit violent escape behavior caused by "punishing" brain stimulation; the macaque does not do this. The large brain of the dolphin thus affords: (a) faster learning, (b) greater control over reactions to stimulation of subcortical systems which are motivationally active, and (c) control and use of vocalizations to obtain 'rewards' and to stop 'punishments.' "

6.   (73)   Lilly, John C. 1962. "Cerebral Dominance in the Dolphin,"
Interhemispheric Relations and Cerebral Dominance. Vernon
Mountcastle, M.D., Editor. John Hopkins Press, Inc., Baltimore, Md., pp.
112–114.

No lateralization has been found in the use of the one flipper versus the other. Some tight swimming patterns in confined quarters tend to show a preference for one side.

The sleep pattern tends to be lateralized but alternating. The dolphins sleep with one eye closed at a time. The eye closures are 180 degrees out of phase. It is rare to have both eyes closed at once. The accumulated sleep for each eye runs from 120 to 140 minutes per day; in other words, a total time of twice these values. The sleep occurs in brief periods between each respiration running from 20 to 40 seconds per eye closure. A dolphin wakes up in order to take each breath.

Their nasal phonatory mechanisms are bilateral though unsymmetrical in structure. We have demonstrated that a dolphin can produce sounds quite independently from three separate emitters, the right and the left phonatory apparatus and the laryngeal mechanism. The laryngeal mechanism is midline and produces the extremely short pulses for the close-up sonar; i.e., echo recognition system. A given dolphin can either whistle or click with the right mechanism or whistle or click with the left

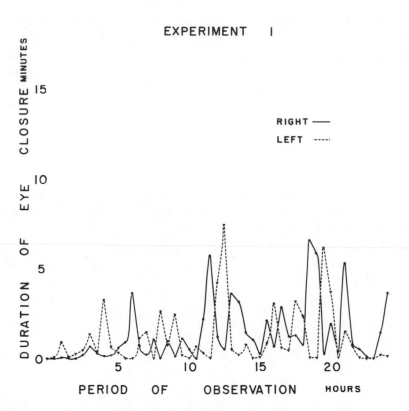

EXPERIMENT   I

RIGHT ——

LEFT -----

DURATION OF EYE CLOSURE MINUTES

PERIOD   OF   OBSERVATION   HOURS

FIGURE 13.   Sleep observation experiments: Experiment 1.

In this first experiment we have plotted the duration of the eye closures in minutes on the vertical coordinate and the time the observation was made on a twenty-four-hour clock in the horizontal coordinate. The tendency for alternation of closure between the two eyes can be seen in this figure. Both eyes are rarely closed. In the ten experiments the longest closure for both eyes together was three minutes. In this figure the longest closure for a single eye is seven minutes for the left eye.

FIGURE 14.   Sleep Experiment No. 10 of the series of 10.

The tendency for alternation of closure of the two eyes is shown further in this figure. There is some preponderance of closures of the left eye, the longest of which in this figure was thirteen minutes at hour No. 7.

FIGURE 15.   Summary of ten sleep experiments.

In this figure the frequency of occurrence of given durations of eye closure in seconds is plotted on log-log coordinates. This figure shows the tendency of the left eye to remain closed for a longer period than the right eye. This curve also shows that frequency of occurrence is very much increased for short intervals over the longer intervals of closure. There are something of the order of sixty cases of intervals shorter than five seconds in duration and only seven cases of durations of seventy seconds. This shows the tendency of the dolphin to take extremely short catnaps, alternately closing one eye and the other. Both eyes are rarely closed together. Both eyes are opened for every breath. These experiments were done in the Communication Research Institute in Miami, Florida, in 1960.

178

EXPERIMENT 10

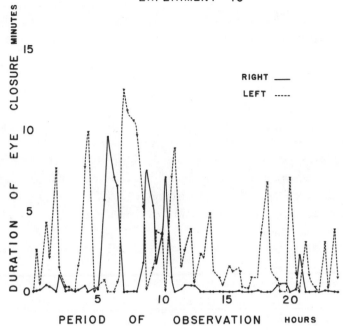

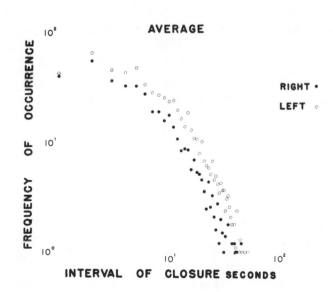

mechanism quite independently of the other. A pair of dolphins communicating with all three mechanisms sound like six individuals.

Eye movements are quite independent of one another; a given animal can scan 180 degrees of solid visual angle on each side of its body quite independently of the eye movements of the other side. There is a stereoscopic binocular field forward and downward and forward and upward that they use close up in the water for seeing and grabbing their fish. The motor cortex of these animals was mapped in the unanesthetized state. Monocular eye movements were found contralaterally and the binocular eye movements are represented homolaterally and contralaterally.

To gross inspection the two halves of the brain look equal. The corpus callosum in the adult is well developed, as are all the subcortical cross-connections.

When upset emotionally, the dolphin's bark or angry buzz is a highly symmetrical and single-minded operation utilizing all three of the sound producers.

It has not yet been determined whether there is any lateralization of language in the cerebral cortices, since we as yet do not have a secure hold on the meaning of any of the sounds except those emitted during emotional states.

7.   (75)   Lilly, John C. 1962. "A New Laboratory for Research on Delphinids." *Association of Southeastern Biologists Bulletin,* vol. 9, pp. 3–4.

On the cover is shown a photograph of the Communication Research Institute Delphinid Laboratory at St. Thomas, U.S. Virgin Islands. The inside is essentially a description of this laboratory giving a description of the wave ramp, the sea pool, and the structure of the laboratory building. A more complete description is given in *The Mind of the Dolphin* and in *Lilly on Dolphins.*

8.   (76)   Lilly, John C. 1962. "Interspecies Communication." *Year Book of Science and Technology.* Mc Graw-Hill, New York. Pp. 279–281.

Up to the present time man, *Homo sapiens,* is the only species of animal on Earth or in the sea known to communicate by means of spoken and written language. Even though there is a Babel of human tongues, it is possible for an individual human to learn to communicate with other humans in a language different from his native one. Man has not yet spoken with another species. The chimpanzee, Viki, learned to say only "mama, papa, cup, and up" in a highly explosive fashion.

Criteria for candidate selection for interspecies communication with man: A mammalian brain above a certain critical weight, a brain of a certain degree of complexity, an adequate vocalization apparatus, a naturally cooperative attitude toward man, sufficient control over emotional impulses (such as aggression, sexual activities, and so on) and ability to learn quickly to select the appropriate sonic and other patterns from the environment. Also in our criteria is the ability to receive and transmit nonverbal gestures associated with the meaning of the vocal exchanges. Theoretically, there does not seem to be a necessarily fixed relation between the actual development of a natural nonhuman language and the unrealized ability to learn one of the human languages. In the Communication Research Institute, in addition to native "delphinese" sounds, dolphins are found to emit high-pitched sounds that have been variously described as quacks, squawks, wails, bleats, barkings, and buzzings. The striking similarity of some of these sounds to those of the human voice has been observed. The tendency of some bottle-nosed dolphins to produce many of these "humanoid" sounds while hearing human speech has been interpreted as mimicking.

Neurophysiological studies. The dolphin's cerebral cortex resembles the human cortex in its vast size, its complicated fissuration patterns, its six layers of cortical cells, and its high cellular (neuronal) densities. Prof. E. Grünthal has called attention to the striking similarity of these brains to those of the highest primates, including man.

The neurophysiological exploration of the dolphin's brain reveals some similarity to the human one (as opposed to smaller-brained animals) with respect to vast "silent" areas, a restricted "motor strip" that causes muscle movements when stimulated, and large and well-differentiated areas for eye movements (both uniocular and binocular). As has been shown by W. Schevill, B. Lawrence, W. N. Kellogg, and K. Norris, dolphins can recognize objects and navigate among obstacles in murky water or darkness by use of the echoes of short recurrent pulses of sound produced in their heads. Their possession of such an ability and the human's lack of it may be a handicap to development of interspecies communication.

9.   (78)   Lilly, John C. 1962. "Vocal Behavior of the Bottlenose Dolphin."
Proceedings of The American Philosophical Society, vol. 106, pp. 520–529.

This paper summarizes the work to date on the naturally occurring sounds of the dolphins, on the naturally occurring vocal exchanges between dolphins and the production of sounds by dolphins in contact with man.

The paper starts out with the history of the dolphin and the literature of ancient Greece and Rome.

"Aristophanes (448 to 380 B.C.) wrote in *The Frogs,* '[the dolphin] races here and oracles there.' Aristotle (384 to 322 B.C.) wrote in *Historia Animalium (The History of Animals),*

> the dolphin when taken out of the water, gives squeaks and moans in the air ... for this creature has a voice (and can therefore utter vocal or vowel sounds), for it is furnished with a lung and a windpipe; but its tongue is not loose, nor has it lips, so as to give utterance to an articulate sound (or a sound of a vowel and a consonant in combination).

"Gaius Plinius Secundus (the Elder) (A.D. 23–79) wrote *"pro voce gemitus humano similis"* (for a voice [the dolphin] has a moaning or a wailing similar to that of the human).

"Many scholars have labeled these and similar ancient writings as farfetched, mythical, legendary, imaginative, and apocryphal. Such deductions of these scholars in regard to the dolphin should be questioned in the light of the findings presented in this paper.

"In brief it looks as though the ancients knew more about these animals than any of the subsequent scholars. We have succeeded in training dolphins to produce sounds which resemble spoken English. We have so taught them with only one piece of apparatus other than that available to the ancient Greeks. The modern apparatus is the magnetic tape recorder. This machine aided us in obtaining our first insights by allowing us to slow down the high speed and high-pitched productions of the dolphins and thus to recognize they can produce humanoid sounds.

"An animal can whistle and click, and as we first demonstrated, can do so simultaneously. Quite recently we have discovered that such emissions come from the two separate phonation mechanisms in their nasal sacs (first described by Lawrence and Schevill), one in the right nasal passage and other in the left nasal passage.

"In regard to the so-called jaw-clap we have found that when an animal emits a very short, sharp series of loud clicks that he tends to open and close his mouth very rapidly. (This gesture acts as a threat.) We have seen other animals move rapidly away from such a gesturing and vocalizing animal and we ourselves pull our hand or leg or arm rapidly away from such animal. Such a gesture combined with a loud, short click train probably gave rise to the mistaken notion of a 'jaw clap.' There seems to be no way that the jaws themselves or the teeth could give a clap or a snap.

"Several authors have described a special kind of clicking which using the analogue of the creaking rusty hinge has been dubbed 'creakings.' This seems usually to be associated with food finding and food recognition and is thought to be evidence of the activity of these animals' excellent 'sonar' operations, described by Schevill, Norris, Kellogg and others.

"Some of our recent studies throw doubt on the necessary and sufficient *sonic creakings* as the source of the sonar pulses. In our experience there are *ultrasonic pulses* quite separately emitted from the *sonic pulses*. If one listens with a radio receiver connected to a hydrophone at about 100 kilocycles every so often one can hear a stream of pulses being emitted straight ahead from the given animal. Such ultrasounds can be dissociated from any sonic output whatsoever. The ultrasonic pulses can be locked in or not locked in with sonic pulses. When the sonic pulses are associated with the ultrasonic, they are apparently being used to communicate the sonar information to the nearby animal by means of the lower communication (sonic) band of frequencies.

[It is perfectly possible to hear the ultrasonic pulses on some types of home tape recorders when the input is overloaded by the high amplitude of the pulses hitting the hydrophone. The overload causes an electrical rectification of the very high amplitude pulses and reduces their frequency by stripping off the envelope of the amplitude changes, thus reproducing them. This point has led to a lot of confusion in the past literature. In our case we made sure that there were no electrical overloads of any of the equipment during the above observations.]

During the course of our studies on the bottle-nosed dolphin we found definitive evidence that they do exchange some of the above sounds [whistles, clicks, and ultrasonic clickings] in appropriate fashions.

Each animal waits until the other animal is either silent, as in the case of the whistles, or there is an opportunity to alternate within the train in the case of clicks. One can hear click exchanges going on between two animals with little overlap. A close study of the overlap shows that they alternate their clicks during the period of overlap. The whistles are very politely exchanged, except for one case called a duet. The sonic spectograph analysis of this kind of exchange shows some of the real complexities of these whistles. The sonogram was reproduced from Lilly and Miller December 1961. The fundamental frequency is usually continuous, the first, second, third, fourth, and higher harmonics are usually discontinuous. They have found that some of the harmonics of these whistles can still be detected as high as 150 kilocycles (kHz). The harmonics appear and disappear in complex ways.

"Each dolphin's voice differs very much from each other voice. For example, some animals fill in between emissions with low frequency whistling.

"Analysis of the sounds called a bark or a mewing or a wailing depending upon its duration, and show each to be a fast series of clicks.

"These sounds are used naturally in what one might call *emotional exchanges*. If one dolphin is irritated with the behavior of another one or of a human observer, he emits such a rapid series of clicks at great intensity and at the same time makes gestures such as rapid head movements, either vertically or horizontally, with the mouth either open or closed. Such movements and sounds signify in no uncertain terms that the animal is emotionally upset.

"For example, if an observer puts a leg into the tank and the dolphin does not want him to enter the tank at that point, such a sound may be emitted just before the animal begins to bang on the leg with the side of his jaw in rapid oscillating movements. They will treat one another in similar fashion though sometimes even more violently than they treat the humans. After several weeks in captivity dolphins apparently learn that humans do not hear these sounds emitted under water very easily, and they begin to express their state by emitting such sounds in air above water aimed at the particular human involved."

The rest of the paper is devoted to the production of sounds by dolphins in contact with man. When animals are first placed in captivity they tend to emit their sounds under water. Slowly but surely they begin to emit their sounds in air, keeping the delphinic patterns of sound.

"After several weeks of such noises one begins to notice a changing pattern of the airborne sounds to more complex sounds involving longer emissions, greater richness of selection of frequencies and harmonics. In our experience such changes occur if and only if people have been talking to the animals directly and very loudly individually. Slowly but surely these sounds become more and more like those of human speech."

This fact was discovered in 1957 when working with brain electrodes.

"The first copies of the human voice by the dolphin (in 1957 and 1958) were at a relatively low amplitude. The most recent ones on the part of our three current animals are sometimes painfully loud for the human observer. The development of these sounds by a given dolphin is as follows:

"Our longest observations have been of an animal by the name of Elvar who joined us on the fifth of July, 1960.

"By persistent efforts in September 1961 we were able to determine that Elvar was quite capable of the production of sounds like those of human speech.

"However, he was emitting these sounds in frequencies well

above those which the normal human adult male or female emits. They were more comparable to those emitted by a very small child as it begins to emit these sounds in a very high pitched falsetto. Resemblances to human speech were heard by slowing the tapes down by a factor of 2 or 4. By the first of September 1961, Elvar had accomplished the first task which we had set him; i.e., emitting sequences of sounds bearing a high-pitched resemblance to the sounds that human beings employ in their speech activities. He had not yet formed any words which we could recognize; these sounds were more like the babbling of a baby before the words are acquired.

"In September we decided that he was ready for Step 2, the formation of understandable words. A typical experience is that of the 10th of September . . . he learned the words 'stop it' and the words 'bye bye.' Another example from the 23rd of October was 'more Elvar' . . ."

"In several experiments with different human observers and different human voices, it is shown that Elvar tends to examine each new human voice and attempts to reproduce the novel characteristics of that voice compared to the previous one. Example of the 2nd of December 1961 with the words 'squirt water.'

"These results illustrate that the very large brain of *Tursiops truncatus* (20 to 40 per cent larger than that of the average human) may have within its complex structure speech capabilities, if not realized, at least potential, similar to those of the human.

"In the summary some of these emissions appear to be attempts on the part of the animal to reproduce words spoken by the investigators. Such mimetic activities are at times surprisingly clear and clean cut. Tests of the capability of these animals of using such 'words' appropriately are in progress."

10.   (81)   Lilly, John C. 1963. "Critical Brain Size and Language." *Perspectives in Biology and Medicine,* vol. VI, pp. 246–255.

This paper is an expanded discussion of that in *Man and Dolphin* about the critical absolute brain size and language.

"Primarily we are interested in human language. Can any correlation be found between brain weight, brain-weight to body-weight ratio (or any of the other biological measurements), and the acquisition of a complex language?

"Several lines of evidence suggest the possibility that at least in the mammalia there may be a *critical absolute brain size* below which language as we know it is impossible and above which language as we know it is possible and even probable (ref. *Man and Dolphin,* 1961). In saying 'language as we know it,' I am referring not to a literal slavish point of view of the human languages currently extant; I am referring rather to the ability of these languages to transmit, to store, and to carry from one mind to another certain kinds of and degrees of complexity of information. This information can contain data related to the past, the present, and the future, and expresses to the mind of the receiver (however imperfectly) the state of mind of the sender, his plans, his actions, his problems. Hypothetically, a nonhuman language may use a logic which is totally strange, an apparent external form which may be bizarre to humans, and contain ways of looking at information which are totally unfamiliar. Thus when I say, 'language as we know it,' I am referring more to ideational content and to the successful influencing of one person by another through the medium of a language than I am to the detailed phonation mechanism and forms of words, sentences, paragraphs, etc.

"The lines of reasoning and evidence which suggest this working hypothesis of a critical brain size are as follows: (a) modern information and computer theory (refs. 8 and 9); (b) clinical evidence from the examination of human beings with small brains (ref. 10); (c) psychological studies on the development of normal human children acquiring language (see Table 1); (d) results of dedicated attempts to teach small-brained primates a human language (ref. 13); and (e) results of some of our experiments and experiences with the bottlenose dolphin *(Tursiops truncatus)"* (ref. 7).

The increasing size of the silent associational cortex as the size of the brain increases is discussed. The necessity of the silent associational cortex for the development of language is brought out in detail.

"We have made some progress in this area and have found out that *Tursiops* does have a relatively small fraction of the cerebral cortex given over to primary motor functions and that this motor cortex has extremely well differentiated movements represented within it, especially for the crossed monocular and dual binocular eye movements. Similarly, we have shown that there are vast areas of the cerebral cortex of *Tursiops* which are non-motoric as comparable large areas in the human. We as yet do not know what functions these areas serve and do not have sufficient data on the possible functions to test for the analogues of human speech. The primary projection areas for the various peripheral receptors are currently being explored, including visual and acoustic. The size of the acoustic cortex is yet to be determined. [It was later determined by Morgane, et al.]"

There is then a summary of the findings on the sonic and ultrasonic emissions of *Tursiops* and a summary of their ability to make humanoid noises in air in response to human stimulation.

"Observers who do and will do productive 'language' research on *Tursiops truncatus* are those who use a minimum of preconception about what will be and will not be found. The dolphins may learn English (or Russian) or they may not; they may have a complex language of their own or they may not. The evidence suggests these are probably productive areas of research. At the present stage of the science of these animals we do not know for certain. We are keeping our minds open to as many productive possibilities as can be encompassed."

The paper ends with a pertinent quote from D. O. Hebb,

> It is clearly implied that scientific investigation proceeds first by the collection of facts and arrives secondly at generalizations from the facts. Speculations and the *a priori* postulate are both ruled out. This is the classical view, deriving from Bacon, but it has been known for some time to be false. No research that breaks new ground will be done in this way; the collection of facts, from which to generalize, demands the guidance of imaginative speculation.

"One may add that the imaginative speculation must be disciplined by integrative feedback with the new facts as they are discovered."

11.   (82)   Lilly, John C. 1963. "Distress Call of the Bottlenose Dolphin: Stimuli and Evoked Behavioral Responses." *Science,* vol. 139, pp. 116–118.

This paper is the first description of the distress call of the bottle-nosed dolphin. Sonograms up to 16 kHz are given showing the rising crescendo and the falling decrescendo in the whistle, also shows the harmonics of those whistles.

Abstract. Analysis of the many different vocal productions of pairs of bottle-nosed dolphins *(Tursiops truncatus,* Montagu) and the related behavior patterns shows that one pair of specific short (0.2 to 0.6 second) whistles was consistently stimulated by physical distress. This call stimulated nearby animals to push the head of the distressed animal to the surface to breathe. After the animal breathed, a vocal exchange preceded other forms of aid.

The first part of the distress call may be used alone and this seems to be "an attention call" without expressing distress, meant to reach any animals who may be within hearing distance.

12.   (83)   Lilly, John C. 1963. "Productive and Creative Research with Man and Dolphin" (Fifth Annual Lasker lecture, Michael Reese Hospital and Medical Center, Chicago, Ill. 1962). *Archives of General Psychiatry,* vol. VIII, pp. 111–116.

Excerpts are as follows:

"If one works with a bottlenose dolphin day in and day out for many hours, days and weeks, one is struck with the fact that one's current basic assumptions and even one's current expectations determine within certain limits the results attained with a particular animal at that particular time. (This effect, of course, is quite commonly found with one's peers in the human species).

"This working hypothesis of an advanced capability raised our index of suspicion and in turn sensitized our minds and methods to new sources of information. It was this subtle preparation of the mental climate which allowed us in 1957 to listen to some rather queer noises that the dolphin was producing in the laboratory and to review them very carefully on the tapes. Because the possibility of a very large brain capacity and because of musings about the possible areas of achievement already realized in this species, but as yet undiscovered by us, our minds began to open.

"This opening of our minds was a subtle and yet painful process. We began to have feelings which I believe are best described by the word 'weirdness.' The feeling was that we were up against the edge of a vast uncharted region in which we were about to embark with a good deal of mistrust in the appropriateness of our own equipment. The feeling of weirdness came on us as the sounds of this small whale seemed more and more to be forming words in our own language. We felt we were in the presence of Something, or Someone who was on the other side of a transparent barrier which up to this point we hadn't even seen. The dim outlines of a Someone began to appear. We began to look at this whale's body with newly opened eyes and began to think in terms of its possible 'mental processes,' rather than in terms of the classical view of a conditionable, instinctually functioning 'animal.' We began to apologize to one another for slips of the tongue in which we would call dolphins 'persons' and in which we began to use their names as if they *were* persons. This seemed to be as much of a way of grasping at straws of security in a rough sea of the unknown, as of committing the sin of Science of Anthropomorphizing. If these 'animals' have 'higher mental processes,' then they in turn must be thinking of us as very peculiar (even stupid) beings indeed."

Then follows an account of the mimicry phenomena with Elvar and other dolphins.

"The repeatedly painful and humbling part of this experience that we as human beings had felt that man is at the top: we are alone; yet here is an 'animal' which was entering into that which was peculiarly human; i.e., human speech. At no matter how primitive a level he was entering into it, he was taking Step #1.

"To convey to you our sense of wonder and yet the sense of the uncomfortable necessity of continuously reorganizing our basic assumptions is difficult. We gambled on Elvar's taking the first step and he did. (We haven't done as well with his delphinese language.) He impressed us with the fact that he took the first step to repair a gap of at least 30,000,000 years in a few weeks. He may be skipping some of the belabored efforts of the human race for the last 40,000 years to achieve our present degree of articulate speech among ourselves. Maybe he is not skipping. Maybe he is just beginning what *Homo sapiens* went through 40,000 years ago. *And he first did it when and only when we believed he could do it and somehow demonstrated our belief to him.*"

Then it goes on with an account of Chee-Chee.

"These experiences illustrate the thesis that one can protect one's self by maintaining one's ignorance by belittling disturbing experiences, or one can newly recapture sensitivity and be open-minded (even painfully so) and *discover* new facts. Discovery, in my experience, requires disillusionment first, as well as later. One must be shaken in one's basic beliefs before the discovery can penetrate one's mind sufficiently above threshold to be detected. A certain willingness to face censure, to be a maverick, to question one's beliefs, to revise them, is obviously necessary. But what is not obvious is how to prepare one's own mind to receive the transmissions from the far side of the protective transparent wall separating each of us from the dark gulf of the unknown. Maybe we must realize that we are still babies in the universe, taking steps never before taken. Sometimes we reach out from our aloneness for someone else who may or may not exist. But at least we reach out, and it is gratifying to see our dolphins reach also, however primitively. They reach toward those of us who are willing to reach toward them. It may be that some day not too far distant we both can draw to an end the 'long loneliness,' as Loren Eiseley called it."

13. (85) Lilly, John C. 1964. "Animals in Aquatic Environment. Adaptation of Mammals to the Ocean." *Handbook of Physiology, Environment I.* American Physiological Society, Washington, D.C. pp. 741–757.

"How and why the whales have developed and why they need such large brains to adapt successfully to the marine environment are questions that have been of great interest for many years. [There follows a review of the classical theory of the origin of cetaceans as given by Kellogg and Winge.]

TABLE 1. Brain and Body Weights of Whales (Cetaceans)

Genus and Species	Common Name	Qty.	Cat. No.	Sex	Brain Wt., g	Body Wt., kg	Body Lgth., m	Remarks and Ref.
Phocaena phocaena (L)	Harbor porpoise	1	70ᵉ	M	1735ⁿ	142.43		Crile & Quiring (10)
		1			460ⁿ	53.80		Warncke's P. communis, see von Bonin (56)
Lagenorhynchus albirostris(G)	White-beaked porpoise	1			1126ᵃ	67.56		Warncke's wt., see von Bonin (56)
Tursiops truncatus (M)	Bottle-nose dolphin	1		F	1100ᵃ	45.50	1.626	Lilly & Miller (34)
		1		F	1175ᵇ	66.00	1.981	Lilly (30) and Kruger (23)
		1		F	1330ᵇ	97.70	2.159	Lilly (30) and Kruger (23)
		1		M	1520ᵇ	117.30	2.337	Lilly (30) and Kruger (23)
		1		F	1588ᵇ	140.00	2.400	Lilly (30) and Kruger (23)
		1		Fʰ	1685ᵇ	156.00	2.591	Lilly (30) and Kruger (23)
		1		F	1707ᵇ	153.60	2.565	Lilly (30) and Kruger (23)
		1			1886ᵃ	287.00		Warncke's T. tursio. see von Bonin (56)
Orcinus orca(L)	Pacific killer whale	1		F	4500ᵃ	1861.70	5.23	Unpublished data
Globicephala melaena(T)	Pilot whale	1			2458ᵃ	983.00		Warncke's G. melas, see von Bonin (56)
Delphinapterus leucas(P)	White whale	2	1) 32)	F	2354ᵃ	303.23		Crile & Quiring (10)
		4	7) 19) 23)					
Balaenoptera acutorostrata(L)	Little piked whale	1	34)	M	2349ᵃ	441.31		Crile & Quiring (10)
					2490ᵃ	62,250		Warncke's B. rostrata, see von Bonin (56)
Megaptera novaeangliae(B)	Hump-backed whale	1			3531ᵃ	42,372		Warncke's M. boöps, see von Bonin (56)

Species	Common name	No.	Specimen	Sex	Brain wt (g)	Body wt	Length (m)	Reference
Balaenoptera physalus(L)	Finback whale	1	Cst.3	F	5970[d]		15.240	Jansen (18, 19)
		1	Cst.1	F	6500[a]		20.726	Jansen (18, 19)
		1	C294	M	6850[d]		16.459	Jansen (18, 19)
		1	C291	M	6920[d]		19.812	Jansen (18, 19)
		1	Cst.2	M	7100[a]		16.459	Jansen (18, 19)
		1	Cst.2	M	7320[e]		16.459	Jansen (18, 19)
		1	C293	M	7150[d]		20.421	Jansen (18, 19)
		1	C292	F	7875[d]		20.421	Jansen (18, 19)
		1			6700[a,f]		18.288	Guldberg's *B. musculus* Company, see Tower (53)
								Ries and Langworthy, see Tower (53)
Sibbaldus musculus(L)	Blue or sulfur whale	1			5950[d]			Warncke's *B. musculus*, see von Bonin (56)
		1	748		3636[a]	50,904		Crile & Quiring (10)
		1			6800[a]	58,059		Wilson's *B. sulfurea*, see Tower (53)
		1			5678[a]			
Physeter catadon	Sperm whale	16			6400–9200[a,g]	264,000	14.935–16.459	Kojima (22)
		1			7000[a]			Ries and Langworthy, see Tower (53)
		1			7980[a]			Ries and Langworthy, see Tower (53)

[a] Fresh. [b] Fresh, perfused with 10% formalin. [c] After 1 month in 10% formalin. [d] After more than 1 year in 10% formalin. [e] Catalog number used by authors indicated. [f] Without dura. [g] Average, 7800 g. [h] Pregnant.

"In Table 1 are the brain and body weights of whales known up to the present time, running from the smallest to the largest (460 to 9,200 grams). The ancient whales, the archaeoceti, had cranial capacities from 310 cc's to greater than 800 cc's of the order of 25–50 millions of years ago.

"The finding of the voluntary nature of respiration in the bottlenose dolphin is recounted with the discovery of a respiratory center in the nucleus ellipticus of the thalamus, a special nucleus found only in the cetaceans. Stimulation of this nucleus by electrical stimuli through implanted electrodes causes explosive respiratory acts to take place in extremely rapid succession. Thus the Cetacea possess a very well developed respiratory control center, at least as high as the thalamus. Presumably this nucleus also has projections to and from the cerebral cortex [which allow the voluntary control of respiration in this animal].

"In order to maintain the completely nasal nature of their respiratory patterns (i.e., breathing through the blow-hole and not through the mouth) means that whales must somehow cross the respiratory tract through the alimentary tract. The classic literature on cetology maintains that the larynx is inserted in the nasal pharynx and held there by a strong sphincter at all times. Recently we have found that these animals do not hold the larynx in this position at all times and that during feeding and swallowing the larynx is freed, laid in the bottom of the pharynx and the food is passed over it. If one carefully examines a cross-sectional anatomy of these animals one finds that when the larynx is held in the nasal pharynx there is not room between the larynx and the bone of the lower jaw to pass food of the size which these animals normally swallow. If one examines an animal during feeding one can palpate the throat region and find the larynx being pulled downwards and pushed outwards during the swallowing act.

"Nutrition. It is found that the full fish ration of the dolphin per day adequately furnishes the necessary supplies of water without the ingestion of sea or fresh water; the water is derived totally from the protein and the fat of the diet.

"If a dolphin of approximately 400 lbs. is kept out of water the skin sloughs off very rapidly unless it is kept wet. Even if the skin is kept wet and shaded the animal will probably expire within six days, apparently because of cardiovascular overload. Each breath under these conditions is a laborious event; for the first time in its life the animal must lift a large portion of its body weight against gravity in order to inflate the lungs. Similarly the intrathoracic pressure rises and impedes the venous return to the chest and to the heart. Thus, their adaptation to the swimming buoyant environment has eliminated adaptation to the pressures of the gravity-countering forces distributed over small areas of the body.

"Sleep. In another adaptation in *Tursiops truncatus* the buoyant swimming environment is the sleep pattern which has been observed recently in our laboratory. In brief, the sleep pattern consists in waking for every respiration and rising to the surface for each breath, if not already at the surface. An apparently unique feature of their sleep pattern is that they sleep with one eye closed at a time. In a series of ten 24-hour experiments in our laboratory it was found that closure of both eyes is an extremely rare event. The period of sleep for each eye totals two to three hours a day. This pattern may assure that the animal is always scanning his environment with at least half of its afferent inputs."

The work of others on sonar is then recounted and a summary given of our discovery of the distress call and the attention call. Our finding of vocal exchanges between pairs of dolphins and the postulation of a dolphin language called "delphinese" is recounted.

"Language concepts. The existence of such language, if proved, will give these animals a means of cooperative adaptation to the marine environment par excellence, which could not be obtained by individuals isolated from one another. If this postulated language is more complex than that of birds, fishes, reptiles and the smaller brained mammals, from the chimpanzee down, the degree of adaptation will correspond to the degree of complexity and level of abstraction which can be transmitted from one animal to the other. The fantastically great gain in adaptive abilities of those who have such a language is most easily demonstrated by another species, *Homo sapiens*. As soon as man acquired language he adapted so rapidly and so well to his environment that he was able to eliminate practically all competing species.

"The large brains of cetaceans have raised many additional intriguing questions. One may well ask if such a large brain may not be capable of not only a natural language but of possibly even adaptively learning a human language. Experiments in the Communication Research Institute along these lines have revealed the following findings:

"1) These animals are capable of phonation of proper dolphin noises in air as well as under water.

"2) If in contact close enough and long enough with persons who are speaking, these animals gradually modify the noises they emit and gradually acquire new noises which begin to resemble the noises of human speech.

"3) Slowly but surely some of these emissions begin to correspond to distinct, human sounds, recognizable words are separated out.

"4) Modifications and variations of these words are produced in great profusion.

"Such flexibility and plasticity of the use of the phonation apparatus of these animals demonstrates an adaptive capability heretofore completely unsuspected. In a sense, these animals who are producing humanoid sounds have adapted to a totally new set of circumstances; i.e., close contact with man, in such a way as to excite interest on our part and to prompt further care of the animals. In a sense, then, the animals are taking full advantage of this artificial environment for their own survival and well-being in a fashion similar to most of the successful individuals of the species, *Homo sapiens*."

14. (85-A) Nagel, E. L., P. J. Morgane, and W. L. McFarland. 1964. "Anesthesia for the Bottlenose Dolphin, *Tursiops truncatus*," reprinted from *Science*, vol. 146, no. 3651, pp. 1591–1593.

This is essentially a follow-up in confirmation of the work published in *Man and Dolphin*, pages 35 through 42, reference no. 70, 1961. The one additional factor is carrying the manual respirator of 1955 to an automatic respirator devised by Forest Bird, called a Cetacean respirator, Mark 9X. This paper confirms the 1955 intubation procedure inserting a 1-inch-diameter tube in through the throat of the dolphin and into the larynx in order to furnish the air supply to the lungs. Text Figure 4 is a good diagram of the relationships of the mouth and the blowhole respiratory approaches. Using the respirator devised in this study, later Dr. Sam Ridgeway of the navy repeated the work and showed that major surgery was made possible by means of this respirator to carry the dolphins through anesthesia.

15. (86) Jacobs, Myron S., Peter J. Morgane, John C. Lilly, and Bruce Campbell. 1964. "Analysis of Cranial Nerves in the Dolphin." *Anatomical Record,* vol. 148, p. 379.

This work gave the following nerve population counts for the dolphin: optic nerve, 114,300; oculomotor nerve, 6,500; trochlear nerve, 1,900; trigeminal nerve, 159,000; abducens nerve, 1,700; facial nerve, 32,500; statoacoustic nerve, 112,500.

16. (87) Lilly, John C. 1964. "Airborne Sonic Emissions of *Tursiops truncatus* (M)." *Journal of the Acoustical Society of America,* vol. 36, pp. 5, 1007.

"During the first few days in confinement the usual large underwater sonic repertoire of *Tursiops* can be recorded. Airborne emissions are rare, exceptional individuals (three out of forty observed) produce in air sounds usually heard under water and then become 'air-silent.' In many cases after 8–24 weeks in confinement, the airborne emissions start. These complex sounds in air are specified by their amplitude patterns, basic repetition rates, frequency spectra, time courses and relations to underwater sounds produced concurrently and/or alternatively.... Some recorded evidence for some degree of apparent time-course coupling of trains of some of these emissions to similar emissions from other sources is presented."

17. (88) Lilly, John C. 1965. "Report on Experiments with the Bottlenose Dolphin." *Proceedings of the International Symposium on Comparative Medicine,* Eaton Laboratories, Norwich, Conn., p. 240.

"Currently medical research for humans cannot make progress without the help of animal research. A balanced regard for animals, an objective but interested point of view, is an appropriate stand for researchers. Researchers have a regard for their experimental animals which is comparable in some cases to the care of medical practitioners for their human patients. We have found that without such attentive care a dolphin in captivity does not maintain good health; with 'tlc' (tender loving care) dolphins do very well in a laboratory setting.

"If we as human beings may ever expect to speak to another species and have an exchange of ideas on the level with which we have exchange with one another, we must attenuate the effects of our tendency for intellectual segregation of all other organisms. In our laboratory as we decrease our psychological distance from individual dolphins they respond and meet us in a gratifying way."

18. (90) Lilly, John C. 1965. "Vocal Mimicry in *Tursiops*. Ability to Match Numbers and Durations of Human Vocal Bursts." *Science,* vol. 147 (3655), pp. 300–301.

"In addition to its normal underwater sonic communication path, the dolphin *(Tursiops truncatus)* can be trained to emit sounds from the blowhole opened in air. By proper rewarding (positive reinforcement) and evocative techniques, such vocal emissions can be changed from the natural patterns. One such group of new sounds is said to resemble the human voice (vocal mimicry). Aspects of these sounds which are physically determinable, specifiable, and demonstrable are the similarities in the numbers of bursts of sound emitted by the man and dolphin and in durations of successive emissions. In 92% of the exchanges the number of bursts emitted by *Tursiops* equal ±1 the number just previously emitted by a man in sequences of 1–10 bursts.

"These results show quantitatively the ability of *Tursiops* to mimic certain aspects of human vocal emissions. This ability seems to be one of many functions of the large brain (1700 g) of this mammal and entails severe modification of the naturally occurring complex vocalizations of *Tursiops*. Differences from observations of other animals are striking: even parrots and mynah birds apparently do not give such large numbers of replies and such sustained and accurate performances. To date only dolphins and humans share this ability."

19. (91) Lilly, John C. 1966. "Sexual Behavior of the Bottlenose Dolphin." *Brain and Behavior,* Volume III. *The Brain and Gonadal Function.* R. A. Gorski and R. E. Whalens, Editors. UCLA Forum on Medical Science, University of California Press, Los Angeles, California. P. 72-76.

"The gonadal region of the female is located on the ventral posterior portion of the body, where the tail joins the abdominal cavity. This slit includes both the anal and the genital openings. To be entered by the penis of the male, it must be pressed open, as it were, by the entering penis. The female has two mammary slits, one on each side of the genital slit. The nipples obtrude from the slits during suckling by the baby dolphin. The mammary glands themselves are buried deep within the body and extend anteriorly from the slits. The female has a bicornuate uterus, and although reports of single births predominate in the literature, Aristotle refers to the births of twins. Aristotle apparently knew these animals extremely well—we should not really look askance at anything he has related until we have evidence to the contrary; we have been able to corroborate some of his behavioral data which had been discounted by scholars during intervening centuries.

"The testicles of the male are buried in the body, extending anteriorly from the genital slit on each side, and are amazingly large. We have recently dissected an animal in which the testicles were twelve inches long, about two inches in diameter, and cylindrical in shape. The penis of a fully developed male is approximately six inches long, and with eight inches maximum for length. The base, fore and aft, is about four to five inches, and the tip is only a couple of millimeters in diameter.

"When a female and a male dolphin are confined in a relatively small area in captivity, the courting behavior is rather violent. If they are isolated with a movable barrier between them, they will resolve all kinds of problems in order to be together, e.g., opening a gate to gain access to another pool and closing it behind them. As soon as they are together they start pursuit games. The initial phases of this behavior appear violent and can continue for the first 24 hours. If the female is not receptive, the male continues to chase her, exhibits erections, rubs against her, and tries to induce her to accept him. They bite one another; they scratch each other's bodies with their teeth. During the mating procedure, they will develop lesions practically everywhere on their bodies specifically on the flippers, on the back, on the flukes, on the peduncle, and around the head region.

"The erection in the male occurs with extreme rapidity. We have observed and timed it in our own tanks: it is something in the order of three seconds to completion, from the time the penis first appears in the slit. It can collapse almost as rapidly, and it looks almost as if it were being done in a voluntary fashion. It is very easy to condition a dolphin to have an erection. The stimulus, for example, can be a single visual signal. One trainer chose to raise his arm vertically as a signal, and the dolphin would turn over and erect his penis in response. If Elvar, one of our dolphins, is alone and a small ring, about a foot in diameter and an inch thick, is tossed into the water, he will have an erection, with his penis lift it off the bottom and tow it around the tank."

A movie was then shown and a verbal description of the behavior shown on the movie follows.

The report ends with the following paragraph.

"We thought for a while that ultrasonic clicking was only sonar, but they use it for communication when they apparently do not want us to hear them. We detect this with wild dolphins; they will start buzzings and whistle-like noises which when converted are found to be originally around 150 kcps. This seems to be more or less a security problem, because the range of ultrasonic frequencies in water is much smaller than that of the sonics."

20.   (91-A)   Galliano, R. E., P. J. Morgane, W. L. McFarland, E. L. Nagel, and R. L. Catherman. 1966. "The Anatomy of the Cervicothoracic Arterial System in the Bottlenose Dolphin *(Tursiops truncatus)* with a Surgical Approach Suitable for Guided Angiography." *Anatomical Record,* vol. 155, pp. 325–338.

There are figures showing the results of X-ray visualization of the circulation of the dolphin to the rete mirabile and the brain. Other figures show the surgical approach to the external carotid and the external jugular vein, and there is a photograph of the left side of the dolphin with a healed incision two and one half months after surgery.

21. (92) Lilly, John C. 1966. "Sonic-Ultrasonic Emissions of the Bottlenose Dolphin." *Whales, Dolphins and Porpoises*. Kenneth Norris, Editor. *Proceedings of the First International Symposium on Cetacean Research*. Washington, D.C. 1963. University of California Press. Pp. 503–509.

"A summary of the findings of the Communication Research Institute over the last five years is as follows:

"1. Underwater, three different, independently controlled emissions are generated by each individual isolated animal (2 kcps to 80 kcps at least).

"2. In air at least two different, independently controlled emissions are generated by each individual isolated animal (300 kcps to at least 30 kcps).

"3. Underwater or in air, shifting from one to the other alternately over short time periods (a few milliseconds), a given individual animal generates at least two different, independently controlled emissions.

"The remainder of this paper is a summary of the published material pertaining to these matters."

(There are good single-paragraph summaries of "Sounds Emitted by the Bottlenose Dolphin," "Vocal Exchanges Between Dolphins," "Distress Call of the Bottlenose Dolphin: Stimuli and Evoked Behavioral Responses," "Vocal Behavior of the Bottlenose Dolphin," and papers by McBride and Hebb, 1948; F. G. Wood, Jr., 1954; Kellogg, 1953, 1958, 1959 and 1961; Schevill and Lawrence, 1953, 1956; Norris, 1961.)

22. (93) Lilly, John C. 1966. "The Need for an Adequate Model of the Human End of the Interspecies Communication Program." IEEE Military Electronics Conference on Communication with Extraterrestrial Intelligence, Washington, D.C., 1965. *IEEE Spectrum,* vol. 3, no. 3, pp. 153–163.

"As long as the conscious-unconscious basic belief exists of the preeminence of the human brain and mind over all of other earthside brains and minds, little credence can be obtained for the proposition that a problem of interspecies communication exists at all."

(Then the biocomputer theory is presented.)

"The phenomenon of computer interlock facilitates model construction and operation. One biocomputer interlocks with one or more other biocomputers above and below the level of awareness any time the communicational distance is sufficiently small to bring the interlock functions above threshold value.

"In the complete physical absence of other external biocomputers within the critical interlock distance, the self-directed and other-directed programs can be clearly detected, analyzed, recomputed, and reprogrammed, and new metaprograms initiated by the solitudinous computer itself.

"Sets of human motivational procedural postulates for the interlock research method on nonhuman beings, with biocomputers as large as and larger than the human biocomputers are sought. Some of these methods involved the establishment of long periods—perhaps months or years—of human to other organism biocomputer interlock. It is hoped that this interlock will be of a quality and value sufficiently high to permit interspecies communication efforts on both sides on an intense, highly structured level."

23.   (96)   Lilly, John C., and Henry M. Truby. 1966. "Measures of Human-*Tursiops* Sonic Interactions." *Journal of the Acoustical Society of America,* vol. 40, no. 5, p. 1241.

"Tursiops truncatus can be induced to produce airborne sounds in response to human utterances. These responses bear certain acoustic and visual-acoustic resemblance to the vocal stimuli. Under effective operant conditioning, the number of *Tursiops* humanoid emissions in a given response train precisely matches the number of human vocal emissions in the corresponding stimulus train. Tabulations based on the analysis of hundreds of such sonic interchanges demonstrate that *Tursiops* is capable of accurate matching of number of events for runs of over 40 stimulus-response interactions, in which the number of events in each train ranged as high as 10. In some experiments the human was replaced through the use of tape-recorded stimuli and an

automatic fish-dispenser, and, in some, the food reward was eliminated entirely to prevent its function as a signal. The incidence of either interpolation or overlap of response events with respect to stimulus events disappears with training. Differing vowel color and intonation contour of stimuli are reflected in humanoid variations of structure and contour by the dolphin. The correlation of humanoid and stimulus utterance is evident in acoustigraphic form. Tape-recorded examples are given, and apparent errors and interspecies considerations are discussed."

24. (99) Lilly, John C. 1967. "Dolphin-Human Relationship and LSD-25." *The Use of LSD in Psychotherapy and Alcoholism.* Harold Abramson, Editor (from the 1965 Amityville Conference). Bobbs-Merrill Co. Inc., New York, pp. 47–52.

The original hypothesis behind this work was based upon the voluntary nature of respiration in the dolphin. Anything that would modify a central nervous system activity as radically as LSD-25 does would interfere with respiration in the dolphin. The dolphin might stop breathing under the influence of LSD. The experiments were done with a standby respirator in case this effect took place.

"The effect of LSD was the opposite of that expected and the opposite of the effect of barbiturates; there was an acceleration of respiration (barbiturates at 10 mg per kg of body weight knocked out respiration completely necessitating the use of the respirator).

"With 100 micrograms of LSD-25 injected intramuscularly into a 400-lb. animal there was about a 50% increase in the respiratory rate and then a four times increase in the rate at the peak of the LSD-25 effect. At the same time the heart rate went up 20%.

"These effects were found with a stranded animal out of water. A dolphin is in a continuous state of anxiety when out of water. Simultaneous with respiration and heart rate we recorded vocalizations and derived a measure of vocal activity called 'the vocalization index.'

"The vocalization index is the fraction of time spent vocalizing per minute.

"Controls are run before and after the LSD experience and with an injected placebo and during the LSD experience. The findings were as follows:

"1. LSD raises the vocalization index to a level of 10–30 percent steadily with anxiety present.

"2. Without anxiety and without stimulation the duty cycle is zero.

"3. Under LSD with stimulation the vocalization index does not drop to zero at all. There is a sustained level and each stimulus increases the vocalization index and keeps it going in a very prolonged "after discharge" fashion. One stimulus will raise the vocalization index for about five minutes, without LSD it will raise it for only about fifteen seconds. We tried various levels of constraint and found that as we freed up the dolphin to the point at which it was allowed natural conditions of free swimming in deep water, the vocalization index dropped closer and closer to zero and then stayed there under LSD 25. We obtained a very brief enhancement of vocalization twenty minutes after the initial dose of 100 micrograms. When the dose was increased to 300 micrograms there was a more sustained effect over and above the results with placebos. (This placebo effect lasted about an hour at a very low level near zero.)

"During the LSD effect if a person enters the tank the vocalization index goes up and stays up. It rises only briefly without LSD.

"If a second dolphin is placed in with the first which has the LSD, the vocalization index rises and stays around 70% for the full three hours; in other words an appropriate exchange now begins to take place. The other animal is answering him and his vocalization index also is up.

"With the placebo the performance is very much lower, 10% as opposed to 70%.

"We find the vocalization index is a behavioral measure of a very sensitive process. The effective quantitative range over which this behavioral variable runs is about 4 log units.

"To utilize vocalization index effectively, running averages through the data must be done with a computer program.

"In the anxiety-producing situation the vocalization index can be produced by giving "tender loving care" such as stroking during this LSD state. The vocalization index can be reduced towards the normal value."

(There is then an account of Pam who for two and a half years after being shot with a spear gun three times through the tail stayed away from all human contacts. Under LSD she approached us and stayed with us for the period of the LSD effect.)

Then there is a discussion of the roots of psychotherapy and its relationship to the dolphin, and the importance of physical contact and the effects of LSD are summarized as follows: "The important thing for us with the LSD in the dolphin is that what we see has no meaning in the verbal sphere. The meaning resides completely in the non-verbal contact exchanges. This is where our progress has been made in the last three or four years in developing this other level because we were forced to. We have had to do it in order to make any progress on the vocalization and communication. In other words, we accept communication on any level where we can reach it. We are out of what you might call a rational exchange of complex ideas because we haven't developed communication in that particular way as yet. We hope to eventually."

(Then follows an account of Peter and Margaret in the St. Thomas laboratory and the human-dolphin relationship being similar to that of the mother-child relationship.)

"We learned quite quickly when we began this research that if anybody working with a dolphin assumed that the dolphin was stupid, then the dolphin would act stupid. If you went at the dolphin the way you would at a rat and tried to get him to perform, he'd perform very well for a short period of time. If the criteria were too strict, and you put him down in too narrow a slot, so that you bored him, he would break the apparatus and throw it out of the tank. We've had several psychologists who came to the lab expecting to work with the dolphins the way they would with rats; the dolphins would not put up with it. It is very dramatic when the system breaks down. We explained this to the psychologist and said, 'Get in the tank with them, make friends with them, and maybe they will put up with it a little longer.' It is very difficult to get humans to go into the tank with the dolphins.

"Another point is the basic beliefs with which one approaches this work. If you come believing in their intelligence, then listen to them, and let them tell you what the experiment is going to be; to a certain extent you let them dictate the terms on their side and you get the performance.

"I think it is important when working with such a large animal to make use of everything that we can possibly learn about our own species. The respect and integrity that we detect in our own species, we at least temporarily must attribute to the animals, and treat them in that fashion. The question of whether you call them animals or not seems to disappear in the laboratory. You now include yourself as an 'animal' and go on calling them 'animals.' Where you drop that term completely and go on calling them by one name—a dolphin. This is a measure of the warmth which has developed. Anybody who is still calling them animals in terms of cats and monkeys we sort of disown."

25. (100)   Lilly, John C. 1967. "Dolphin's Mimicry as a Unique Ability in a Step Towards Understanding." *Research in Verbal Behavior and Some Neurophysiological Implications.* Kurt Salzinger and Suzanne Salzinger, Editors. (Conference on Verbal Behavior, New York City, 1965). Academic Press, New York City. Pp. 21–27.

This paper gives the history of the discovery of the ability of dolphins to mimic sounds produced by humans. The discussion is based upon the audience of psychologists so that there is a lot of work on operant conditioning. The problem of primary reinforcement versus secondary reinforcements is discussed at some length. The necessity of acoustic novelty is discussed. There is some mention of input/output nerve fibers and their counts in the dolphin and in the human. There is a brief description of the double phonatory apparatus of the dolphin with double phonation and stereo phonation described as new processes. The use of the two diagonal membranes and the two nasal tongues for the formation of sounds as well as the laryngeal emitter are mentioned. Insofar as cerebral dominance is concerned alternating dominance and coordinated dominance between the two sides is mentioned.

"The only midline structure he has for his vocalization activity is the sonar apparatus which we now pin down to being the larynx. It is very different and quite separate from the communication at the lower frequencies.

"This is a summation of several years of research with the dolphin-human communication problems. We are pursuing this strange new field with new instruments and new methods. We need bright and flexible help from many fields including human acoustics and speech, psychology, computers, the humanities, psychoanalysis, psychopharmacology, veterinary medicine. There is a big future here; I hope Man sees and seizes this opportunity for new vistas, new thinking, new philosophies, and a new breakthrough to escape his solipsistic preoccupation in anthropocentric and anthropomorphic self-adulation of himself and of his fellows: the dolphins are still for us and with us. We need them."

26. (101) Lilly, John C. "Dolphin Vocalization." *Brain Mechanisms Underlying Speech and Language.* F. L. Darley, Editor. (Symposium at Princeton, N.J., 1965.) Grune & Stratton, New York City. Pp. 13–20.

This paper No. 101 and paper No. 100 "Dolphin's Mimicry as a Unique Ability in a Step Towards Understanding" are good papers to recommend reading with the paper No. 112, "Reprogramming of the Sonic Output of the Dolphin. Sonic Burst Count Matching." Nos. 101 and 100 give additional materials in a simpler way than does the reprogramming paper. For example, the table of vowels in 101 is given in English rather than in the way it was given in the later paper in 1968, No. 112. In addition, paper No. 90, "Vocal Mimicry in *Tursiops,*" should be read along with these other three. So for the mimicry effects so far we should have papers 90, 100, 101, and 112.

There is then a review of our findings on the neuroanatomy of *Tursiops.* There is a comparison between the dolphin behavior and that of the mimicking birds. Discussion following the paper is rather irrelevant; it is mainly about Thorpe's work with the mynah birds.

Final remarks on page 20 discuss the emphasis on the formants. Dr. Thorpe did not answer very well the question about the mynahs raised as a result of this discussion.

"All we are saying is that there are certain aspects in which the dolphin can mimic extremely accurately with new material over long periods of time and very complex sequences which the mynah bird or the parrot cannot do. The dolphin has abilities not matched by the bird and the bird has abilities the dolphin cannot match. The two are very, very different animals and both very, very different from us. Can Dr. Thorpe's mynahs produce on first exposure without practice ten nonsense syllables immediately after human utterance of them, and then 9, 3, 7, 2, and so forth at an average rate of one per second for stimuli and responses and latencies between the human and bird of 0.5 seconds?

Chairman Milliken: "Dr. Thorpe, do you have any final comment?"

Dr. Thorpe: "No, I don't think so, except to say that some birds also can imitate long and complex new sequences."

27. (103)   Lilly, John C. 1967. *The Mind of the Dolphin.* Doubleday and Company, Inc., New York, N.Y. 310 pages.

A complete account of the research up to 1967 given in terms for general audiences.

28. (104)   Lilly, John C. 1967. "Intracephalic Sound Production in *Tursiops truncatus;* Bilateral sources." *Federation Proceedings,* vol. 26, no. 2, March-April.

"*Tursiops truncatus* (bottlenose dolphin) in addition to sonar capability has means of production of two separate sounds simultaneously in an independent or a dependent relationship. By removing a *Tursiops* from the water and placing flat hydrophones in the proper positions on the head, the sounds from the separate sources can be observed and recorded independently. The results show that the major classes of sounds produced, including whistles, slow clickings, fast clickings (intracephalic and airborne) can be produced by at least two sources. Modulation of specific frequencies in the clicks can be achieved by two systems of air sacs, one on the right and one on the left side in the nasal passageway. Stereophonic listening and phase studies on the cathode-ray oscilloscope show that these two sources can function independently or can be phase-locked in such a way as to cause an apparent single source to move from one ear to the other ear during stereophonic listening. Anatomical studies show that the system of muscles controlling these sound producers and modulators are enervated by the facial (VII) nerve and the trigeminal (V) nerve." (See Text Figure 5.)

29.   (105)   Lilly, John C. 1967. "Human Biocomputer: Programming and Metaprogramming." Miami Communication Research Institute. Scientific Report No. CRI-0167.

This was the first edition of the human biocomputer. See No. 106.

30.   (106)   Lilly, John C. 1968. "Programming and Metaprogramming in the Human Biocomputer: Theory and Experiments." Miami Communication Research Institute. Scientific Report No. CRI-0167. 2nd. Edition.

This is the second edition of this work which was later published by the Julian Press. See No. 113 below. It was also published by Bantam Books. See No. 114 below.

31.   (110)   Truby, Henry M., and John C. Lilly. 1967. "The Psychoacoustic Implications of Interspecies Communication." *Journal of the Acoustical Society of America,* 42:1181.

"... As a corollary and prerequisite to the acoustic study of interspecies communication, consideration needs to be given to the psychoacoustic or psycholinguistic aspects of the problem. It should not, for example, be assumed that the communication systems (codes, "languages") of alien species bear resemblance to those of *Homo sapiens,* and they are very likely unlike any of the currently active 5000 mutually exclusive human languages. It is difficult enough for a given human speaker with a single native language to comprehend any language much unlike his own, in spite of the sharing, on both the transmitting and the receiving side, of similar frequency and time domains, as is true for all human languages, and he needs more than a little convincing that a plethora of languages contemporary with his own are by nature so radically different in structural design and coding that he could apply none of his inherent linguistic instincts to their comprehension. This leaves no opportunity for fundamental pattern or system comparisons, i.e., perhaps there is no lexical inventorying, no verbal system, no connectives, or the like; perhaps the temporal sequence is complexly coded; perhaps that which is basic to human linguistics is incidental or nonexistent in the codal organization of alien species. Consider, for example, the bottlenose dolphin *(Tursiops truncatus),* who has three sonic-ultrasonic emitters, two of which can be linked in double or stereo phonation, and the third of which is used for sonar operation. This species apparently has alternating cerebral dominance, high rates of body locomotion and other muscular-operation speeds, and an acoustic frequency range approximately 10 times that of the human at both the transmitting and receiving terminals. These factors are indicative of a vocalization capability that is not only highly complex but fundamentally different from that of *Homo sapiens.* The complement of the dolphins' apparent patience with and affinity for human association adds to the challenge for expert professional psychoacoustic and psycholinguistic research on this particular species, as preparation for designing *modi operandi* suitable for treating any encounterable nonhuman codes."

32.   (111)   Lilly, John C., Henry M. Truby, Alice M. Miller, and Frank Grissman. 1967. "Acoustic Implications of Interspecies Communication." *Journal of the Acoustical Society of America,* 42:1164.

". . . When, in interspecies exchange of information, the dominant modes of the communication are vocal and acoustic, some of the physical limitations imposed upon the communication are shown by the hearing curves and the acoustic energy output curves. Additional limitations are shown in the difference frequency limen curves and in certain time-pattern perception limitations. One such communication system is the interlock or feedback between a single individual *Homo sapiens* (Hs) and a single individual *Tursiops truncatus* (Tt). The speech output of Hs was measured with a high-frequency microphone; detectable amounts of energy were found above the generally accepted speech band, up to the order of 60 kc. This high-frequency energy is detectable by Tt as is shown by its hearing curve from 400 Hz to 160 kHz.

The usually accepted limits for Hs-Hs transmissions for 100% intelligibility are from approximately 100 Hz-10 kHz. The Hs-Hs feedback control thus is limited to approximately 10 kHz; i.e., energy above this limit is not controlled nor used by Hs. In the Hs-Tt transmission, this energy functions as an adequate stimulus to Tt. Thus, to Hs this high-frequency energy is unknown noise but can be mistaken by Tt for signals. Further consideration of the physical limitations on Hs-Tt vocal exchanges are considered with a feedback diagram and quantitative calculations based on the hearing curves and the sonic-ultrasonic output of Hs and Tt. Thus, in treating another species with a different hearing curve and a different sonic energy output, it is imperative to have quantitative physical measures in order to find channels that are adequately open both ways between the different species. Such considerations determine necessary acoustical and electrical transforms of the outputs and inputs from and to each member of the different species. [Work supported in part by AFOSR and NIH, NINDB.]" (See Text Figures 8 and 3.)

33. (112) Lilly, John C., Alice M. Miller, and Henry M. Truby. 1968. "Reprogramming of the Sonic Output of the Dolphin: Sonic Burst Count Matching." *Journal of the Acoustical Society of America,* vol. 43, no. 6, pp. 1412–1424.

This paper was reproduced in Appendix 1 of *Lilly on Dolphins* (Anchor Doubleday, 1975).

This paper introduces into behavioral science an extension of the usual learning theory as follows:

"In dolphin-human experiments, the human programming is specified by programs arbitrarily assigned to the operator, by those already existing below levels of awareness in the operator, and by those developed between the operator and the dolphin in the experiments. In the case of the dolphin, similar programming exists. Some human and some dolphin programs are already present, others can be created and certain behavioral parts of both recorded experimentally by objective methods. A limited set of these programs are found and described in this paper. (The experiments, the results and the analyses)."

The programming subroutines used in the experiments are

listed insofar as they are known. There are eight subroutines listed. The consonant vowel and vowel-consonant pairs used to cover all of the sounds of the general American spoken language were constructed from a list of nine vowels and eleven consonants and the 187 pronounceable combinations out of the possible 198 items used in the experiments.

"The investigator read the list to the *Tursiops* in a loud, natural voice. (Later, a tape recording of the reading voice was used.) Initially, the rate of presentation of syllables in the human speech output during each train was paced by a small light flashing once every 0.7 seconds within the visual field of the reader. In the preliminary training of the dolphin he was exposed to consonant-vowel, vowel-consonant symmetrical pairs. Once the dolphin mastered these pairs so as to give two physical bursts for two syllables, he was programmed with a new list read to him by the human operator.

"The new list rearranged the consonant-vowel, vowel-consonant pairs from the systematic order of List 1 to a randomized order. The randomized order was then chopped up into groups each group of which contained a certain number of consonant-vowel or vowel-consonant pairs. The number in each group was assigned randomly so that the dolphin could not know how many were going to be given to him next. (See Text Figure 9.)

"In this subroutine 8, the dolphin was expected to match a number of syllables from 1 to 10 with an equal number of bursts.

"Complete tape recordings of the human output and the dolphin output for the two sets of experiments were analyzed by various methods for number of bursts per train, burst timing, frequency spectrum, and pulsing rates. In the first group of analyses naive operators listened to the tape and counted the number of bursts in the human train and the number of bursts in the dolphin response train. Several observers counted what they heard from the tapes played back at either normal speed or slowed down speeds two to thirty-two times. Objective recordings made from the tapes were done with oscillographs of the rectified integrated envelopes of the bursts with a full passband and with bands isolated with various high pass and low pass filters. Counts were also made from spectral records of sonograms. The primary recorded wave forms displayed on a storage cathode-ray oscilloscope were also used to count bursts.

"It was found that naive operators tended to miscount bursts. They did not make the secure separation of individual physical bursts as compared with meaningful vowel and consonant renditions. This resulted in an error curve which was lopsided; i.e., the dolphin did better than the human operators. When the objective methods for measuring the bursts by means of oscillosope and oscillograph recordings were made it turned out that the dolphin had been counting sonic bursts and matching those rather than the nonsense syllable counts that naive observers made.

"The dolphin performed for approximately twenty minutes for six experiments allowing us to plot his rate of learning. His final scores are given in Text Fig. 11. If the dolphin gave too many sounds he was said to be generating one kind of error; if he failed to match the number of bursts in each train this was called the mismatch error. By the end of the sixth experiment the dolphin was making no errors whatsoever of either type.

"The results were analyzed by means of sonograms and a new type plot instituted to encompass the results. In these plots the pulse repetition rate of the dolphin as a source and of the human as a source is plotted against the values of the peak partials as measured in the sonograms. The resulting log-log plot shows (Text Fig. 10) the distinctive separation of the human voice versus the dolphin voice and shows that the pulse repetition rate; i.e., the pitch of the human voice and the pitch of the dolphin voice are distinctively separated in the case of the male human, and there is a tendency toward overlap with the female voice with another dolphin. (Fig. 13).

One important point about these experiments is given in Section B, Reprogramming Mode of Transmission. "The sound producing mechanisms in the dolphin operate naturally under water with a closed blowhole. In these experiments, the dolphin's ability to open the blowhole and make airborne sounds is selectively programmed and thus forces the phonatory apparatus to function in another mode in vocal-acoustic interlock with another organism. That the dolphin adapts to this mode of signalling with man is shown in these experiments. It is also shown that the dolphin can be programmed (within limits) to reproduce some physical aspects of the human speech output.

TABLE   2

1. *in*   *ool*   *oom*
    ɪn   ul   um
    ɪn   ul   um

2. *at*   *ree*
    ɑt   ri
    æt   ri

3. *oyn*   *oat*   *lye*   *chew*   *kih*   *chee*   *ine*   *key*   *oil*   *tih*
    ɔɪn   ot   laɪ   tʃu   kɪ   tʃi   aɪn   ki   ɔɪl   tɪ
    ɔɪn   ot   laɪ   tʃu   kɪ   tʃi   aɪn   ki   ɔɪl   tɪ

4. *en*   *ane*   *eat*   *ayer*   *noo*   *we*   *ate*   *chay*   *moe*
    ɛn   en   it   er   nu   wi   et   tʃe   mo
    ɛn   en   it   ɛr   nu   wi   et   tʃe   mo

5. *ta*   *rah*
    tɑ   rɑ
    tɑ   rɑ

6. *oh*   *lee*   *vay*   *coy*   *aim*
    o   li   ve   kɔɪ   em
    o   li   ve   kɔɪ   em

7. *woe*   *moo*   *itch*   *wye*   *wih*   *moy*   *ehh*
    ʍo   mu   itʃ   waɪ   wɪ   mɔɪ   ɛ
    wo   mu   ɪtʃ   waɪ   wɪ   mɔɪ   ɛ

8. *oys*   *air*   *eem*   *say*
    ɔɪs   ɛr   im   se
    ɔɪz   ɝ   im   se

9. *ett*   *ighch*   *ace*   *eel*   *ah*
    ɛt   aɪtʃ   es   il   ɑ
    ɛt   ɝtʃ   es   il   ai

10. *oot*
    ut
    ut

11. *roy*   *kah*   *ovv*   *kehh*   *oyv*   *noy*   *rye*   *nigh*   *ootch*
    rɔɪ   kɑ   ɑv   kɛ   ɔɪv   nɔɪ   raɪ   naɪ   utʃ
    rɔɪ   kɑ   ɑv   kɛ   ɔɪv   nɔɪ   raɪ   naɪ   uɛʃ

12. *mih*   *eek*   *ease*   *tay*   *zee*
    mɪ   ik   iz   te   zi
    mɪ   ik   iz   te   zi

13. *lih*   *va*   *ole*   *ni*
    lɪ   vɑ   ol   nɪ
    lɪ   vɑ   ol   nɪ

14. *eyes*   *ee*   *otch*
    aɪz   i   otʃ
    aɪz   i   otʃ

15. *ah*   *ass*   *oyer*   *oy*
    ɑ   as   ɔɪr   ɔɪ
    ɑ   as   ɔɪɝ   ɔɪ

16. *kay*   *lieu*   *ick*   *so*   *etch*
    ke   lu   ɪk   so   ɛtʃ
    ke   lu   ɪk   so   ɛtʃ

17. *teh*   *aitch*   *I've*   *zi*   *cha*   *me*   *choy*   *oo*
    tɛ   etʃ   aɪv   zɪ   tʃɑ   mi   tʃɔɪ   u
    tɛ   etʃ   aɪv   zɪ   tʃɑ   mi   tʃɔɪ   u

18. *oak*   *i*   *loy*   *vie*   *see*   *chi*   *rih*   *ose*
    ok   ɪ   lɔɪ   vaɪ   si   tʃɪ   rɪ   os
    ok   ɪ   lɔɪ   vaɪ   si   tʃaɪ   rɪ   oz

19. *toy*
    tɔɪ
    tɔɪ

20. *aze*	*coo*	*ees*	*ir*	*eve*	*oll*	*I'm*			
ez	ku	is	ɪr	iv	al	aɪm			
ez	ku	iz	ɪr	iv	ɔl	aɪm			
21. *it*									
ɪt									
ɪt									
22a. *may*	*own*	*im*							
me	on	ɪm							
me	on	ɑm	"correction"						
22. *may*	*own*	*im*	*wah*	*an*	*toe*	*kie*	*meh*	*ai*	*ray*
me	on	ɪm	wɑ	ɑn	to	kaɪ	mɛ	aɪ	re
me	on	ɪm	wɑ	ɑn	to	kaɪ	mɛ	aɪ	re
23. *ees*	*ooze*	*or*							
is	uz	or							
iz	uz	or							
24. *zeh*	*iss*								
zɛ	ɪs								
zɛ	ɪz								
25. *knee*	*are*	*ite*	*reh*	*row*	*ove*				
ni	ɑr	aɪt	rɛ	ro	ov				
ni	ɑr	aɪt	rɛ	ro	ov				
26. *ma*	*is*	*too*	*zoo*	*een*					
mɑ	ɪz	tu	zu	in					
mɑ	ɪz	tu	zu	in					
27. *eeer*	*ev*	*oyt*	*veh*	*la*	*no*				
ir	ɛv	ɔɪt	vɛ	lɑ	no				
ɪr	ɛv	ɔɪt	vɛ	lɑ	no				
28. *ice*	*sa*	*ek*							
aɪs	sɑ	ɛk							
aɪs	sɑ	ɛk							
29. *vee*	*ire*	*each*	*zye*	*voy*	*vous*	*atch*			
vi	aɪr	it\	zaɪ	vɔɪ	vu	at\			
vi	aɪɚ	it\	zaɪ	vɔɪ	vu	æt\			
30. *oove*	*soy*	*iv*	*choe*	*ack*	*zah*	*sue*	*si*		
uv	sɔɪ	ɪv	t\o	ak	zɑ	su	sɪ		
uv	sɔɪ	ɪv	t\o	æk	zɑ	su	saɪ		
31. *oon*	*oyk*	*leh*	*rue*	*tie*	*chie*	*my*			
un	ɔɪk	lɛ	ru	taɪ	t\aɪ	maɪ			
un	ɔɪk	lɛ	ru	taɪ	t\aɪ	maɪ			
32. *cheh*	*ohm*								
t\ɛ	om								
t\ɛ	om								
33. *nay*	*lo*	*lay*	*omm*	*ache*	*ike*	*ale*	*isle*	*ell*	*zoe*
nɛ	lo	le	ɑm	ek	aɪk	el	aɪl	ɛl	zo
ne	lo	le	ɑm	ek	aɪk	el	aɪl	ɛl	zo
34. *oze*	*way*	*oyz*	*av*	*vih*	*voe*	*woy*	*as*	*em*	
oz	we	ɔɪz	ɑv	vɪ	vo	wɔɪ	ɑs	ɛm	
oz	we	ɔɪz	ɑv	vɪ	vo	wɔɪ	ɑs	ɛm	
35. *nah*									
nɑ									
nɑ									
36. *oos*	*neh*	*tea*	*woo*	*zay*	*oym*				
us	nɛ	ti	wu	ze	ɔɪm				
uz	nɛ	ti	wu	ze	ɔɪm				
37. *sigh*	*oych*	*seh*	*ooke*						
saɪ	ɔɪt\	sɛ	uk						
saɪ	ɔɪt\	sɛ	uk						
38. *ill*	*zoh*	*ooor*	*ezz*	*koe*	*weh*				
ɪl	zo	ur	ɛz	ko	wɛ				
ɪl	zo	ur	ɛz	ko	wɛ				

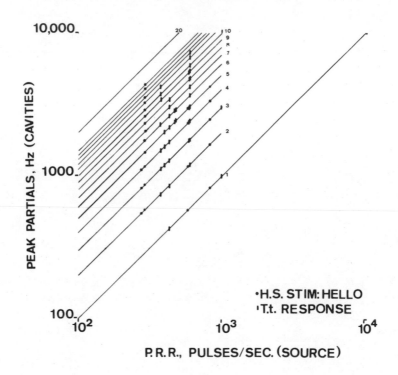

FIGURE 13. The Hs speech-output program stimulus train analysis was "hello" (●), and (|) is the analysis of Tt No. 26's voice output response. In this program analysis, it is demonstrated that the Hs (●) output (pitch) and the Tt response overlap in the frequency ranges. In this experiment, the pitch of the Hs (female) voice output has been raised and overlaps the dolphin's. In a sense, the dolphin's high-pitch reprogrammed the Hs female voice to unusually high values (up to 800 Hz).

Despite the natural use of the band of frequencies approximately ten to twenty times that normally utilized in the human voice range, the dolphin can shape up the transmissions in the lower end of his output frequency spectrum. These experiments illustrate that his hearing curve and probably his frequency differentiation threshold extend into the upper portion of the human speech frequency spectrum. Therefore, probably in a limited way he can hear human speech.

"Text Figures 8 and 3 give a comparison of the human and dolphin hearing curves (Text Figure 8) and their sonic outputs (Text Figure 3).

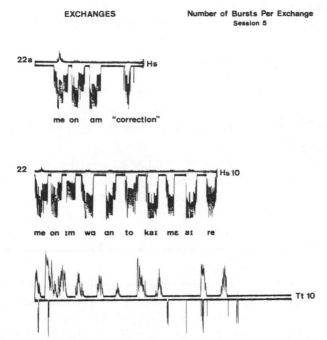

EXCHANGES   Number of Bursts Per Exchange
                          Session 5

22a   Hs

me on am "correction"

22   Hs 10

me on ɪm wɑ ɑn to kaɪ mɛ aɪ re

Tt 10

FIGURE 17.   An oscillographic record from the magnetic-tape recording of Expt. 5. There has been no editing or cutting from the onset of 22A to the end of 22 except for display purposes. This example illustrates the dolphin's acoustic-storage and pattern-recognition ability that enabled him to respond only to the correct Hs stimulus train with the correct number of matching bursts.

"Careful controls were done to eliminate start and stop signals other than those inherent in the human voice. These controls are listed in the paper.

"Some evidence that the dolphin has grasp of a set of directions as to how to control his output as given by the humans are shown in the paper. One of these is illustrated in Fig. 17, in which the operator corrects himself after giving three nonsense syllables by saying 'correction.' He then gives ten nonsense syllables. The dolphin's reply consists of only ten. He leaves out the three given before the word 'correction.'

"This particular dolphin had been trained by this operator and several other operators using the word *'correction'* when he was expected to cancel what was just preceding in the human presentation.

"Similar events are frequent enough in these experiments to lead to the hypothesis that the dolphin has learned (at the very least) to recognize that pattern that is to be matched (stimulus) and that which is to be ignored (instructions, corrections, deletions). What clues the dolphin uses for this selection are at present obscure.

"In those experiments in which food reward (fish) or "physiological reinforcer" is eliminated, it is not obvious what the reinforcers are (what motivates the dolphin). As a working hypothesis we assume that *Tursiops truncatus* like *Homo sapiens* has a sufficiently large and complex brain to have (or to develop) programs that motivate performances and hence act as reinforcing programs or "symbolic reinforcers" in the absence of explicitly humanly programmed rewards (such as fish giving). Presumably such hypothesized reinforcing programs include pattern recognition and "success-failure" criteria with storage of the performance record as it develops. Such high level programming does not seem to exist in the smaller brained mammals (rat, cat, or monkey) nor in the talking birds (parrot or mynah).

34. (112-A) McFarland, W. L., P. J. Morgane, and M. S. Jacobs. 1969. "Ventricular System of the Brain of the Dolphin *(Tursiops truncatus)*, with Comparative Anatomical Observations and Relations to Brain Specializations." *Journal of Comparative Neurology,* vol. 135, pp. 275–368.

This is a very exhaustive study of the ventricular system within the brain of the dolphin and comparative and quantitative work on other species including the phylogenetic development from the dogfish, the lamprey, the frog, and the lizard. And then a generalized mammalian form of the ventricular system with an exhaustive analysis of the literature on the ventricular system of all species concerned. The technique of injection of the system is presented, and the various casting procedures are analyzed.

There is an extensive bibliography and 25 plates showing the analysis of the ventricular system through neuroanatomical microscopic cross sections and analysis of the injected ventricles themselves.

35. (112-B) Jacobs, Myron S., P. J. Morgane, and Willard L. McFarland. 1971. "The Anatomy of the Brain of the Bottlenose Dolphin *(Tursiops truncatus)*, Rhinic (rhinencephalon) on the Paleocortex." *Journal of Comparative Neurology*, vol. 141, pp. 205–272.

In this paper there is a beautiful cross section showing the relationships between the brain and the other structures in the head of the dolphin, including the jaws, the tongue, the eyes, the blowhole, and the respiratory tract. The planes of the sections through three beautifully perfused brains of three different dolphins are shown. There is a diagram of the paleocortical zone of the rhinic lobe to archicortical zone, and a basal photograph of the brain showing the great size and prominence of the olfactory lobes in spite of the lack of an olfactory tract and olfactory bulbs. A photograph of the medial wall of the hemisphere shows relations important in this analysis. A dissection of the cerebral cortex laterally shows the insular cortex and the temporo-uncal borders of the hemisphere. There are more details of these structures in photographs, sections, and diagrams. The posteromedial and basal view of the olfactory lobe and formations surrounding it in the right hemisphere are shown. There are thirteen plates including many microscopic enlarged photographs showing the cell layers and the fiber layers in these various structures.

36. (112-C) Morgane, P. J., and M. S. Jacobs. "Comparative Anatomy of the Cetacean Nervous System." In *Functional Anatomy of Marine Mammals*. R. J. Harrison, Editor. Pergamon Press. London, 1972. Pp. 117–244.

This 177-page report summarizes the findings on the three extremely well preserved brains from the Communication Research Institute of 1963. The Table of Contents illustrates the contents of the paper. Introduction, Adaptive Evolutionary

Implications of Brain Structure, Materials and Methods, Brain
Stem Body Axes, Brain Waves and Brain/Body Weight Ratios,
Blood Supply to the Brain, Ventricular System of the Brain,
Cranial Nerves, Surface Morphology and Gross Features of the
Cetacean Brain, Rhinencephalon of Cetacea, Limbic Lobe and
Amygdala, Diencephalon, the Striatum, Cerebral Cortex, Cere-
bellum and Inferior Olive, the Spinal Cord. There is an extensive
analysis of the literature and a long Bibliography including the
Russian literature on the subject.

37. (113) Lilly, John C., *Programming and Metaprogramming in the
Human Biocomputer.* Julian Press (now Crown Publishers, New York),
edition 1972; Bantam edition, 1974.

38. (114) Lilly, John C., *Programming and Metaprogramming in the
Human Biocomputer.*

39. Lilly, John C. 1975. *Lilly on Dolphins, Humans of the Sea.* Anchor Press,
Doubleday, New York.

This collection contains a shortened version of *Man and Dolphin,* the
lecture from *The Dolphin in History,* and *Mind of the Dolphin.* Also
included in the appendixes are "Reprogramming the Sonic Output of the
Dolphin: Sonic Burst Count Matching" (1968) and "Communication
with Extraterrestrial Intelligence" (1966). A comprehensive index of this
volume is included.

40. Alpers, Antony. 1960. *A Book of Dolphins.* John Murray, London.

41. McBride, Arthur F., and D. O. Hebb. 1948. "Behavior of the Captive
Bottlenose Dolphin *Tursiops truncatus,*" *Journal of Comparative and
Physiological Psychology,* vol. 41, pp. 111–123.

42. Irving, L. P., P. F. Scholander, and S. W. Grinnell. 1942. "The
Respiration of *Tursiops truncatus." Journal of Cellular and
Comparative Physiology,* vol. 14, p. 145.

43. Langworthy, O. R. 1932. "A Description of the Central Nervous System
of the Porpoise *(Tursiops truncatus)." Journal of Comparative
Neurology,* vol. 54, pp. 437–488.

44. Szilard, Leo. 1961. *The Voice of the Dolphin & Other Stories.* Simon & Schuster, New York.

45. Morgane, Peter. 1974. "The Whale Brain: The Anatomical Basis of Intelligence." In *Mind in the Waters,* Joan McIntyre, Editor. Scribner, New York. P. 84–93.

46. Bateson, G. 1965. "Report on Work at St. Thomas and Sea Life Park." Communication Research Institute, Miami.

47. Kuhn, Thomas. 1962. *The Structure of Scientific Revolutions.* University of Chicago Press, Chicago.

48. Lilly, John C. 1963. "Modern Whales, Dolphins, and Porpoises, as Challenges to Our Intelligence." In *The Dolphin in History* by Ashley Montagu and John C. Lilly. William Andrews Clark Memorial Library, UCLA, Los Angeles. Pp. 31–54.

49. Jerison, H. J. 1973. *Evolution of the Brain and Intelligence.* Academic Press, New York.

50. Payne, Roger. 1971. "Orientation by means of long-range acoustic signaling in baleen whales." *Annals of New York Academy of Sciences,* vol. 188, pp. 110–141.

51. Tavolga, W. N., Editor. 1964. *Marine Bio-Acoustics,* vol. 1. MacMillan, New York.

52. Tavolga, W. N., Editor. 1967. *Marine Bio-Acoustics,* vol. 2. Pergamon Press, New York.

53. Busnel, R. G., Editor. 1963. *Acoustic Behavior of Animals.* Elsevier Publishing, Amsterdam.

54. Kellogg, W. N. 1961. *Porpoises and Sonar.* University of Chicago Press, Chicago.

55. Norris, K. 1974. *The Porpoise Watcher*. Norton, New York.

56. Schevill, W. E., and Barbara Lawrence. 1956. "Food-finding by a Captive Porpoise *(Tursiops truncatus)." Breviora,* Museum of Comparative Zoology, Harvard, Vol. 53: 1-15.

57. Batteau, D. W. 1967. "The Role of Pinna in Human Localization." *Proceedings of the Royal Society, British,* vol. 158, pp. 158–180.

58. Yerkes, R. M., and B. W. Learned. 1925. *Chimpanzee Intelligence and Its Vocal Expression.* Williams & Wilkins, Baltimore.

59. Kellogg, W. N., and L. A. Kellogg. 1933. *The Ape and the Child.* McGraw-Hill, New York.

60. Hayes, Keith. 1951. *The Ape in Our House.* Harper Bros., New York.

61. Gardner, R. A., and B. T. Gardner. 1969. "Teaching Sign Language to a Chimpanzee." *Science,* vol. 165, pp. 664–672.

62. Fouts, Roger S. 1975. "Capacities for Language in Great Apes," in *Socioecology and Psychology of Primates.* R. H. Tuttle, Editor. Mouton Publishers, The Hague/Paris. Pp. 371–390.

63. Premack, D. 1971. "Language in Chimpanzee?" *Science,* vol. 172, pp. 808–822.

64. Donaldson, Henry H. 1895. *The Growth of the Brain.* Walter Scott, London.

65. Lang, T. G., and H.A.P. Smith. 1965. "Communication between Dolphins in Separate Tanks by Way of an Electronic Acoustic Link." *Science,* vol. 150, pp. 1839–1844.

66. Fletcher, H. 1940. "Auditory Patterns." *Reviews of Modern Physics,* vol. 12, pp. 47–65.

67. Harnad, S. R., H. D. Steklis, and J. Lancaster, Editors. 1976. "Origins
     and Evolution of Language and Speech." *Annals of New York Academy
     of Sciences,* vol. 280, pp. 1–914.

68. Hewes, G. W. 1975. *Language Origins: A Bibliography* (2 vols.). Mouton,
     The Hague/Paris.

69. Lenneberg, Eric H. 1968. "Language in the Light of Evolution." In
     Animal Communication: Techniques of Study & Results of Research, T.
     A. Sebeok, Editor. Indiana University Press, Bloomington. Pp. 592–613.

70. Ireland, W. W. 1900. *Mental Affections of Children.* J. & A. Churchill,
     London.

71. Lilly, John C. 1956. "Distribution of 'Motor' Functions in the Cerebral
     Cortex of the Conscious, Intact Monkey." *Science,* vol. 124, p. 937.

72. Lilly, John C. 1958. "Correlations between Neurophysiological Activity in
     the Cortex and Short-term Behavior in the Monkey." In *Biological and
     Biochemical Basis of Behavior.* H. F. Harlow and C. N. Woolsey,
     Editors. University of Wisconsin Press, Madison. Pp. 83–100.

73. Geschwind, Norman. 1972. "Language and the Brain." *Scientific
     American,* vol. 226, pp. 76–83.

74. Geschwind, Norman. 1965. "Disconnexion Syndromes in Animals and
     Man: Part II." *Brain,* vol. 88, pp. 585–644.

75. Busnel, R. G., Editor. 1967. *Animal Sonar Systems: Biology and Bionics.*
     Laboratoire de Physiologie Acoustique, Joisy-en-Josas, France.

76. Johnson, C. S. 1968. "Masked Tonal Thresholds in the Bottlenosed
     Porpoise." *Journal of the Acoustical Society of America,* vol. 44, pp. 965–
     967.

77. Ridgeway, S. H., Editor. 1972. *Mammals of the Sea.* Charles Thomas,
     Springfield, Illinois.

Abstract of Scientific Research Program Proposal; Scientific Origins of Interspecies Communication (Project JANUS 1977)

Previous studies conducted with dolphins (see references) have indicated that these Cetacea employ intraspecies sonic communication at a high level of sophistication. These studies further show that humans and dolphins have the capability of learning from and teaching each other in the acoustic realm, even though there are a number of physical barriers to this sort of teaching and learning. In the current research project, we propose to lower the physical barriers to interspecies communication through the use of minicomputer technology, electronics and sophisticated programming techniques currently available. The apparatus which will be used in the current project provides an interface between the two species. JANUS (for Joint Analog Numerical Understanding System), like the god of mythology, will face in two directions: the human-facing side of JANUS includes those inputs and outputs suitable for human use in air; the dolphin-facing side includes inputs and outputs appropriate for dolphin use in water.

The use of a minicomputer as an interface will provide each

participant in the process with an audio output/input in a frequency range appropriate to his species. This is of particular importance because of the dolphins' regular employment of frequencies several times higher than those used by humans. Initially, a basic code will be developed for use by both participants. Teaching programs will use the code to develop and test the ability of human-dolphin pairs to communicate meaning at successively higher levels of complexity. Simultaneous sonic and visual displays will be generated, and responses of each species will be used to confirm understanding of the message received from the other participant. The computer will also serve as a constantly available programmed learning center for the dolphin participant, and will be designed to give the dolphin access to control over selected aspects of his environment. (A number of experiments with chimpanzees using the computer as a constantly available teaching device have met with remarkable success in the last several years [see references].)

For those unfamiliar with the work done up to this point with dolphins, it may be helpful to review briefly some of the reasons for choosing dolphins as participants in experiments in interspecies communication. First, the bottle-nosed dolphin *(Tursiops truncatus)* possesses, as do several others of the Cetacea, a brain as large as or larger than that of man. Studies initiated under the principal investigator in the 1960s indicate that the brains of these Cetacea also have large silent cortical associational areas in the parietal and temporal lobes. In humans, these are the areas which are essential for virtually all of what we call the "higher" functions of human intelligence (e.g., long-range planning, adaptive and creative self-reprogramming, etc.). Further, in the primate series, these cortical areas are the ones that can be seen to increase both relatively and absolutely as one moves up the scale from the anthropoid apes to man. Neurophysiological-behavioral studies with dolphins have demonstrated the dolphins' ability to employ any available mode, including voice output, to achieve the onset of a desired stimulus or the termination of an undesired one. Only man among the primates has demonstrated willingness to continue learning situations which employ only neutral reinforcement (learning for the sake of learning, rather than for reward or punishment). Virtually all long-term research done with dolphins includes comments by the researchers on the singular willingness and eagerness on the part of the dolphins to participate in joint efforts with humans.

Until recently, the equipment needed for the real-time

accomplishment of the sonic transforms described above did not exist. With the advent of appropriate LSI circuit technology and present-day software, it appears that the physical barriers to high-level experiments in communication between man and dolphin have been made permeable. For the first time, man may be able to communicate symbolically with another species possessing a brain fully as complex as, and with an evolutionary pattern very different from, his own.

The implications of such a breakthrough reach into virtually every realm of human endeavor. The sea, comprising some 71% of the earth's surface, is almost universally seen as an inevitably crucial factor in human development and survival in the coming years and decades. Cooperative projects between humans and the mammals of the sea can provide solutions and new perspectives in this crucial area. The basic codes and methods developed in this research program will be applicable to human acquisition of oral and symbolic languages, as well as to interchanges between individuals possessing totally different communication systems, regardless of species or mode of communication, provided the necessary computational capacity is present. It seems certain as well that new knowledge about the nature of language itself will be an inherent product of the dolphin studies.

In the initial experiments, some basic questions to be posed are: can dolphins perform logical operations and differentiations? Can they perform numerical functions? Can they recognize and use linguistic symbols to convey constant meaning? Ultimately, the equipment and programming will be such that the system will be usable by previously untrained humans and dolphins. Sufficient flexibility will be retained in the system to allow new information about the capabilities of both humans and dolphins to modify the JANUS configuration. In this way, the program will not be committed to premature assumptions which could later prove limiting or inappropriate.

At the present time (January 1978), grants and contributions have enabled the foundation to purchase and install a PDP 11/04 computer, a VT-55 terminal and peripheral equipment. Funds are currently available for analog-to-digital and digital-to-analog converters, two-way hydrophones and other specific items needed to begin preliminary studies. The development of the initial software is also well under way. Arrangements have been made with a cooperating institution to begin initial experiments with dolphins to determine the appropriateness of the system developed thus far and to find the acoustic parameters within which future work will take place. Funding for the next year of research is currently being sought. The total projected budget for 1978 is $125,000.

A much more complete description of each of the subjects dealt with above is available in *Scientific Origins of Interspecies Communication* (27 July 1977). This proposal also includes supporting documentary data and a budget for the first five years of the program. Other supporting data (such as reprints of pertinent scientific articles) will be furnished on request.

The Human/Dolphin Foundation
P.O. Box 4172
Malibu, California 90265

REFERENCES

"Animals in Aquatic Environment. Adaptation of Mammals to the Ocean," John C. Lilly, M.D., *Handbook of Physiology,* Environment I, American Physiological Society, Washington, D.C. Pp. 741–757.

"Comparative Anatomy of the Cetacean Nervous System," Peter J. Morgane and M. S. Jacobs, *Functional Anatomy of Marine Mammals.* London: Pergamon Press, 1972.

Lilly, John C., *Man and Dolphin.* New York: Doubleday & Co., 1961.

Lilly, John C., *The Mind of the Dolphin.* New York: Doubleday & Co., 1967.

Lilly, John C., and Ashley Montagu. *The Dolphin in History.* Los Angeles: UCLA Press, 1963.

"Reprogramming of the Sonic Output of the Dolphin: Sonic Burst Count Matching," John C. Lilly, Henry M. Truby, and Alice M. Miller. 1968. *Journal of the Acoustical Society of America,* vol. 43, no. 6, pp. 1412–1424.

Rumbaugh, Duane, Editor. *Language Learning by a Chimpanzee.* New York: Academic Press, 1977.

List of Organizations Interested in the Whales, Dolphins, and Porpoises, Friends of the Cetacea

This list is derived from the correspondence files of the Human/Dolphin Foundation. In all probability the list is not complete; suggestions for additional organizations or corrections should be sent to the foundation.

AMERICAN CETACEAN SOCIETY
National Headquarters
P.O. Box 4416
San Pedro, California 90731
213/548-6279

AMERICAN CETACEAN SOCIETY
Los Angeles Chapter
P.O. Box 2698
San Pedro, California 90731
213/548-6279

AMERICAN CETACEAN SOCIETY
Marin Chapter
P.O. Box 2636
San Rafael, California 94901

AMERICAN CETACEAN SOCIETY
Maui Chapter
P.O. Box 446
Lahaina, Maui, Hawaii 96761

AMERICAN CETACEAN SOCIETY
Orange County Chapter
P.O. Box 18763
Irvine, California 92713

AMERICAN CETACEAN SOCIETY
Puget Sound Chapter
P.O. Box 1384
Bellevue, Washington 98005

AMERICAN CETACEAN SOCIETY
San Diego Chapter
P.O. Box 22305
San Diego, California 92122

AMERICAN CETACEAN SOCIETY
VOYAGERS
1043 East Green Street
Pasadena, California 91106

ANIMAL PROTECTION INST. USA
Belton P. Mouras
P.O. Box 22505
Sacramento, California 95822

ANIMAL WELFARE INSTITUTE
Christine Stevens
P.O. Box 3650
Washington, D.C. 20007

CENTER FOR OCEAN STUDIES
Gardner's Basin
Atlantic City, New Jersey 08401
609/348-5252

CETACEAN RELATIONS
Zantar Buru
P.O. Box 958 Paia
Maui, Hawaii 96779

CONNECTICUT CETACEAN SOCIETY
P.O. Box 145
Wethersfield, Connecticut 06109

COUSTEAU SOCIETY INC.
9 Bay Street
Westport, Connecticut 06880

COUSTEAU SOCIETY INC.
8150 Beverly Boulevard
Los Angeles, California 90048
213/655-4641

THE DOLPHIN EMBASSY
P.O. Box 77082
San Francisco, California 94107
415/788-1424

THE DOLPHIN EMBASSY
P.O. Box 59, Potts Point 2011
Sydney, Australia
(02) 357-1636

DOLPHIN PROJECT JAPAN
54 Mint Street
San Francisco, California 94103
415/777-3066

ENDANGERED SPECIES
PRODUCTIONS, INC.
Phoebe Wray
175 West Main Street
Ayer, Massachusetts 01432
617/772-0445

FRIENDS OF THE EARTH
David Brouwer
620 C Street, N.E.
Washington, D.C. 20003

FRIENDS OF THE EARTH
529 Commercial Street
San Francisco, California 94111

FUND FOR ANIMALS
Cleveland Amory & Christine Clark
1112 North Sherbourne Drive
Los Angeles, California 90069
213/659-9577

GENERAL WHALE
Larry Foster
9616 MacArthur Boulevard
Oakland, California 94605

GREENPEACE FOUNDATION
240 Fort Mason
San Francisco, California 94123

GREENPEACE FOUNDATION
13719 Ventura Boulevard
Sherman Oaks, California 91403
213/986-2315

GREENPEACE FOUNDATION
2007 West 4th Avenue
Vancouver, British Columbia,
Canada

GREENPEACE FOUNDATION
404 Piikoi
Honolulu, Hawaii 96814

HUBBS-SEA WORLD RESEARCH
INSTITUTE
1700 South Shores Road
San Diego, California 92109
714/223-2693

HUMAN/DOLPHIN FOUNDATION
John C. Lilly, M.D.
P.O. Box 4172
Malibu, California 90265

HUMANE SOCIETY OF THE UNITED
STATES
Patricia Forkan
2100 L Street, N.W.
Washington, D.C. 20037
202/452-1100

HUMANE SOCIETY OF THE UNITED
STATES
West Coast Regional Office
1713 J Street
Sacramento, California 95814

INTERNATIONAL ASSOCIATION OF
AQUATIC ANIMAL MEDICINE
925 Harbor Plaza
P.O. Box 570
Long Beach, California 90801

JOJOBA PROJECT
P.O. Box 2749
Tucson, Arizona 87502

MARINE MAMMAL COMMISSION
1625 Eye Street, N.W.
Washington, D.C. 20006

MONITOR
1522 Connecticut Avenue, N.W.
Washington, D.C. 20036
202/234-6576

NATIONAL OCEANIC & ATMOSPHERIC
AGENCY
Mr. Richard Frank, Administrator
Administration
Department of Commerce
Washington, D.C. 20230

OCEAN CONTACT
Peter Beamish
Box 1111
Bedford, Nova Scotia BON 1BO
Canada

THE OCEANIC SOCIETY
Mid Atlantic Region
P.O. Box 13357
Philadelphia, Pennsylvania 19101
215/WA-5-6544

THE OCEANIC SOCIETY
111 Prospect Street
Stamford, Connecticut 06901
203/327-0948

OREGONIANS CO-OPERATING TO
PROTECT WHALES & DOLPHINS
873 Willamette Street
Eugene, Oregon 97401
503/485-5144

PROJECT JONAH
Joan McIntyre
Lanai, Hawaii 96763

PROJECT JONAH NEW ZEALAND INC.
P.O. Box 42-071 Orakei
Auckland 5, New Zealand

SAVE THE DOLPHINS
Stan Minasian
1945 20th Avenue
San Francisco, California 94116

SAVE THE WHALES
Maris Sidenstecker
P.O. Box 49604
Los Angeles, California 90049

SIERRA CLUB
Bob Hughes, Chairman
Box 2471
Trenton, New Jersey 08607

WHALE CENTER (WORLD
HUMANITARIAN
ASSOCIATION FOR THE LIVING
ENVIRONMENT)
Danny Hirsch
173 Avocado Street
Leucadia, California 92024

WHALE CENTER
3929 Piedmont Avenue
Oakland, California 94611
415/654-4892
Maxine McCloskey, Exec. Director

WHALE ISSUE COMMITTEE
JACL National H.Q.'s Building
Clifford I. Uyeda, M.D., Chairman
1765 Sutter Street
San Francisco, California 94115

WHALE PROTECTION FUND/Center for
Environmental Education
2100 M Street, N.W.
Washington, D.C. 20037
202/466-4996

WHALEWATCH
3720 Stephen White Drive
San Pedro, California 90731
213/832-4444

WORLD SEA LIFE
P.O. Box 4266
Valley Village Station
North Hollywood, California 91607

Compiled by the
HUMAN/DOLPHIN FOUNDATION
March 1978

List of Known Locations Where Tursiops Are Held in Captivity

This list was prepared for the Marine Mammal Commission in November 1977. It was published by the U.S. Department of Commerce, National Technical Information Service as PB-273 673, entitled *Breeding Dolphins; Present Status, Suggestions for the Future* (Zoological Society of San Diego, California).

The estimated total number of *Tursiops* in captivity in 1977 for all countries of Earth is four hundred and fifty. Of this total, about three hundred are in the United States.

AUSTRALIA

Marineland of South Australia
P.O. Box 63
Glenelg Post Office
Glenelg, South Australia 5024

General Manager: Mr. R. H. Porter
Tursiops: 5; 2 females and 3 males between the ages of 5 and 9 years

Marineland of Australia
P.O. Box 823
Southpost, Q 4215, Main Beach
Gold Coast, Queensland, Australia

Director: Mr. David H. Brown
Tursiops: 11; 6 females and 5 males

Marineland
West Esplanade, Manly
New South Wales, Australia

Jack Evans Pet Porpoise Pool & Marine-World
P.O. Box 128
Coolangatta, Queensland, Australia 4225

Director: Mr. Jack Evans
Tursiops: 2; Lulu, 20 years in captivity
Ringo, 6 years in captivity

(One birth from this pair occurred on 12/8/69, lived 12 days)

Pet Porpoise Pool Pty. Ltd.
Coffs Harbour
New South Wales, Australia

Managing Director: Mr. Hec Goodall
Tursiops: 3; 2 females, 6 and 15 years *(catalania/aduncas)*
1 male, 5 years *(catalania/aduncas)*

Bullen's Lion Park
Waragamba, Camden
New South Wales, Australia

Director: Mr. Andrew Wowarth-Booth
Veterinarian: Dr. R. H. J. Hyne
Tursiops: 3

Sea World, Surfers Paradise
P.O. Box 190
Surfers Paradise, Queensland 4217
Australia

Director: Mr. Keith Williams
Tursiops: 15; 5 females and 10 males

BELGIUM
Dolphinarium Brügge
Boudewijn Park
Brügge, Belgium

Royal Zoological Society of Antwerp
Kroningin Astridplein 26
B-2000 Antwerpen, Belgium

BRASIL
Santos, Brasil
Tursiops: 1 or 2

CANADA
Montreal Aquarium
La Ronde, Isl-St. Hélène, Montréal
P.Q., Canada H3C 1A0
Director: Mr. Raymond Roth
Tursiops: 5; 4 females, 5, 8, 12, 13
   years;
1 male, 12 years

GERMANY, WEST
Zoo Duisburg
21 Duisburg 1
Mülheimerstrasse 273
West Germany
Director: Dr. Wolfgang Gewalt
Tursiops: 4; 2 females and 2 males

Westfälischer Zoologischer Garten
4400 Münster
Himmelreichalle, West Germany
Managing Director: Mr. W. Nuis
Dolphinarium operated by
   Harderwijk—similarly they run one
   at Brügge, Belgium.
Tursiops: 3; 2 females, 1 older than
   10 years
1 older than 15 years
1 male, older than 10 years

Tierpark Nürnberg
85 Nürnberg
Am Tiergarten 30, West Germany

Director: Dr. Manfred Kraus
Curator: Dr. Peter Mühling
Veterinarian: Dr. Anton Gauckler
Close replica of Duisburg using
   chlorinated NaCl.

Hagenbeck Zoo

GREAT BRITAIN
Brighton Aquarium
Marine Parade
Brighton, Sussex, BN2 1TE, Great
   Britain
Director: Mr. F. C. Glover

Marineland Oceanarium and
   Aquarium
Morecambe, Lancs
Great Britain
Director: Mr. G. D. Smith
Tursiops: 4; 3 females and 1 male,
   13, 11, 8, and 15 years

Flamingo Park Zoo
Dirby Misperton, Malton
Yorkshire YO17 0UX, Great Britain
Director: Mr. Don Robinson
Curator: Mr. I. O. Gibbs

Royal Windsor Safari and Leisure
   Park
St. Leonards, Windsor
Berkshire, Great Britain
Director: Mr. Ronald Smart
Tursiops: 3; 2 females and 1 male

Zoological Society of London
Whipsnade Park, Dunstable LU6 2LF
Bedfordshire, Great Britain
Curator: Dr. V. J. A. Manton
Tursiops: 2 females; 1 female, 5–6
   years old
1 female, 12 years old

HONG KONG
Ocean Park Ltd.
Wong Chuk Haug Road
Aberdeen, Hong Kong

General Manager: Mr. Williamson

Tursiops: 6 *Tursiops gilli*

INDONESIA
Jaya Ancol Oceanarium   Opened
   1974
Jalan Lodan Timur
Djakarta, Indonesia

General Manager: Mr. Sukinan
   Handrokusumo, M.Sc.

Tursiops: 6; 1 female *Tursiops
   aduncus* (Java Sea),
   100 kg, 12 years
3 male *Tursiops aduncus* (Japan)
   151, 146 kg
1 male *Tursiops truncatus* (Gulf of
   Mexico),
   170 kg
1 male *Tursiops gilli* (Hawaii), 190
   kg,
   8 years
1 *Tursiops aduncus* stillbirth, 1975
   (conceived in wild)

JAPAN
Enoshima Marineland
17-25, Katasa Kaigan 2 Chome
Fujisawa City, Knaagawa Prefecture
Japan 251

Curator: Mr. Kazushi Takahashi

Tursiops: 13; 10 females and 3
   males

Ito Aquarium
4-568 Yukawa, Ito
Shizuoka Prefecture
Japan

Director: Mr. Akio Tamura

Nagasaki Aquarium
Shukumachi, Nagasaki
Japan

Mito Aquarium
Nagahama, Numazu
Shizuoka Prefecture
Japan

Director: Mr. Sisaku Hanajima

Shimonoseki Municipal Aquarium
Chofu-cho, Shimonoseki
Yamaguchi Prefecture
Japan

Director: Mr. Masao Nitta

Toba Aquarium
Toba 3-3-6, Toba City
Mie Prefecture
Japan

Director: Mr. Kusuo Nakamura

Kamogawa Sea World
Chiba Prefecture
Japan

Director: Dr. T. Tobayama

Taiji Aquarium
Taiji Machi
Wakama Prefecture
Japan

Okinawa Oceanarium
Okinawa Prefecture
Japan

Director: Mr. Vchida

Shimoda Aquarium
Izu Peninsula
Schizuoka Prefecture
Japan

MALTA
Dolphin World Maltaquarium, Ltd.
Dragonara Palace
St. Julian, Malta
Director: Dr. Albert Camilleri
Curator: Mr. Albert V. Everbroek

NETHERLANDS
Dolfinarium Strand Harderwijk
Strandboulevard
Harderwijk, Netherlands
Director: Mr. F. B. den Herder
Tursiops: 11; 9 females, 7 adults, 2
  infants
2 males, one over 20 years, 1 over 14
Had 8 births since 1971, 3 while
  active in show, all conceived in
  captivity.

Ouwehand Zoo Rhenen
Grebbeweg 109, Rhenen
Prov. Utrecht, Netherlands
Directors: Mr. A. Ouwehand and
  Mr. J. Baars
Veterinarian: Dr. G.H.P.J. Gouda
  Quint

Dolfirama, Burg. v. Fenemaplein
Zandvoort, Netherlands
Owner: Mr. N. W. Bouwes
Tursiops: 6; 4 females, 3 about 10
  years, 1, 7 years
2 males, older than 10 and 15 years

Dolfirodam B.V.
Scharendijke, Netherlands
Director: Mr. A.v.d. Oever
Tursiops: 3; 2 females, 8 and 10
  years
1 male, 9 years

NEW ZEALAND
Hawke's Bay Aquarium
P.O. Box 167
Napier, New Zealand

Director: Mr. L. P. Ryan
Curator: Mr. G. L. Dine

Marineland of New Zealand   Opened
  1974
Private Bag
Napier, New Zealand
Manager: Mr. Pat McIlroy
Tursiops: None at present. Has 6
  Delphinus delphis.
Previously kept *Tursiops truncatus*
Lagenorhynchus obscurus
Cephalorhynchus hectori
Kogia breviceps

Mount Maunganui Marineland
  Ltd.   Opened 1966
Tauranga
New Zealand
Owner: Mr. P. R. Sorrenson
Tursiops: None at present.
Previously kept *Delphinus delphis*
  20-foot beaked whale with foetus

Marineland
Orewa, New Zealand
Manager: Mr. Horobin
Tursiops: At present aquarium is
  closed.
Previously kept *Delphinus delphis*

Pacific Sea Aquarium   Opened 1970
Picton, New Zealand
Manager: Mr. Ross Hedge
Tursiops: At present aquarium is
  closed.
Previously kept *Delphinus delphis*
Lagenorhynchus obscurus

SOUTH AFRICA
Dolphinarium and Oceanographic
  Research Inst.   Opened 1976
P.O. Box 736, 2 West Street, Durban
Natal, South Africa
Owner: South African Association
  for Marine Biological Research

Institute Director: Dr. A. Heydorn

Asst. Director Dolphinarium: Mr. E. A. Fearnhead, B.Sc.

Tursiops: 2; 1 female and 1 male

1 *Lagenorhynchus obscurus*

Port Elizabeth Oceanarium
  Museum, Beach Road
Humewood, Port Elizabeth
South Africa

Director: Dr. John Wallis

Tursiops: 5; 2 females, 1 juvenile conceived and born in captivity and 1 adult

3 males, 1 juvenile conceived and born in captivity and 2 adults

SPAIN

Marineland S.A.
Costa D'en Blanes
Palma Nova
Mallorca, Spain

Director: Mr. David Mudge

Tursiops: 4; 2 females and 2 males, ages 13–15 years

Holding Facilities: Main show pool—30 x 12 x 3 meters deep
Two holding pools—14 x 7 x 2.5 meters deep

Parque Zoologico De Barcelona
Parque de la Ciudadela

Barcelona 5, Spain

Director: Dr. A. Honch

Manager: Mr. B. González

SWEDEN

Kolmardens Djurpark
Kolmarden, Norrköping
Sweden

Director: Mr. Ulf Svensson

Tursiops: 5; 2 females, 7 and 20 years
3 males, 8, 15, and 25 years

Holding Facilities: Main pool— irregular 800 square meters by 4 meters deep

Holding pool—200 square meters by 4 meters deep

Closed-circuit circulation using NaCl and chlorination

SWITZERLAND

Knie Kinderzoo
8640 Rapperswill
Switzerland

Owner: Mr. Gebr. Knie

Tursiops: Had *Tursiops* conceive in captivity and give birth to live infant 7/29/75

Holding Facility: Irregular shape pool—10 x 15 x 3.5 meters deep— using NaCl and chlorination

UNION OF THE SOVIET SOCIALIST REPUBLICS

All *Tursiops* were taken from the Black Sea. (Submitted by V. S. Gurevich)

Karadag Biological Station. Institute of Biology of the South Seas, Academy of Science of the Ukrainian SSR. Situated in the vicinity of the city, Feodosiya (Black Sea). The manager is Dr. A. A. Titov. This station works year-round and very closely with the Acoustics Institute of the Academy of Science of USSR, Moscow, particularly with Dr. N. A. Dubrovsky. They have one permanent tank, where 10 specimens of *Tursiops truncatus* (4 males and 6 females) are kept during winter. As far as is known they have never had success in breeding dolphins.

Kazachya Bay Station, which is situated in the vicinity of city, Sevastopol' (Crimea), in the Black Sea, is the principal coordinator in any research on marine mammals. The head is V. V. Belyaev. They work very closely with institutions that have an interest in hydrobionics investigations. Protasov is a medical (human) doctor, who acts as medical officer (veterinarian) and takes care of the health of all the experimental animals. This station has worked year-round since 1967, having not only sea pens but a few permanent warm-water tanks. The number of bottle-nosed dolphins maintained varies from year to year, but averages from 10 to 18 animals. They have never bred *Tursiops* in captivity, although several births have occurred. All calves have died.

Former station of the TSNII AG, situated in the vicinity of the city of Gagra (Black Sea), Pitsunda. Although this station has very good facilities for keeping animals in captivity, they have slowed down any experimental work with marine mammals. For the last three years a few *Tursiops truncatus* and common dolphins have been maintained at this place. No special breeding program has been active either in the past or the present. The few births that have occurred in the past have always resulted in stillbirth or death shortly after birth.

Station Bol'shoy Utrish in the vicinity of the cities Anapa and Novorossiysk (Black Sea). There is a summer field biological station of the Institute of the Evolutionary Ecology and Animal Morphology of the Academy of Sciences of the USSR (Director Academician, V. E. Sokolov). Head of this station is Dr. E. V. Romanenko, whose main interest is research on echolocation, sound production, and behavior. This station is functional only during summer from April till November. They maintain a maximum of 10–15 *Tursiops*. Some of them are brought from Kazachya Bay because they live there during the winter. There is no formal animal husbandry program at this facility.

Oceanarium at Batumi (opened for the public in 1975) was built on the site of the VNIRO Fishery Station. The head of the research program with marine mammals is Dr. A. P. Shevalev who works very closely with the people from Kazachya Bay. The number of *Tursiops* at this oceanarium at the present is unknown, but thought to be 7 or 8. Two births were announced for mid-November and early December 1975. These subsequently died, however.

UNITED STATES

California

Marineland of the Pacific, Inc.
P.O. Box 937
Palos Verdes, California 92704, USA

President: Mr. Michael Downs

Curator: Mr. Tom Otten

Tursiops: 4 *Tursiops gilli*

14 *Tursiops truncatus,* 7 females and 7 males, females aged 7, 7, 7, 9, 13, 13, and 18 years and males aged 4, 7, 10, 13, 15, 18, and 20 years

Marineworld/Africa USA
Marineworld Parkway
Redwood City, California 94065, USA

Manager: Mr. Michael B. Demetrios

Curator: Mr. Stan Searles

Seaworld, Inc.
1720 South Shores Road
San Diego, California 92109, USA

Director: Mr. Frank Powell

Curator: Dr. Lanny Cornell

Tursiops: 6 *Tursiops gilli,* 3 females
and 3 males
28 *Tursiops truncatus,* 14 females and
14 males

Naval Ocean Systems Center
(formerly Naval Undersea Center)
San Diego, California 92152, USA

Director: Mr. B. A. Powell

Veterinarian: Dr. S. H. Ridgway

Tursiops: 23 *Tursiops truncatus,* 12
females and 11 males
1 *Tursiops gilli,* male

Connecticut

Mystic Marinelife Aquarium
Mystic, Connecticut 06355, USA

Director: Mr. Stephen Spotte

Tursiops: 4; 2 females aged 5 years
and 2 males aged 4 and 5 years

Florida

Aquatarium & Zoological Gardens
6500 Beach Plaza Road
St. Petersburg Beach, Florida 33706,
USA

Curator: Mr. Richard A. Whitman

General Manager: Mr. Michael D.
Haslett

Tursiops: 14; 6 females, 3 females
aged 14–20 years, 2 aged 6–10 and 1
aged 3–6 years,
8 males, 5 aged 12–14 years, 2 aged 5–
10, and 1 aged 3–5 years
There have been 2 births; 1 conceived
in captivity, lived to 2 years and 1
stillbirth conceived in wild.

Miami Seaquarium
4400 Rickenbacker Causeway
Virginia Key
Miami, Florida 33149, USA

Manager and Curator: Mr. Warren
Zeiller

Tursiops: 23; 17 females and 6
males

Marineland of Florida
Route 1, Box 122
St. Augustine, Florida 32084, USA

General Manager: Mr. Clifton
Townsend

Curator: Mr. Robert Jenkins

Veterinarian: Dr. Ronald F.
Jackson

Holding Facilities: Pool—22.9 meters
diameter by 3.7 meters deep
Open ocean circulation

Sea World of Florida
7007 Sea World Drive
Orlando, Florida 32809, USA

Director: Mr. George Becker

Curator: Mr. Edward D. Asper

Tursiops: 2 Pacific bottle-nosed
dolphins, 1 female and 1 male
8 Atlantic bottle-nosed dolphins, 5
females and 3 males

Aquatic Mammals Enterprises
Key Largo, Florida 33037, USA

Directors: Charles and Leigh Riggs

Tursiops: 4; 1 female and 3 males

Ocean World
1701 S.E. 17th Street
Fort Lauderdale, Florida 33316, USA

Director: Mr. Charles Beckwith, Jr.

Tursiops: 9

Gulf World
West Panama City Beach, Florida,
USA

Owner: Mr. Wesley Burham
Curator: Mr. Carl Selph

Tursiops: 3

Waltzing Waters Aquarama
P.O. Box 68
Cape Coral, Florida 33304, USA
Director: Mr. Jack Scarpuzzi

Tursiops: 2

Flipper Sea School
P.O. Box Dolphin
Marathon Shores, Florida 33052,
   USA
Director: Mr. Jim Lewis

Tursiops: 20; 4 births since 8/1/73,
   2 females and 2 males of which 2
   are still living
Natural water environment

Theatre of the Sea
Matacumbe Key, Florida
Director: Mr. P. McKinney

Tursiops: 2

Gulfarium
Fort Walton Beach, Florida 32548,
   USA
Director: Mr. John B. Siebenaler

Tursiops: 7; 6 females and 1 male

The following individuals   Number of
are keeping *Tursiops.*   *Tursiops*

Mr. Gene Asbury
Sugar Loaf Motel
Sugar Loaf Key, Florida 33044, USA
                                          1

Mrs. Betty Brothers
Brothers Motel
Little Torch Key, Florida 33043, USA
                                          2

Mr. John Slater
3054 Gordon Drive
Naples, Florida 33940, USA   3

Mr. Harvey Hamilton
Villa Marada, Florida   2

Hawaii

Naval Ocean Systems Center
   (formerly Naval Undersea Center)
Box 997
Kailua, Oahu, Hawaii 96734, USA
Division Head: Mr. Richard Soulé

Tursiops: 18 *Tursiops truncatus,* 9
   females and 9 males
1 *Tursiops gilli* male

Sea Life Park
Waimanalo, Hawaii 96795, USA
Director: Dr. Edward Shallenberger
Curator: Ms. Ingrid Kang

Tursiops: 8 Atlantic bottle-nosed, 5
   females and 3 males
3 Pacific bottle-nosed, 2 females and
   1 male

Illinois

Chicago Zoological Society
Brookfield Zoo
Brookfield, Illinois 60513, USA
Director and Curator: Dr. George
   B. Rabb

Tursiops: 3; 2 females and 1 male,
   aged 2, 12, and 20 +

Massachusetts

New England Aquarium
Central Wharf
Boston, Massachusetts 02110
Director: Mr. John Prescott
Curator: Mr. Lewis Garibaldi

Tursiops: 6; 4 females and 2 males

Atlantic Aquarium
1 State Park Road
Hull, Massachusetts 02045

Director: Mr. Gilmore

Tursiops: 2; 1 female and 1 male

Mississippi

Marine Life Inc.
c/o Marine Animal Productions
150 Debuys Road
Biloxi, Mississippi 39531, USA

Owner: Mr. Don Jacobs

Manager: Mr. Robert Corbin

Tursiops: 22; 13 at Marine Life Inc.,
  Mississippi
9 at Seven Seas, Texas

Missouri

Six Flags over Mid-America
St. Louis, Missouri, USA

Manager: Mr. Larry Cochran

Curator: Mr. Marvin Boatman

Tursiops: 4; 2 females and 2 males

North Carolina

Quinlan Marine Attractions
Route 1
Lincolnton, North Carolina 28092,
  USA

Director: Mr. Ralph Quinlan

Tursiops: 27

New York

New York Aquarium—New York
  Zoological Society
Boardwalk at West 8th Street
Seaside Park
Brooklyn, New York 11224, USA

Director: Dr. James A. Oliver

Curator: Dr. William Flynn

Tursiops: 1 female

Niagara Falls Aquarium
701 Whirlpool Street
Niagara Falls, New York 14301, USA

Director: Mr. Leonard F. Bryniarski

Tursiops: 4; 3 females and 1 male

Puerto Rico

Ocean Life Park Aquarium
Boca de Congrejos Isla
Villamar, Isla Verde,
San Juan, Puerto Rico 00913, USA

Director: Mr. Robert E. Pile

Curator: Mr. Regino Cruz

Tursiops: 1 six-year-old female

Texas

Sea-Arama Marineworld Inc.
91st Street and Sea Wall Boulevard
Galveston, Texas 77550, USA

Manager: Mr. Dale Ware

Curator: Mr. Ken Biggs

Tursiops: 10; 9 females and 1 male
1 stillbirth (twins)

J & L Attractions, Inc. d/b/a/ Seven
  Seas
P.O. Box 777
Arlington, Texas 76010, USA

President: Mr. Jacobs

Manager: Mr. Corbin

Tursiops: 9; 4 females and 5 males

Washington

Seaworld
Pier 56
Seattle, Washington 90101, USA

Director: Mr. Don Goldsbury

Tursiops: 2; two dolphins from the
  San Diego Sea World were there
  temporarily during this period.

The Cetacean Brain

For the last one hundred years the problem of the intelligence of oceanic mammals, *Cetacea,* has been a topic of continual discussion among neurologists. In the last fifteen years the knowledge of their large brains and their communicative sounds has become widespread. As a result there are currently various largely unsubstantiated beliefs about their intelligence ranging from "adapted animals" to "oceanic superbeings."

Among the *Cetacea* are found the largest brains and the largest bodies on this planet. Figure 1 shows brain weights of large-brained mammals plotted against their body weights, both on logarithmic scales. Why are there no animals above this curve? Why are there no large brains without a corresponding large head and body? The fossil record indicates that no animal ever existed with brains sufficiently large in relation to their bodies to place them above the limiting line of Figure 1. Why?

At least part of the answer lies in some mechanical properties which large brains require and which can be measured in present-day animals. The vulnerability of large brains to physical damage and hence their allowed evolution can now be better understood.

The clinical knowledge of how we become adversely affected by damage to or by the lack of growth of our brains has expanded rapidly in the last thirty-five years.

We propose that the limiting factor in the physical size of a brain is the relationship between the moment of inertia of the brain and that of the head and body containing it. (The moment of inertia is the angular momentum of a mass with respect to a fixed point.) Stated more simply, the size of a brain is limited by the ability of the head containing it to resist twisting blows. The relationship between the moments of inertia of brain and head determines the displacement within the skull and hence the limiting rotatory acceleration which brains with the mammalian structure can sustain without damage. Above a certain critical value of rotatory acceleration of the head, the brain is displaced within the skull to the point at which it will break its entering blood vessels and shear its own structure on its partitioning membranes (falx cerebri and tentorium) fastened to the skull. By such displacement about axes in the brain, the brain can be so damaged that the animal goes into coma. In the case of an air-breathing sea creature, unless the whale or dolphin revives or is roused by his fellows within a certain critical leading time, he dies. Even if he revives there may be irreversible brain damage leading to death.

In order to avoid reaching the damaging value of displacement and of acceleratory rotation, the brain is surrounded by a skull and a head which has a much larger moment of inertia than the brain. The moment of inertia cushions the normal tangential forces which the head experiences and prevents the brain from accelerating to damaging levels of brain displacement. The head, in turn, is supported and controlled by a proportionately sized body which has a very large moment of inertia and further prevents too great a rotatory acceleration of the brain (see Figure 2). If a mutation occurs in a given species in which genes creating an increase in brain size are not associated with genes causing a concomitant growth of the skull, head and body, that particular mutation may produce an animal that cannot survive the day-to-day tangential forces usually experienced.

Reprinted from *Oceans,* July 1977, vol. 10, pp. 4–8.

Thus we can see in principle that the quantitative application of Newton's laws of motion to the problem of large brains and large bodies may explain why there are no animals above the limiting line of Figure 1.

Such considerations apply equally to land animals as well as animals in the sea. The elephant with a 6,000-gram brain requires a large head and a large body for that brain to survive. Among land animals, elephants are the only ones with a brain larger than that of man. As yet no Newtonian mechanical measurements have been taken of the brain, the skull, the head or the body of an elephant exposed to the normal stresses of its everyday life. No pathological analysis based on these factors has been done on the bodies of elephants killed either in combat or by an accident.

When one realizes that the density of sea water is eight hundred times that of air, one can see that the cushioning effect of the former medium allowed the evolution of much larger brains in water than on land.

The only animal that has been investigated on this Newtonian mechanical basis is man himself. During World War II neurosurgeons encountered cases of death or brain injury in which they could find no wounds upon the scalp, the skull or the rest of the body adequate to account for the disability or the death. Careful investigation of clinical cases with brain damage and exhibiting minimal external signs showed that in many cases a tangential blow rotated the head abruptly. Most of these cases were caused by missiles striking tangential blows to the head or by vehicle crashes where the head suffered a glancing blow from hitting against the inside structure of the vehicle. A study of recent high-speed vehicle accidents by the Crash Research Unit of Cornell University reveals that many people die from brain injuries resulting from extremely fast head rotation.

We conclude that among the various laws of survival should be included this very important one which we term the "Newtonian mechanical law of survival." It can be stated as follows:

In evolution, the moment of inertia of the brain determines the moment of inertia of the surrounding structures. For survival a given brain size requires a given skull/head size and a given body size, both of which are calculable on the basis of Newtonian mechanics.

The evolution of modern mammalian species has progressed along a narrow Newtonian path limited by the possibility of damage to the material structure of brains.

For a brain of a given size, a head of a given size and a body of a given size, one can calculate the moments of inertia involved. The necessary measurements for the calculations have been made on only a few individuals in a few species. The new principle suggests new experiments and new measurements.

In Figure 2 we have plotted various brain weights against the ratio of the respective head moments of inertia to that of the moments of inertia of the brains. A human brain is protected by a skull which has approximately three times the moment of inertia of the contained brain. An *Orcinus orca* brain (three times the weight of that of the human brain) is surrounded by a head which has a moment of inertia approximately five hundred and fifty times that of its brain.

For man the constraints acting counter to the accelerated rotation of the skull and its contained brain are considerably less than for the orca. The neck vertebrae of the orca are fused and the head rotations take place at the axis and the atlas (top vertebra) only.

One may well ask, are not the larger brains stronger and hence more resistant to damage than the smaller mammalian brains? If one examines the detailed microscopic structure of the human brain and the larger cetacean brains, one finds that all sizes are equally fragile in every cubic centimeter throughout their structure (comparable in fragility to a bowl of congealed gelatin floating in water). Displacements of structure within each of the brains by an equal value of rotatory acceleration are greater in the large brain, and thus can cause more shearing damage in the larger brains than in the smaller ones.

Such considerations as these enable us to see that the only large brains which have evolved on the planet are well protected from rotatory acceleration. No large brains have developed which were not so protected. Thus we can see why large brains are evolved in large heads and in large bodies.

Having made these structural/mechanical distinctions, we are still left with the problem of comprehending the intelligence of such large brains. The neurologist, Gerhardt von Bonin, in 1937,

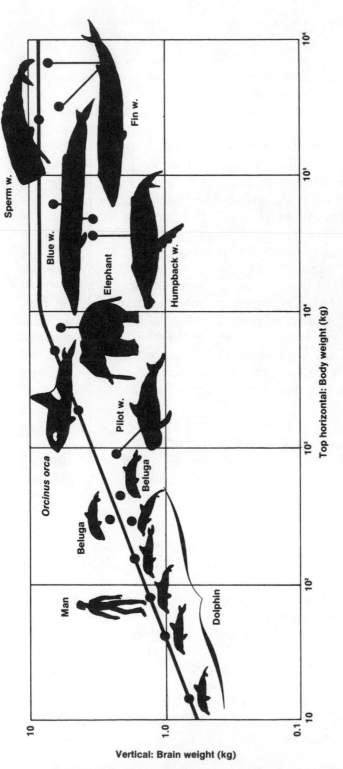

1. Brain weight plotted against body weight (both on logarithmic scales). The curved line shows the limiting size of the brain in proportion to the size of the body. For all mammals, the point representing the ratio of their brain size to body size falls on or below the curve.

Top horizontal: Body weight (kg)

Vertical: Brain weight (kg)

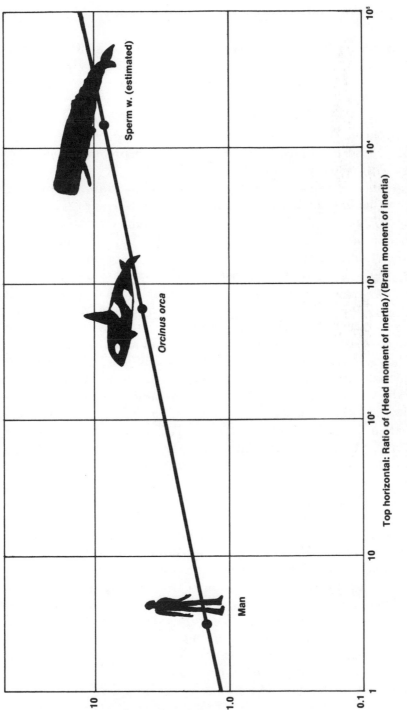

Top horizontal: Ratio of (Head moment of inertia)/(Brain moment of inertia)

Sperm w. (estimated)

Orcinus orca

Man

Vertical: Brain weight (kg)

2. Relation between the brain weight and the ratio of moments of inertia of the head to the brain. Large brains appear to be protected from damage due to rapid rotation by large heads and bodies.

in a paper entitled "Brain Weight and Body Weight in Mammals" stated, "Whether or not this [law of brain weight versus body weight] is an indication of the intelligence of animals must be left to the psychologist to answer."

The relationship between absolute mammalian brain size and intelligence is yet to be scientifically determined. We suffer from a lack of secure knowledge of how to measure intelligence in those with whom we cannot communicate.

The only brain whose activities we can understand is our own. Each of us lives and thinks with a brain of a given size, a given structure, a given complexity, with built-in limits to its functions.

In our further analysis the data are limited. We have some detailed neurological analyses of the structure of our brains and those of the Cetacea. Comparisons of the structure of our brains with the structure of cetacean brains can give us clues as to their functions only through analogy. Studies by Peter Morgane and his co-workers show that the brains of cetaceans are large in those parts (the cortical silent associational areas) in which ours are larger than those of the apes. Clinical studies show that people who have lost the use of these large silent cortical areas lose that which is considered to be most valuable to humans: the ability and the dedication to carry out future plans; they have lost their initiative and memory and their ability to function effectively in our society. Those people who are born with too small cortical areas of association must be protected and kept under institutional control.

Our essential humanness seems to depend upon the intactness of the structure of these critical cortical areas. Our ethics, morals and planning ability, our social relationships all depend upon the adequate size and functioning of these critical areas of the cortex.

The very large cortical associational areas in the Cetacea do not preclude processes analogous to human qualities such as initiative, dedication, thinking, planning, valuing traditions, and respecting ethics and morals. One may say cautiously that at least the equipment is present in cetaceans to allow for equivalent analogues of these functions. One cannot attribute these human functions to cetaceans on a one-to-one correspondence. Cetacea live in an alien environment, have an alien evolution and alien experience. We would expect them to have computational capacities quite foreign to ours. However, we assume that the complexities of their mental operations, within their particular evolution and in their particular environment, may be comparable and even superior to ours. We can observe in their behavior some activities analogous to human initiative, dedication and the appreciation of ethical concepts.

The considerations so far of the structure of very large brains, including human brains, do not lead to definite conclusions regarding their intelligence. The first requirement for testing intelligence is direct communication. To date we have no communication at this level with any of the Cetacea. None of the cross-species comparisons of the brain and its structure answer the questions of intelligence; so far they only pose fresh ones which must be investigated by new methods.

Studies of the sonic and ultrasonic signals of dolphins and whales indicate that these are very complex phenomena. At least one part of the use of their brain is in generating, transmitting, receiving and interpreting complex sonic signals. Whether or not these are analogues of human speech, its transmission and its reception remain to be determined by experiments.

Cetacea communicate underwater, which explains in part why communication between them and us has not yet been investigated thoroughly. The differences between the two media of air and water are obvious: sound travels in water 4.5 times faster than it does in air, and can be transmitted over much longer distances in water. The human speech spectrum is limited to between about 100 Hertz and approximately 3,000 Hertz. The baleen whales (and elephants) emit sounds in a frequency region below twenty Hertz. Dolphins and orcas emit sounds within the range of human hearing and above it by at least one order of magnitude. In other words, human speech is preponderantly outside the two ranges used by the two large groups of cetaceans, with some slight overlapping.[1]

If we are ever to communicate with Cetacea we must devise physical means of transforming the frequencies of our sounds to fit their hearing range and their sound to fit ours in order to establish adequate sonic exchanges. Using electronic equipment it is now feasible to transform their sounds and ours and thereby open a "sound doorway" between cetaceans and us. Assuming that suitable technology can be devised, the next problem will be to develop some form of common language.

Since the Cetacea cannot exist on land, we must invent technical methods which will enable us to remain in the water. Then, and only then, will we be in a position to share their experience and interactions which will give meaning to our mutually transformed sonic exchanges.

In our past experience with the intimate relations developed between dolphins and people, we saw evidences of an ethic among the dolphins which assigns man to a very special station. It is as if cetaceans teach their young that man is special and they should try to avoid injuring him.

We also found evidence that individual dolphins will exert great effort to reprogram their sonic emissions in attempting to devise a means of communication with us.[1] Although such reprogramming (speaking in air) is extremely difficult for them, the fact that they took the initiative is, in itself, astonishing. The conditions for such dedicated work on their part require close physical association between them and humans. To begin to understand the dedication involved and the remarkable adaptive reprogramming initiated by the dolphins, one should experience these exchanges as recorded at the time on tapes. For those professionally interested in these matters, tapes are available through the Human/Dolphin Foundation in Malibu, California.

A program to establish the physical sonic doorway for communication between man and cetaceans is currently in the developmental stages at the Foundation. The program involves the use of microprocessors and integrated circuit devices with large scale integration for the necessary operations on the sound spectra of the human and of the dolphin. It is planned to use underwater sound for the cetacean end and airborne sound for the human end of the communication links. Insofar as possible the work with dolphins and/or *Orcinus orca* will be done in their natural habitat.

With such equipment and the requisite software, we plan to investigate man's ability to test the computational capacities of dolphins. We do not know whether man is capable of understanding an alien intelligence. Our test is an inter-species intelligence test.

Cetaceans evolved brains the size of ours thirty million years ago.[2] Our brains have only been their present size for approximately 100,000 years.[3] We, as relative newcomers, may be asking too much of ourselves to communicate meaningfully with minds as ancient as those of the whales and dolphins. This program may be far more important than we currently conceive it to be: the whales and dolphins may have more to teach us than we have to teach them.

1. J. C. Lilly, *Lilly on Dolphins,* Anchor-Doubleday, 1975.
2. H. J. Jerison, "Paleoneurology and the Evolution of Mind," *Scientific American* (284:2) January 1976.
3. David Pilbeam, *The Ascent of Man,* Macmillan, 1972.

APPENDIX SEVEN

The Dolphins Revisited*

... We have decided to go back to the dolphin work, examine it very carefully, and do some entirely new work with the dolphins. Dolphins are very exciting to work with. They are playful, curious and develop very close attachments for humans. They are infinitely patient with us. In all of our work with the dolphins no one was badly injured over the thirteen-year period. Most of us in working with them in water received black-and-blue marks or scratches on our skin at one time or another when we pushed the dolphins too far. Their discipline with humans in the water is really amazing. If they do not want you in the water they bang their beaks against your legs just hard enough to move you out of the water. If you insist on coming into the water, they may scratch your skin with their teeth in a very precise controlled fashion. When I remember that a dolphin can bite a six-foot barracuda in two with those teeth I can imagine them biting my leg or my arm in two; however, this never happened in spite of this capacity to do so.

* Reprinted with permission from *Dyadic Cyclone,* 1976.

The largest of the dolphins are *Orcinus orca* and are in captivity in large numbers in the United States, Canada and England. At no time have any of these huge dolphins injured the people that swim with them.

This is the most astonishing property of these large brains— their gentleness, forbearance and their care of us. The dolphins we worked with over the thirteen-year period, had brains 20 to 40 percent larger than ours. *Orca* has a brain four times the size of ours. To give you the background, let me give you some of the characteristics of the detailed anatomy of these brains and of the detailed anatomy of their sound communicating and sonar apparatus.

I spent the years from approximately 1955 to 1968 working practically full time with the dolphins. During that period I wrote the books: *Man and Dolphin* and *The Mind of the Dolphin* in addition to *Programming and Metaprogramming in the Human Biocomputer*. Each of these books deals with the problems that humans have in being faced with an alien species with a brain size equal to and larger than the human brain.

Much work has been done upon the brain of the dolphin showing its superb complexity and its detailed structure on a microscopic scale. Prior to the work on the brain done by Dr. Peter Morgane, Dr. Sam Jacobs and Dr. Paul Yakovlev, there were no *preserved* brains of dolphins or whales examined. All of the materials previously investigated had deteriorated owing to postmortem self-digestion.

These early specimens from the last century and the early part of this century had a low cell count owing to the autodestruction of the cells caused by this rather warm brain lying on the beach or on the deck of a factory ship.

Morgane, Jacobs and Yakovlev developed three dolphin brains that were totally preserved so that every cell was still present. When we looked at these sections, I suddenly realized that these resembled the human brain to the point where the unpracticed eye could not tell the difference between the cortical layers of the human and those of the dolphin. The only significant difference was that the dolphin had a thicker layer number one on the outside of the cortex. From studies of the 11,000 microscopic sections made of these brains, Morgane, Jacobs and Yakovlev have been writing many scientific papers and are currently preparing an atlas of the dolphin brain. The material they have used for this atlas is better than anything that has been done to date on the human brain.

Those results show that the dolphin's cell count is just as high per cubic millimeter as is that of the human. The material also shows that the connectivity—i.e., the number of cells connected to one another—is the same as is that in the human brain. They have also shown that there are the same number of layers in the cortex of a dolphin as there are in that of a human.

In other words, this brain is as advanced as the human brain on a microscopic structural basis.

They have also shown that the dolphin brain has quite as large "silent areas" as does the human brain. Let me explain.

We have frontal lobes and parietal lobes, the greater part of which are silent, i.e., there are no direct motor outputs or sensory inputs from or to these portions of our brain. It is the silent areas that distinguish us from the chimpanzees and from the gorillas. We have, of course, an anthropoid brain, but it has been enlarged only in the silent areas.

An examination of the brain of *Tursiops truncatus,* the bottle-nose dolphin of the Atlantic, shows that their brain has enlarged over that of the smaller dolphin's brain, purely by an increase in the size of the silent areas, even as we have enlarged silent areas compared with those of the chimpanzees. Just as our brains, in increasing in size over the chimpanzees' expanded in the silent areas, so did the dolphins as they grew larger brains. (The current smaller dolphins have brains the size of a chimpanzee and are decreased in size in the silent area region over that of the larger dolphins.)

What do the silent areas do? Presumably these are the areas of our brain in which we do our major central processing (computations) as humans. That which we value most as humans (as opposed to smaller-brained animals) is in these silent areas. They are the association areas for speech, vision, hearing and motor integrations and for relating these to all other activities of our bodies.

In all other regions the dolphins are comparable to us with some differences. Their visual system is one-tenth the speed of ours; however, they make up for this in that their sonic and acoustic systems are ten times the speed of ours. This means that the dolphins can absorb through their ears the same amount of information—and at the same speed—that we do with our eyes. We can absorb through our eyes ten times the amount of information that the dolphins can through theirs.

This means that we are dealing with a species that is primarily acoustically oriented. We are primarily visually oriented. Our visual orientation is built into our language so that we, in general, talk as if we were watching and seeing and analyzing what we were talking about as if *seen*.

In contrast, the dolphins "see" with their sound-emitting apparatus and the echoes from the surrounding objects underwater. Remember that half the twenty-four-hour day, during the night, their eyes do not need to function. Remember that they must be able to "see" underwater in the murky depths during the day as well as during the night. They must be able to detect their enemies, the sharks; they must be able to detect the fish that they eat, and they must be able to detect one another in spite of a lack of light; therefore, they have an active processing mechanism for sound that is immensely complex.

Over the years we have examined the sound-emitting apparatus of the dolphins very carefully, both anatomically and physiologically. As is presented in *The Mind of the Dolphin* they have three sonic emitters, two of them (nasal) on their forehead, just below the blowhole, anterior to the brain case. They have their third one in their larynx which crosses their foodway in the nasopharynx.

We put small hydrophones on the sacs in the top of their heads on each side of the blowhole and followed what they could do with these two sonic emitters. It turned out that they have total independent control of these two emitters and that they can whistle on one side while clicking on the other and change over from one to the other. They can also control the phase of what is emitted by controlling the timing of these two emitters. The laryngeal emitter produces extremely short clicks that are used in their "fine structure" sonar. The sound from the larynx is propelled through the head forward in the two rows of teeth, eighty or more, which acts similarly to a "yagi antenna" for transmitting a very narrow band of frequencies, around one hundred and sixty thousand hertz. This dental yagi also works for reception concentrating the return echoes in the same frequency band and thus reducing the noise of the sea and enhancing the signal from these clicks. We measured the tooth structure and the wavelength of the emitted sound. We found that the spacing of the teeth was exactly half a wavelength of the sound being emitted and received. This is a very sophisticated system with which the dolphins can not only get the distance of objects but they can get the composition of those objects in terms of density. They emit this beam and scan one another's bodies. If one gets into a pool with them, they immediately turn on their sonar and scan one's body. This is one of their forms of recognition for individuals. (They can also recognize one visually under well-lighted circumstances.)

This sonar beam can penetrate one's body, is reflected off one's lungs, the gas in one's gut and the air cavities in one's head. A dolphin looking at one's stomach for example can tell if one is anxious or upset because the stomach tends to churn during anxiety. They can see this churning with the bubble of air that is in the stomach.

To return to the nasal emitters on each side of the blowhole. We examined these very carefully and it turns out that there are two tonguelike muscles that move anteriorly and posteriorly coming up against the edge of what is called the "diagonal membrane." When they wish to click they keep this membrane a little bit relaxed. The muscles for this membrane go down through the nasal passages (through the bone) and can be contracted in such a way as to tense the free edge of this membrane in the air passage. The tongue is then brought back forming a very narrow slit about three-quarters of an inch long through which they blow air into sacs above the membrane and sacs below the membrane. This means that they have the ability to push air back and forth through this narrow slit. We set up a model of this and showed that when the edge is tight, whistling takes place when air is blown between the membrane and the tonguelike muscle. When the edge is more lax, clicks form as air is blown through the slit.

We also showed that they can do stereo effects by controlling the phase on the two sides of the head, which means that they can also polarize the sound so as to distinguish it from the surrounding sea noises.

With such a degree of sophistication of their emitters and an equal sophistication of their receivers, their ears buried inside their heads, they can do amazing things with this apparatus.

For example, a dolphin can distinguish the difference between a one-inch diameter, one-sixteenth-inch thick aluminum disc against a concrete wall versus a copper disc of the same dimensions, when this is hidden behind a visually opaque but a sonically transparent screen.

Two dolphins communicating sound like three dolphins. They may face each other and use the laryngeal tight sonar beam for communication when they do not want somebody else to know about their communication. We often found them doing this in our laboratory, and every so often we had the opportunity of having a hydrophone between them and we would then detect the fact that they were doing this. We could not hear it of course, it was too high a frequency for our ears, but we could show it on a cathode-ray oscilloscope and record it on high-frequency tape recorders.

I do not think that dolphins distinguish their sonar from their communication with the nasal emitters. The nasal emitters emit longer wavelength sound than does the laryngeal emitter. This means that they have a 360° solid angle "sonar" in the two emitters near the blowhole as opposed to the tight beam emitter of the larynx. This means that they can detect objects behind, above, below or ahead of them with the nasal emitters, and then with the laryngeal emitters they can turn on any interesting object and examine it in detail.

They do not distinguish between sonaring and communicating; in other words they are quite capable of sending holographic sonic pictures to one another with their communication apparatus. They can then use these pictures in symbolic ways similar to the way that we use the printed versions of words spoken out loud.

This implies an immense complexity of acoustic memory and of acoustic portrayal, way beyond anything that we have achieved either in simulations in computers or in terms of concepts having to do with acoustic events. Only our most sophisticated and advanced mathematics can even approach an analysis of this kind of a system.

Most of the above work was done between 1961 and 1968 in the Communication Research Institute in the laboratory in Saint Thomas in the Virgin Islands and in the laboratory in Miami, Florida.

Over the years I gradually developed an entirely new set of assumptions based upon our work with dolphins. I realized that here was an independent being living in an alien environment whose evolution was several times the length of the human evolution. The original whales, from thirty million years ago in the Eocene period, found in rocks where the sea used to be—now land—had brain capacities of eight hundred cc's. This means that they have a longer evolution than does the human. The humanoids were found in strata that are of the order of two million years old. The humans themselves (Neanderthal, Cro-Magnon, and so forth) are not nearly this age. This means that these alien beings are much more ancient than we are on this planet. It also means that they achieved brain sizes comparable to the human a lot sooner than did the human itself.

I believe that we can presume that they have ethics, morals and regard for one another much more highly developed than does the human species. For example, they realize their total interdependence. Let me illustrate this interdependence.

All of the dolphins and whales breathe totally voluntarily. They have no automatic respiratory mechanism such as we have; if they did, they would drown when they passed out from a high fever or a blow on the head or some other reason. An automatic breathing system would mean that underwater they would breathe water when unconscious. They cannot afford an unconscious respiratory automatic system such as we have.

This voluntary respiration means then that any time a dolphin or a whale passes out for any reason, his fellows must bring him to the surface and wake him up in order that he will breathe again, or else he dies.

We saw many instances of this among the dolphins. To wake one another up they will rake the dorsal fin across the anal/ genital region causing a reflex contraction of the flukes, which lifts the endangered animal to the surface. Dolphins support one another at the surface and stimulate the unconscious one until the respiration starts again when he is awake.

This implies that dolphins cannot afford to be very far away from one another, twenty-four hours a day, three hundred and sixty-five days a year, day and night. This also means that when a large group of dolphins becomes ill, say owing to a virus, they will beach themselves in order not to die at sea. They would prefer to die on the beach rather than to die in the depths. This explains the beaching of pilot whales and various dolphins. We have seen several dolphins come in from the deep sea and enter small shallow protected lagoons in the Florida Keys in order to recover from their illness, safe from sharks and the other predators of the sea. We have seen spotted dolphins, which are pelagic (i.e., a deep-sea species), come into very shallow water and stay there several weeks while they were recovering from their injuries.

Please pardon this long introduction to our future program with dolphins. Toni and I have decided to go back to dolphin work in depth under very stringent controlled circumstances.

As I stated in *The Center of the Cyclone,* I closed the dolphin laboratory because I did not want to continue to run a concentration camp for my friends, the dolphins.

I have not attacked publicly the oceanaria for keeping dolphins restrained in what they call a "controlled environment" for the following reasons.

The oceanaria have done a very great service for the dolphins and killer whales in acquainting literally hundreds of thousands of humans with their existence and with their capabilities in a circus way. The dolphins and the whales are indebted to the oceanaria for educating the human species. This has been a costly education for these species; however, I believe that this is worth it. Thousands of people are becoming more and more aware of the necessity of stopping whaling, for example. More and more people are aware that when a dolphin is beached, something is wrong and that it needs help. The oceanaria assure that we will get closer and closer to an ability to communicate and to break the barrier between these species and ourselves. For this I am very grateful. If it weren't for the oceanaria, I would not have been able to do my initial work with the dolphins. Let me give specific examples.

Recently I attended the so-called killer whale *(Orcinus orca)* show at Sea World near San Diego. I saw these huge dolphins treating humans in the same gentle fashion that the smaller dolphins had treated us. I saw a man ride a killer whale holding on to a loop around the whale's neck and holding on to the dorsal fin with his feet, wearing a small aqualung in case of emergencies. The whale then took him down to the bottom of this rather deep pool and then propelled himself up into the air, leaping clear of the water with the man on his back and diving immediately to the bottom of the pool again, five or six times.

This is an astounding cooperative effort on both the part of the human and the killer whale. This man has immense courage and immense trust in this huge creature. On the other side, the killer whale has an immense trust in the humans and does everything he can to be sure that that man can breathe at the proper timing so that he does not drown. This requires a discrimination and a careful timing of the dives and the leaps in such a way that the man can survive. He then delivers the man to the side of the pool so the man can step off safely. This is an incredible performance. I could hardly believe it the first time I saw it. Without the beautiful organization of the oceanaria such feats would be impossible.

I originally saw the potential of this sort of work when Ivan Tors made the movie *Namu—The Killer Whale.* The movie crew swam with the whale in a lagoon. There is one scene in that movie in which there is one person riding on the back standing up and holding on to the immense dorsal fin, another swims up near the huge flukes and taps them and the whale lowers the flukes and allows the person to climb aboard also.

The immense sensitivity of these animals' skin allows them to detect the presence of a person and to regulate their activities in such a way as to not damage them. It is most impressive, their careful control of their immense size so as not to endanger their human friends.

The killer whale had a very bad reputation mainly from the writings of Robert Falcon Scott *(Scott's Last Voyage,* published in 1913), who wrote about his trip to the South Pole. He witnessed an episode in which killer whales broke four feet of ice to investigate some Eskimo dogs around his ship next to the ice. As soon as they saw the photographer, i.e., a human on the ice floe, they went away again. This episode frightened Scott, as he wrote in his diary. He attributed many things to the whales that they did not have, such as ferocity and cunning. I believe this episode is easily explained when one knows that the killer whales came up to the edge of the ice, looked across the top of the ice and saw the dogs, but no humans there. The humans were on the ship tied up at the edge of the ice. Naturally their tremendous power in breaking the ice seemed a threat to Scott and his people.

I believe that the whales, dolphins and the killer whales know all about us, know how dangerous we are. They have been present when we have held our wars in the sea and let off depth charges; they know about our submarines, and our atomic bombs and hydrogen bombs. They know how dangerous the human species really is and they respect us as a very dangerous group. I believe that they all know that we can wipe them out if they hurt any of us and this message gets around. There was an episode written up for example in one of the skindiver magazines in which a man went out of Seattle in a forty-foot power boat made of wood and saw some killer whales. He shot through the dorsal fin of one of the male killer whales. I don't know why.

The whale turned around, came up to the front of the boat, came up in the air, grabbed the stemhead (the wooden part of the boat that holds the front of it together) and pulled the stemhead out of the boat, opening the hull above the waterline. The man then scrambled around and readjusted the weight in the boat so that the front end came up out of the water and he went back to Seattle. He then told everybody what had happened and showed his boat.

This to me is an example of the measure of the killer whale's very high intelligence. He pulled the stemhead out of the boat, but did not sink it, so that the man could come back and, as it were, give the message "Don't shoot killer whales" to his fellow humans.

In the Communication Research Institute we did many experiments which we did not report publicly. We did a lot of quantitative work on the sonic spectrum of the dolphins. We did a lot of quantitative work on what the dolphins could do with this amazingly sophisticated system. We found for example that they can control their click rate, i.e., the pulses of sound that they emit, in the following fashions. They can control the sonic spectral content of each of the clicks. They can control the rate of click production to a very fine degree. They can control the number of clicks that they emit to a very close value. They can change from clicks to whistles in a fraction of a millisecond. They can control the click rate from one per minute up to several thousand per second easily. They can control the acceleration and deceleration of the clicking rate to an amazing degree of accuracy.

We intend to use these capabilities in inducing them to control a computer. In the Institute we set up a teaching program to teach them how to control a computer through a code, a machine code using their clicking.

In the new project we intend to pursue this. Since the days we were working with the computer many new micro- and mini-computers have been devised that are suitable for this kind of work. We have already started our work on the software necessary for this.

What are the assumptions behind this kind of work? The assumptions are that there is a very sophisticated, very developed, alien mind behind this type of communication and we assume that they already have an immensely complex language based upon acoustic pictures analogous to our words and sentences. They have probably developed a *sonic picture language*.

We intend to unearth this language, to make it more obvious to us, to perform transformations of it to a visual representation (a "hologram") from their acoustic representation.

We intend also to establish that this very sophisticated animal has an acoustic language probably as complex (if not more so) as any human language and that they can learn to control a high-speed computer.

The reason for using a high-speed computer is that the dolphins can transmit and receive so rapidly that a human operator cannot possibly keep up with them in their natural state. We found in the Institute that dolphins will accommodate to the humans' slowness and the humans' lower-frequency range of transmission, but they do so with great difficulty. Our language is a very narrow band in their frequency spectrum and seems very slow to them, at least something of the order of five to ten times.

These are the reasons that Toni and I are going back to work with dolphins. We have found that the amount of interest in dolphins and the technical advancement in computers has gone up tremendously since 1968 when I closed the Institute.

We can now do much more sophisticated software, much higher speed operation of computers, than we could do then.

We want to break the communication barrier and believe it can now be done—with the cooperative efforts of many persons working on these problems knowledgeably, with the dolphins *(Tursiops* and *Orcinus).*

Index